D-40-96-D

TRY
AND STOP ME

A Collection of Anecdotes and
Stories, Mostly Humorous

By Bennett Cerf

ILLUSTRATED BY CARL ROSE

New York, 1945
SIMON AND SCHUSTER

ABOUT THE APPEARANCE OF BOOKS IN WARTIME

A recent ruling by the War Production Board has curtailed the use of paper by book publishers in 1944.

In line with this ruling and in order to conserve materials and manpower, we are co-operating by:
1. Using lighter-weight paper, which reduces the bulk of our books substantially.
2. Printing books with smaller margins and with more words to each page. Result: fewer pages per book.

Slimmer and smaller books will save paper and plate metal and labor. We are sure that readers will understand the publishers' desire to co-operate as fully as possible with the objectives of the War Production Board and our government.

TO

ALL THE PEOPLE

WHOSE WIT,

OR LACK OF IT,

MADE THIS VOLUME

POSSIBLE

CONTENTS

FOREWORD

I HAVE ALWAYS had a hitherto useless knack for remembering hundreds of unrelated anecdotes about unrelated people. In the minds of some this has constituted me a "raconteur"; in the mind of my wife, who has had to listen to the same yarns a hundred times, it has inspired justifiable thoughts of mayhem. It is not always possible to avoid her eyes and put boyish zest into a "That reminds me of a funny thing that happened just yesterday" at the same time. If it does nothing else, this book may persuade Mrs. Cerf that remembering stories isn't a complete waste after all.

To supplement my own memory, I have pored through countless issues of The New Yorker, Time, Life, Newsweek, Variety, Reader's Digest, and Coronet in quest of additional anecdotes. I have devoured reams of columns by Winchell, Lyons, Sobol, Wilson, Skolsky, Hoffman, and their fellows. I have listened to radio programs until I thought that one more singing commercial would destroy my sanity entirely. Some of the choicest material comes from new books and old ones. I have tried to give credit wherever possible, but anecdotes are bandied about so generally and new stories sweep the country so quickly that it is often impossible even to discover who put a story into the public prints first, let alone find out who actually originated it.

Column conductors and radio comics are engaged in a highly competitive business, and their anxiety to establish the originality of their material is thoroughly understandable. It has always struck me as faintly ridiculous, however, for them to cry "Thief! Thief!" at rivals who very possibly overheard the gem in dispute at the same night-club table or in the same gentlemen's room. They seem to forget that they actually create very few of the bright quips and amusing anecdotes they chronicle, and that the

ix

people who tell them *their stories probably repeat them to a dozen others that very evening.*

One of the most amusing features of my research for this volume was the frequency with which certain classic yarns bobbed up with entirely different casts of characters. In one instance, Bernard Shaw had said something to H. G. Wells; in another, Ilka Chase had delivered the same bon mot to Hedda Hopper. An identical witticism was credited to Oliver Wendell Holmes, Winston Churchill, and Charles Boyer. A Dorothy Parker sally of 1936 found its way into a feature story about Gypsy Rose Lee in 1944. Columnists and "raconteurs" (odious word) discovered long ago that the public laughs harder and is more impressed when a line is delivered by somebody whose keen sense of humor is already established. Any honest celebrity who subscribes to a clipping service will admit that he learns about some of his cleverest punch-lines for the first time when he reads that he has delivered them. This is a harmless and amiable practice and generally flattering to the beneficiaries, but it makes the business of tracking anecdotes to their actual source complicated indeed.

Many of the paragraphs in this volume appeared originally under my name in my weekly "Trade Winds" column in the Saturday Review of Literature, *and in* Esquire, Coronet, Liberty, American Mercury, Reader's Scope, *and* Town and Country. *You will recognize dozens of them. For every new anecdote, I have included two that are hoary with age. I did not make them up; I collected them. If they remind you of some good ones you had forgotten; if they add a few more to your repertoire; above all, if they provide a few honest thrills and belly-laughs, this volume will have achieved the purpose for which it was compiled.*

BENNETT CERF
New York,
May 25, 1944.

TRY AND
STOP ME

Chapter One

SHOW CASES

HURRAH FOR CAPT. SPALDING AND
THE OTHER MARX BROTHERS

WHAT THIS country needs is a new show for the Marx Brothers. It's all very well to recall their patter of years gone by, and chuckle reminiscently over it, but something fresh along the lines of *The Coconuts* or *Animal Crackers* would give Broadway an unbelievable fillip. The funniest lines usually fell to Groucho. He revived on the radio the other night his "I never forget a face —but I'm willing to make an exception in your case."

One of his funniest routines concerned his African hunting trip which began with "Did I ever tell you how I shot a wild elephant in my pajamas? How he got into my pajamas I'll never know. Getting his tusks off was quite a problem. In Alabama the Tuscaloosa." He came home in a rickshaw. The meter registered $11.40. "Confound it," he roared to the driver. "Didn't I *tell* you not to go through India?"

Then there was the skit where Groucho and Chico served as opposing lawyers. Chico became tongue-tied when it was his turn to question the witness. The judge thundered, "Well, ask your witness some questions." "All-a-right," said Chico. "What's a big-a da animal wid four legs an' a trunk in da front?" "That's irrelevant," screamed Groucho. "Dat's a right," agreed Chico. Groucho crossed the stage, planted his portfolio on the judge's bench, and declared, "I rest my case."

And the time when Groucho proposed to that wonderful foil, Mrs. Rittenhouse. "Your eyes shine," he told her, "like the seat of my blue serge pants." "But you'll have to get out of that house you're living in," he added. "I don't like Junior crossing the tracks. In fact, come to think of it, I don't like Junior."

The weak sister of the Four Marx Brothers on the stage was Zeppo, but when he quit the greasepaint and became an agent, he ended with more pelf than the other three put together. Harpo, who never says a word on the stage, is the wittiest conversationalist in private life, and was one of Alexander Woollcott's favorite companions. Harpo once flew all the way from Hollywood to Bomoseen, Vermont, for a week-end to surprise Woollcott. He painted himself from head to foot with hideous hues, paddled to the Island, and howled like a banshee. Nobody was frightened, however. In fact, nobody was on the Island. Another time, Harpo appeared in a broken-down Model-T Ford. "What on earth do you call that?" scoffed Woollcott. "This is my town car," said Harpo grandly. "Yes," answered Woollcott, "and the town is Pompeii."

Chico's wife invited an elderly relative to spend a few weeks at his house one time. The visitor was very charming, but her English was on the sketchy side. When Irving Thalberg and his wife, Norma Shearer, were coming for dinner, Chico took the old lady aside. "When Mr. Thalberg says 'pleased to meet you,'" he instructed her, "all you have to do is answer with one word: 'likewise.' " The old lady repeated the word several times, and swore that she would uphold her end without mishap. The Thalbergs arrived. "Pleased to meet you," said Thalberg as expected. The old lady beamed at him. "Wise guy," she said.

The Marx Brothers once became the managers of a prize-fighter. He was a lumbering giant named Cohen, and richly earned the nickname of "Canvasback" by an invariable custom of getting himself knocked cold in Round One of every fight. The boys had a great time with Canvasback Cohen until one day, according to legend, Groucho knocked him out in a gymnasium workout. That was too much. Harpo claims that Canvasback started as a lightweight, but was hit so many times that he swelled out into a heavy.

As long as I have rambled on this far about the Marx Brothers, I'd better quote a few other of their more famous lines, if only to avoid the wrath of thousands of enthusiasts who remember their dialogues almost word for word and are ready to fight at the drop of a wisecrack. In *Horse Feathers*, Groucho informed his son, "I'd horsewhip you—if I had a horse."

His secretary interrupted him to announce, "Jennings has been waiting to see you for hours, and he is waxing wroth." Groucho's reply to this was, "Tell Roth to wax Jennings for a change."

When Chico entered the scene, Groucho commented, "Hey, you look a lot like a guy I know by the name of Ravelli." "I am Ravelli," declared Chico. "Aha," said Groucho, "that accounts for the resemblance."

In *Monkey Business*, Groucho discovered a large automatic pistol and near it a few small pearl-handled revolvers. "This gat," announced Groucho, "had gittens." Almost immediately after that deduction, the ship's captain hove into view. "I've got a complaint," roared Groucho. "What is it?" said the captain testily. "Last night when I was in bed in my cabin, who do you think came tiptoeing along the corridor and tapped on my door?" The captain said he didn't know. "Nobody did," declared Groucho, "and that's my complaint."

Marx Brothers addicts will never forget their burlesque of Madame Du Barry. Groucho, essaying the role of high minister, was feverishly embracing Du Barry when Chico came charging into the scene. "Who are you?" snarled Groucho. "King of France," averred Chico. "What?" said Groucho. "You the king? And I the prime minister? France is certainly in one hell of a fix!"

* * *

Vaudeville lovers remember with some affection the old comedy team of Sweeney and Duffy, which invariably brought down the house—whenever Duffy, a rather vague character, remembered to show up. A distraught stage manager found him luxuriating in a Turkish bath one afternoon when he should have been on the Orpheum stage. "For God's sake, Duffy," he spluttered, "what are you doing here? You're on now!" "I am?" said Duffy. "How'm I going?"

Sweeney and Duffy's act didn't please the burghers of Memphis, Tennessee, on one memorable occasion. Joke after joke fell flat as a pancake. Duffy stood the chill silence just so long. Then he strode to the footlights and declared, "Citizens of Memphis! This is one of the proudest and happiest moments of our lives! Your tumultuous reception has overwhelmed us! And now, if you all will just remain seated a few moments longer, my partner, Mr. Sweeney, will pass down the aisle with a baseball bat, and beat the be-Jesus out of you."

That was the end of the act known as Sweeney and Duffy.

* * *

During a rehearsal of a John Barrymore play, the leading lady aroused the star's ire, an incautious procedure, to say the least. Barrymore gave a pungent lecture on her paternity and nocturnal pursuits. "Kindly remember," interpolated the actress, "that I am a lady!" "Madam," snapped Barrymore, "I will respect your secret."

* * *

John Barrymore once confounded an audience with a somewhat similar stunt—right in New York, at the height of the run of *Redemption*. There was an epidemic of coughing throughout the first act. When it broke out again in the second, Barrymore was all set. He suddenly yanked a five-pound sea-bass from under his coat and flung it over the footlights. "Busy yourselves with *this*, you damned walruses," he bellowed, "while the rest of us proceed with the libretto!"

* * *

John Barrymore and Richard Bennett, reports Gene Fowler, spent an evening together in London that included liquid refreshments of many descriptions and copious quantity. Bennett woke up the next morning, gingerly felt his head, and wondered if Barrymore had gotten to his home without bodily injury. He phoned him, and, when several seconds passed without an answer, called angrily into the instrument, "Hello! Hello!"

Barrymore's voice, very sleepy, replied, "Hello."

"Are you all right?"

"I'm fine. How are you?"

"Fine. But I've had the devil of a time getting your room. Are you in it, or down in the lobby?"

"I don't know."

"What in hell do you mean, you don't know? Where *are* you then?"

"Here, I suppose," said Barrymore, poking his head out from beneath Bennett's own bed.

* * *

June Havoc, musical comedy star, and, incidentally, sister of Gypsy Rose Lee, was taken to a tea at the sedate Columbia Faculty Club by a learned and curious admirer. Miss Havoc took a despairing look at the venerable professors who decorated the premises and sighed, "My, my! I've never been with such a lot of extinguished gentlemen before in all my life."

* * *

One of the costliest musical comedy failures of recent years was a show called *Allah Be Praised!*, produced by Al Bloomingdale, a scion of the well-known department-store magnate. During the Boston try-out, an experienced "play doctor," Cy Howard, was summoned to give first aid to a palpable crack-up case. He watched the show in silence. When the final curtain fell, Bloomingdale asked anxiously, "Well, what do you think?" Howard put his hand on the other's shoulder. "Al," he advised, "close the show, and keep the store open nights."

* * *

Eugene O'Neill, America's leading dramatist, has long since completed his brilliant new play entitled *The Ice Man Cometh*, but has forbidden its production until he is on the scene to check every detail. He has a sound reason for this decision. Only once in his career was a play done without his personal direction. That was *Dynamo*, in 1929, and, says Mr. O'Neill bitterly, "The only thing anybody seems to remember of the entire production is that Claudette Colbert wore a red dress and had beautiful legs." *The Ice Man Cometh* will have to wait until the author is good and ready to come to New York and brave once more the rigors and heartbreaks of rehearsals and out-of-town try-outs.

The new play is based on that period of Mr. O'Neill's turbulent youth when he lived in a grubby little rooming-house over a saloon just off the Hudson River waterfront. It was known as "Jimmy the Priest's." Those were the days when he sailed before the mast, and underwent the experiences that were poured into *The Long Voyage Home* and his other early plays of the sea. A little later they were produced by the Provincetown Playhouse. George Cram Cook, Eleanor FitzGerald and Jimmy Light ran the Provincetown then. They remember the day when O'Neill appeared in tow of a burly chap who was no less self-conscious because he was temporarily out of funds. He was Howard Scott, but his magic Technocracy was still around the corner.

O'Neill never could stand the ordeal of his own first nights. On the memorable occasion of the premiere of *Strange Interlude,* he wandered unrecognized down Broadway. Unrecognized, that is, by all but a single passerby, who clapped him on the back and boomed, "Eugene O'Neill, by all that's holy! Haven't seen you since we shipped together on the *Southern Cross!* What on earth ya been doin' with yourself since?"

* * *

Joe Cook spent an entire season in a musical revue that co-starred the oft-married Peggy Hopkins Joyce. His billing for her was "that somewhat different virgin."

* * *

One of the sharpest and most devastating wits in the theatre is the property of Beatrice Lillie, in private life Lady Peel. She was virtually unknown in America in 1924 when an unpretentious musical called *Charlot's Revue* opened, and made stars overnight not only of Miss Lillie, but of her co-players Gertrude Lawrence and Jack Buchanan.

Years later Bea Lillie was being fitted for a number of dresses by a leading Chicago modiste. A lady who had married into the Swift hierarchy was next on the appointment calendar, and fussed and fumed because she was being kept waiting. "Tell that actress in there," she said very loudly, "that she is delaying Mrs. Swift!" This tactic, of course, resulted only in Miss Lillie's taking a half hour longer in the fitting room. Finally she tripped blithely out and, as she passed the fuming Mrs. Swift, said airily to the modiste, "Tell that butcher's wife that Lady Peel has finished now."

The only time Miss Lillie's *sang-froid* deserted her behind the footlights was at the final New York performance of *The Third Little Show.* The revue had enjoyed a long and prosperous run, and both the cast and the management were in high good humor. Howard Dietz, who had composed the lyrics, bought the entire first row of the orchestra that night, and distributed the tickets among mutual friends of Bea Lillie and himself. She was in the middle of a solo number when, by prearranged signal, everybody in the row, men and women alike, bent down and donned long whiskers of every conceivable shade and pattern—bright red, green, pink, zebra, plaid, and polka dot. The sight was too much for Bea Lillie, who stopped in the middle of her song, pointed helplessly at the solemn and oblivious first row, and ran howling to the wings. By the time Dietz reached her dressing room she had regained control of the situation. "Nobody can appreciate my voice anyhow," she reminded him, "when I sing above a whisker."

* * *

Phil Baker, master of ceremonies of the popular radio show called *Take It or Leave It,* recently received a letter—possibly from his press agent—which read, "Dear Phil: Here's a real $64 question for you. Will you lend me $64?"

THE GREAT NOSEPIECE

JIMMIE "SCHNOZZOLA" DURANTE's recent ascent to heights he had never before known is one of the most soul-satisfying comebacks in show business. The "Schnoz" had been bogged down for years by atrocious Hollywood material, but once he turned back to his own wacky song creations, and the inimitable routine that had first won him favor, he was back in lights in no time flat.

Durante is a product of the sidewalks of New York and beer joints in Coney Island. There he learned to maltreat a piano, make capital of a nose Cyrano would envy, and warble ditties like "I Ups to Him," "Could Broadway Do Widout Me" and "The Hot Pertater" in a voice that sounds like a foghorn off Sandy Hook. For years, his partners were Clayton and Jackson. Then he had a girl stooge for a while. Her name was Martha Raye. Regardless of his associates, the backbone of his act involved storming about the floor of a night club, throwing hats at the musicians, mangling the King's English, and working himself up into a monumental dudgeon at nothing in particular. The trumpeter was "playin' wid only one lip." The waiters were "tryin' to horn in on the act." The customers were walking out at the wrong time. "Remember, mister," Jimmie told one of them, "I never fergits a back!" "I know dere's a million good-lookin' guys," he explains, "but I'm a novelty."

At the Copacabana, Jimmie packed them in so deep that, he declared, the star customers had to be satisfied with a table behind a *small* post. He dropped a collar-button one night, and before he could recover it, "a waiter threw a table cloth over it and seated five people." "Dose waiters," he ranted. "Assassins! Twelve-fifty for a load of ice wid three olives! If you don't tip 'em five dollars more, de Union calls 'em out on strike! Let 'em touch dis nose, however! I'll sue de jernt and turn it into a bowlin' alley!"

Some years ago Russel Crouse and Howard Lindsay, producers of *Life with Father* and *Arsenic and Old Lace,* signed Jimmie Durante to co-star with Ethel Merman in a musical play called *Red Hot and Blue.* When the day for the first rehearsal came round, they were horrified to learn that the "Schnoz" was in Italy. They

called Lou Clayton, now acting as Durante's manager. "What's this about Jimmie being in Italy when he ought to be here rehearsing?" they demanded. "Naw, he's not in Italy," said Clayton patiently. "He's in Rome. Tomorrow he gets to Italy."

Jimmie came home exuberant about the sights he had seen. "Dat day in Rome was de best of all," he reported. "How could you possibly do Rome justice in one day?" asked Lindsay. "One day?" said Jimmie. "Why, I didn't know what to do wid myself all afternoon!"

A great fuss developed over which name was to go first on the billing: Mlle. Merman's or Monsieur Durante's. The agents kicked up more of a row than the stars themselves. "Merman's got to go first," said her representative. "The lady's name *always* goes first." "Yeah?" said Jimmie. "How about 'Mister and Missis'?"

For a while it looked as though the whole show would be called off. Eventually a settlement was effected. The names were crossed:

Jimmie's wartime experiences were "humiliatin'" and "colossial." He volunteered to drive his neighbors to work but "Share-the-Ride Schwartz" and other rotund guests kept crowding him over farther and farther in his jalopy. "Suddenly I'm standin' on de corner waitin' for a streetcar!"

In Congress, he saw senators pass a bill voting eighty millions to the Army and sixty to the Navy. "Den I hears a great commotion. A Senator starts tearin' around screamin', 'I dropped a nickel out of my pocket, and not one Senator leaves dis room till I finds it.'" He met a Colonel and cried, "Hello, chum." "Hello, chump," was the answer. "De Colonel," Jimmie explained, "speaks more distinct dan I do."

In private life, Jimmie is so friendly, unassuming, and generous that everybody in show business loves him. Fred Allen calls him "The Riff-Raff's Caruso." "His voice," reports Allen, "can only be described as a dull rasp calling its mate, or an air-raid signal blasting through two layers of gravel." He hasn't much hair left, and refers to himself as "The Surrey with the Fringe on Top." He wears glasses now ("to read de racin' form"), plays piano duets with men like Professor Einstein and Deems Taylor, and explores esoteric dishes at exclusive restaurants. He had his first cheese soufflé at an expensive French eatery not long ago. After one bite, he registered ecstasy, and summoned the head waiter. "Where has dis been all my life?" he demanded. The waiter looked very pained. "I do not know, sir," he apologized.

* * *

Drama critics have to see so many horrible "turkeys" in the course of a season that they may be excused if they occasionally forget their manners in print.

Brooks Atkinson wrote the shortest review on record. It read: "Such-and-such opened last night. Why?" Another critic declared that a musical "arrived in town after an insufficient number of postponements." "The picture version of *Panama Hattie* needs a certain something," wrote David Lardner, and added pensively,

Actor's-eye view of three dramatic critics *

"Possibly burial." Burton Rascoe announced that a certain actress' performance "sickened him." The next day she sent him a bottle of castor oil.

Percy Hammond closed a review with "I have knocked everything except the knees of the chorus girls, and nature anticipated me there." David Lardner is credited with "The plot was designed in a light vein that somehow became varicose." A Detroit music reviewer contributed: "The Blank Quartet played Brahms last night. Brahms lost."

Somebody met George Kaufman after a particularly gruesome opening. "What did you think of it?" ventured the stranger. "It's

* (Left to right) Brooks Atkinson, Wolcott Gibbs, Kelcey Allen.

not quite fair for me to say," Kaufman assured him. "I saw it under peculiarly unfortunate circumstances. The curtain was up."

* * *

Kelcey Allen, the dean of New York's present-day dramatic critics, composes his essays on the theatre for a paper called *Women's Wear Daily*. His reading audience is composed chiefly of the garment trade and buyers in town to have a time for themselves, and he guides himself accordingly.

A woeful production of *Macbeth* in modern dress once came close to turning New York into a one-night stand. Somebody in the audience was heard to mutter, "Lay on, Macduff; lay off, McBride." For years this witticism was credited to Kelcey Allen, but now Wolcott Gibbs comes along to say that it really was coined by Harry Hershfield.

One afternoon Russel Crouse was sitting in the Astor lobby when Allen approached with a man whom he identified as a doctor. "Don't bother getting up," he added hastily. "He's only a dentist." The play *Amphitryon 38* was always "Amferon 56" to him. Allen has an amiable habit of falling sound asleep in the middle of a show. One evening he began to snore in a spirited tempo. Walter Winchell whispered, "I see that Kelcey is writing his review early."

Allen was one of the prime spirits in the founding of the New York Critics' Circle. He makes no bones about his motives. "It's the only way," he says, "that I thought I might ever get to meet George Bernard Shaw in person."

* * *

Paul Muni, whose real name is Muni Weisenfreund, served his apprenticeship in the Jewish theatre. One of the roles that brought him stardom was that of a coal miner. In the second act finale, he led a delegation to plead for higher wages from a flint-hearted mine owner, who threw him out, but got what he deserved in a rousing third-act climax. One night Muni's entire family attended the show, and the young star put everything he had into the performance. So eloquent, in fact, was his description of the starving wives and babes of the miners that, at the height of his plea, the actor who was playing the owner suddenly burst into tears, and cried, "Stop! Stop! You're breaking my heart. Of course, you can have a raise!" They got the curtain down somehow or other, and the manager had to explain that just before the third act began the wicked owner had experienced another change of heart, and decided to lock the miners out after all.

* * *

When William Collier died, his old friend, Joe Laurie, Jr., jotted down a few reminiscences. It was Collier who originated a now-familiar theatrical jibe when, asked how he had liked a newly opened show, he replied, "The play was a success but the audience was a failure."

He met Al Wilson, a German comedian, at a railroad station and noted that Wilson was at one end of the platform, his company at the other. "I never speak to my company," explained Wilson. "I saw your show," said Collier, "and I don't blame you."

Collier opened one of his own plays, *The Patriot,* in New York on December 30th. January 2nd he advertised: "Second Year in New York." Meeting the oft-married DeWolf Hopper at the Friars Club, he grumbled, "Wolfy, I wish you'd invite me to one of your weddings now and then."

He was toastmaster at a banquet where first an admiral, and then a general, talked on and on while the audience writhed. Collier restored everybody to good humor by his comment: "Now I know what they mean by the Army and Navy Forever."

* * *

Ilka Chase's first husband was the actor, Louis Calhern. Miss Chase describes their brief romance very frankly in her autobiography, *Past Imperfect.* After their divorce Calhern married Miss Julia Hoyt. A month or so later Ilka found in her trunk a

box of beautiful calling cards engraved, "Mrs. Louis Calhern."
"It seemed a pity to waste them," relates Miss Chase, "so I mailed
the box to my successor. But, aware of Louis' mercurial marital
habits, I wrote on the top of one, 'Dear Julia: I hope these reach
you in time.' I received no acknowledgment."

* * *

Louis Shurr, the corpulent theatrical agent, is the hero of many
Broadway fables. Shurr is said to own a sable coat and an em-
erald necklace with which he adorns his lady of the evening.
When he bids her good night, he takes the wrap and necklace
home with him.

Shurr is hard to impress. An actor is said to have burst into his
office one day; when he took off his hat, Shurr observed that four
daisies and a stalk of asparagus were growing right out of his
head. "I think I've got something for Ripley," said the actor.
"Why?" said Shurr.

A vaudevillian proposed a novel turn to him on another occasion. "I dive off a gallery box onto the stage," he explained, "com-
mitting suicide right in front of the audience. It'll wow them."
"Could be," agreed Shurr, without too much enthusiasm. "But
what'll you do for an encore?"

* * *

There was a scene in Sherwood's *Reunion in Vienna* that Alexander Woollcott particularly loved. It was played by the returning Hapsburg (Alfred Lunt) and the old beldame who ran the
Vienna restaurant (Helen Westley). Lunt speculated idly as to
whether she still wore her old red flannel drawers, and at an op-
portune moment lifted her skirt to see. One night the unpredictable Miss Westley forgot to put the red flannels on. Lunt gazed in
horror, and choked over his next line, which read, "Well, thank
God there is one thing in Vienna that hasn't changed!"

KAUFMAN AND HART

T HE COMBINATION of Kaufman and Hart has become as familiar
to Americans as ham and eggs. In the theatre it is the hallmark
of themes so timely, dramatic construction so instinctively perfect, and dialogue so crackling that in their particular field the
collaborators are simply beyond competition. One magazine or
another is always writing pieces about them. They are wonderful
copy; both have said so many funny things that a writer has only
to string a lot of them together to convince himself—and his
editor—that he has turned out a sparkling and highly original
piece of work.

Kaufman has been called "the gloomy dean of Broadway wits."
He is nervous, short-tempered, abrupt. "I'm never sure," said one

famous actress, "whether George is smiling at me or baring his teeth." Moss Hart soon discovered, however, that beneath his acidulous manner there beats a heart of purest marshmallow. Hart himself looks like a benevolent Mephistopheles. His warmth and charm of manner have endeared him to hostesses all over the country. A hundred highly eligible girls have set their caps for him, but when it comes to matrimony, elusive is the word for Mossy. He entered the Stork Club one evening with Miss Jane Doe, a charming actress whom he was squiring at the moment. Somebody remarked, "Here comes Moss Hart with the future Jane Doe."

Kaufman and Hart are ideal collaborators, close neighbors in Bucks County, and inseparable companions. For a long time their lives were so closely interwoven that nobody even talked about them separately. In the past couple of years, however, they have gone about some separate affairs of their own, Hart to write *Lady in the Dark* and *Winged Victory*, Kaufman to direct *Doughgirls* and *Over Twenty-One* and to collaborate with J. P. Marquand in a dramatization of *The Late George Apley*. Before they intertwine again in an inevitable future collaboration, let us take gun and camera in hand, and explore a few of their vagaries:

GEORGE S. KAUFMAN...

George Kaufman is allergic to vegetables, dogs, hats, and typical New York first-night audiences. He favors bright-hued neckwear from Charvet, snappy bridge and gin rummy games, croquet, and being by himself. He can disappear from crowded cocktail parties and stuffy dinner groups with the speed of a meteor. "He shies at the slightest display of emotion," confides Hart, "as most men flee from smallpox. At our first meeting I was wide-eyed with hero worship; Kaufman recoiled in horror. Later, however, everything worked out fine; we married and had several beautiful children."

Kaufman was born in Pittsburgh in 1889, studied law for a few months, loathed it, sold hatbands and ribbons on the road for a year, and loathed that even more. He then settled down for a spell as a newspaper columnist, under the aegis of Franklin P. Adams, who had been deeply impressed by contributions he had received from "G.S.K." In 1917, he journeyed to Rochester to act as best man at a wedding. Another member of the bridal party was Beatrice Bakrow. Kaufman married her on the spot. The young couple were short on cash but long on hope, good humor, and friends who, like themselves, were bound for places in a hurry. Furthermore, Kaufman caught the press agent of a swank metropolitan hotel cadging his material; in retribution the hotel boarded the Kaufmans free in an elegant suite for the first months of their married life. Mrs. Kaufman's introduction to the literary

and theatrical set that she now rules in queenly fashion (they were known as "the Algonquinites" in those days) came when George and Frank Adams took her to a cocktail party, introduced her to numerous persons who said "hello" and then forgot her, and deposited her on a cane-bottom chair in the corner. The cane-bottom collapsed, and the new Mrs. Kaufman found herself imprisoned in the framework, her posterior drooping to the floor

like a loose coil of rope. There was a sudden hush while everybody turned to stare. Adams added to her confusion by remarking, "I've told you a hundred times, Beatrice: that's not funny!"
Today Mrs. K. would take a thing like that in her stride. Not long
ago, Mrs. Kaufman met so many relatives and friends from her
home town in a walk up Fifth Avenue that she reported, "All
Rochester seems to be in New York this week." "What an excellent time," commented George, "to visit Rochester."

From columning, Kaufman drifted into the drama department
of the *New York Times;* he clung to his well-loved job of drama
editor long after his plays were netting him a fortune on Broadway. His first smash hit, *Dulcy,* was written with Marc Connelly;
so were *To the Ladies* and *Merton of the Movies.* Before he met
Hart, he also collaborated with Edna Ferber, Katherine Dayton,
Ring Lardner, Alexander Woollcott, Morrie Ryskind, and Herman
Mankiewicz. On the side he became one of the best directors of
our time, and turned many an indifferent entry into a solid success by adroit doctoring during the out-of-town try-outs. In all
his spectacular career he has written only one play alone: *The
Butter and Egg Man,* produced in 1925.

Kaufman traces his ancestry back to Sir Roderick Kaufman,
who, he claims, went on the Crusades—as a spy. After the playwright's success was assured, he was plagued with the usual
swarm of stock salesmen and insurance agents. One gold-mine
promoter told him his stake was so rich that it was unnecessary
to dig for the gold; it lay around right on the surface. "What?"
grumbled Kaufman. "You mean I'd have to stoop over to pick
it up?" He and his cronies used to play cards once a week above
the swanky Colony Restaurant in New York. Harpo Marx ordered
a ham sandwich; roared indignantly when his bill came to $1.50.
"Isn't there *anything* you can get for a quarter in this restaurant?"
he inquired. "Sure," Kaufman assured him. "Twenty cents." When
his daughter Anne informed him that a friend of hers at Vassar
had eloped, George remarked, "Ah! She put the heart before the
course."

When Kaufman is in the throes of composition, a slow and careful picking of lint from the carpet, Moss Hart discovered, is generally the forerunner of the emergence of a particularly effective line. Sometimes he removes his shoes and stretches full length on the floor. Then he performs gymnastics that would make "The Daring Young Man on the Flying Trapeze" turn green with envy. He is afraid of genuine satire, which he defines as "something that closes Saturday night," and does not welcome suggestions from outsiders. "Possibly you don't realize who I am?" grumbled one self-appointed critic when he was brushed aside. "That's only part of it," Kaufman assured him.

On an opening night, Kaufman broods in the rear of the orchestra, and glares at the limelight-hoggers who arrive late on purpose so that everybody may see them parade to their seats. He says that his farewell to the theatre will be a production of *Noah's Ark* in modern dress. The curtain won't go up until the last straggler is in his seat. Then Noah will appear and say, "Now it's going to rain for forty days." At this point the audience will be drenched with water from the ceiling of the theatre. Kaufman promises to stand at the door with a hose to catch any stray who may have escaped the general inundation. Another of his whimsical notions is *Othello* in blackface. Every character will be black except Othello himself, who will be played by somebody like Clifton Webb or Frank Sinatra. His will, he swears, provides that he be cremated and his ashes thrown in the face of a certain Hollywood producer.

Ruth Gordon once described a new play to him. "There's no scenery at all," she explained. "In the first scene, I'm on the left side of the stage, and the audience has to imagine I'm eating dinner in a crowded restaurant. Then in Scene Two I run over to the right side of the stage and the audience imagines I'm home in my own drawing room." "And the second night," nodded Kaufman, "*you* have to imagine there's an audience out front." During the abbreviated run of *Let 'Em Eat Cake*, an unsuccessful sequel to *Of Thee I Sing*, a disappointed backer spied Kaufman in the lobby and mistook him for George Gershwin. "How could you let a thing like this happen, Mr. Gershwin?" he complained. "My score is perfect," answered Kaufman, suddenly restored to high good humor. "The whole trouble is with Kaufman's book!"

He keeps a close check on his productions, lest the actors let down, as they do so frequently in long-run successes. Late in the run of *Of Thee I Sing* he sent a wire to one of the stars, William Gaxton, which read, "Am watching show from rear of orchestra. Wish you were with me." In another hit, the leading actor began to change his part to suit himself. Kaufman brought him back to scratch with a note that began, "Your performance grows more scintillating every evening. Sorry I can't say the same about the lines."

The Kaufmans recently went in for chicken-raising on a substantial scale at their country place. George made an inspection tour, and fourteen hundred chicks, expecting to be fed, came flocking toward him. He remarked: "I believe these chickens expect me to say a few words." He mounted a crate and exclaimed, "Chickens of the world, unite!" At this point a Connecticut bantam bit him on the ankle.

A guest expressed concern at the fate of all the women war workers when the boys came marching home. George had a ready solution. "Keep the women on the job," he suggested, "and let the men stay home and have the babies. All that is necessary is a certain amount of retooling."

Brooks Atkinson sums up George Kaufman's contribution to the theatre: "He has done the best work he could on every occasion;

he is master of the destructive jest; he has made the wisecrack part of our language; he has given something distinctive, compact in form, dynamic in tempo, to American drama." Furthermore, George Kaufman is one of the few important figures in the theatre who have resisted the blandishments of Hollywood. Except for the briefest of intervals, he has declined fantastic offers from picture studios, in order to stay in the legitimate theatre, where he belongs. He has helped to keep the American drama on its course when it was floundering desperately.

. . . AND MOSS HART

"I was born on Fifth Avenue," says Moss Hart grandly, but adds in a whisper, "at the wrong end." It was 107th Street as a matter of fact, and the whole family was desperately poor. He went to public school in the Bronx. At the pinnacle of success he couldn't resist going back to impress his old principal, who had not regarded him too highly as a scholar. The principal looked him over coldly. "Moss Hart?" he mused. "Oh, yes, I'm sorry, my good fellow, but I can't do a thing for you." "This prodigal son business," concluded Hart, "is strictly bunk." He got his first look at Broadway one November day in 1918. People were dancing in the streets and embracing one another indiscriminately; ticker tape was cascading from every window. Young Hart decided then and there that Broadway was his oyster, a conviction that remained unshaken even after he learned that what he had witnessed was the Armistice celebration. The Astor Hotel looked to him like a palace in fairyland; he spent the night there after the opening of *Once in a Lifetime;* it was a dream come true. So many others of his boyish dreams have come true that you'd think Moss Hart would be the happiest man in the world. He isn't. Vague and undefined fears dog his waking hours, a result, possibly, of early privations and inhibitions. Psychoanalysis is gradually ironing out the kinks in his unconscious. Such treatment costs most men a fortune; it's characteristic of Hart that he turned it to a handsome profit. He can patronize psychoanalysts to his heart's content for the rest of his life on the royalties from *Lady in the Dark*.

From the Bronx, the Hart family drifted to Brooklyn, and then to Sea Gate, on the fringe of Coney Island. Moss became a director of amateur theatricals, and a "host" at summer resorts on the "Borscht Circuit." It was his job to keep the guests happy. This involved whipping up entertainments, strumming guitars, crooning love ballads, and donning grease paint himself. It soon developed that he was a willing donner. A half-inch beneath the suave Hart exterior is a layer of pure ham. To this day he is ready to dash on-stage at the drop of an understudy.

When he wrote the first draft of *Once in a Lifetime* the Hart exchequer was in its usual state of non-existence. Irving Berlin read it and suggested that it be made into a musical with music and lyrics by himself. Ninety-nine out of a hundred struggling young writers would have swooned at an opportunity like this. Not Moss Hart, however. "Nothing doing," he declared. Berlin was flabbergasted but impressed. He told George Kaufman of the minor miracle. A meeting was arranged. Kaufman and Hart became a going concern. At first Moss was scared to death by his famous collaborator. His terror increased when Kaufman visibly shuddered every time he entered the room. Later he found that it was because of the aroma of his five-cent cigars. Today he smokes a pipe so regularly that several people have mistaken him for a book publisher.

Once in a Lifetime opened at the Music Box Theatre on September 24, 1930. George Kaufman was a member of the cast, so he couldn't moan around the back of the theatre, convincing himself and Hart that the show was a failure. It was so evident a smash hit, in fact, that after his ecstatic night at the Astor Hotel, Moss taxied out to Sea Gate, rounded up his family, and moved them en masse into a suite in the Ansonia Hotel, on upper Broadway. The furniture and everything else were left behind in Sea Gate; for all Hart knows, they are still there. Life began anew for the Harts, with no leftovers from the seedy days. Papa Hart, who came to be known as "the Commodore" for no apparent reason, decided he was a song-writer. He has written a song for every one of Moss' plays, *The Man Who Came to Dinner* being his favorite. Irving Berlin, uncowed by his previous rebuff at the hands of an impetuous Hart, ventured to suggest a variation in one of the Commodore's melodies. "You stick to your song-writing," spluttered the Commodore, "and let me stick to mine." He called up Moss from Florida last winter to sing his latest composition, a little number called "Carrie from Toledo, Ohio." Moss told him it wasn't quite up to his usual standard. "Don't forget," said the undaunted Commodore, "that I'm singing it without my teeth."

With Moss' theatrical star steadily in the ascendant, his brother Bernie became a Broadway fixture too. At the moment he is stage manager of *The Doughgirls* and one of the best in the business. Moss' mother, until her death, gloried in her son's success, and couldn't keep up with the gifts he showered upon her. Once he phoned her from California that a friend was coming East to lie low in his apartment until a front-page domestic entanglement blew over. Mrs. Hart entered the conspiracy with the zest of a Borgia. The following morning she wired him, "Coast clear. Have left K. with the J." Moss Hart finally figured out that she had left the key with the janitor. "We Harts," he boasted, "rise to our greatest heights in other people's crises."

Moss Hart was now fully embarked upon what he terms his "gold garter period." All the things he had dreamed of owning when he was a penniless kid he bought—usually in triplicate. His wardrobe became so varied and authentic that his impeccable butler consented to patronize the Hart tailor and bootmaker. Edna Ferber remarked that he was "monogrammed in the most improbable places." Probably his greatest extravagance—but one that gave him the most genuine happiness—was the remodeling of an old brick house on a tract he purchased in Bucks County, Pennsylvania. With a prodigal hand, he turned a run-down old farm into a model estate. Whole forests were uprooted and re-planted with gay abandon. "Look," he said to Wolcott Gibbs, "I've moved this oak so that it shades my library." "It just goes to show you," muttered Gibbs, "what God could do if He only had money."

Bucks County merchants are accustomed to bargaining over their transactions; when they quoted Moss a price of ten dollars on an article, they fully expected to be beaten down to five. Moss usually confounded them, however, by exclaiming, "Only ten dollars! How can you afford to sell a thing like that for so little?" A landscape artist gave him an $11,000 estimate for a particular job. Moss would have okayed it without question, but fortunately Beatrice Kaufman was on the premises that day. "Mr. Hart will give you exactly $7000 for this job," she said firmly. "Done and done," agreed the landscape man without a second's hesitation. Hart had a beautiful swimming pool constructed on the grounds; it was quite finished before he discovered that there wasn't enough water to fill it. His guests that first summer dodged enough drilling equipment to supply a Texas oil field; water finally was uncovered about three hundred feet down.

All these didoes confounded the simple Bucks County folk for a while, but he soon won their hearts with his unfailing friendliness and kindnesses. Now they stand and gape at the steady succession of Hollywood stars and Broadway celebrities who come to visit him. A typical bowling expedition to the near-by alleys at Lambertville will include Moss, Barbara Stanwyck, Robert Taylor, Darryl Zanuck, Gertrude Lawrence, his butler Charles, and his general supervisor Raymond. "What's your score?" Moss asked Taylor at the end of four frames one evening. "Forty-seven," said Taylor. "Hah!" exulted Hart. "I'm sixty-three." "You look it," said Taylor. The neighbors liked it, anyhow.

In fourteen years of successful playwriting, Moss Hart has

earned over a million dollars. In the same period, he has spent over a million dollars. His *Winged Victory*, written as a noble contribution to the Army Air Forces Fund after a 28,000-mile air

tour of the country's training centres, has netted him untold glory but left him strapped. Nobody—least of all himself—doubts that his next effort will put him right back in the big money. About him is the ineffable aura of success. He does everything in a big way. When he goes to the dentist, he stays in the chair for fifteen hours and has three experts tinkering with his molars. He has their signed affidavit to prove it. At the moment, happier than he has ever been, he is the spiritual guide of the boys in the cast of *Winged Victory*. When he goes to a party he takes sixty or seventy of them with him. They sing Army Air songs, eat and drink everything in sight, go their way with the blessings of their startled and unprepared hosts. Kaufman calls him "Forked Lightning." Broadway is waiting for him to strike again.

* * *

S. N. Behrman, whose plays contain some of the wittiest and most polished dialogue in the American theatre, has been called "the Boswell of the overprivileged" by Irving Drutman, "a man who writes like a silk herring" by Fanny Brice. Not for Behrman the problems of the lowly proletariat; in *The Second Man, Biography, No Time for Comedy, The Pirate,* and a half-dozen other successes he has probed the neuroses and peculiar problems of the well-heeled, putting wittier dialogue into their mouths than ever was heard in Newport or Palm Beach. Ina Claire, who often appears in his plays, once heard that she had only three weeks to learn a new Behrman part. "Three weeks!" she echoed in horror. "I can't even learn what some of Sam's lines *mean* in three weeks!"

Behrman is now a famous personage in Hollywood. The first script that he wrote there, however, failed to win the approval of the tycoon who had hired him. "It stinks," he pronounced flatly. "Ah," said Behrman, "a master of innuendo." His greatest admirer on the Coast today probably is Greta Garbo. One day when he had finished his current Hollywood stint, he interrupted Garbo on her set to say good-bye to her. She embraced him passionately, and cried, "Come back soon, my darling!" He was just closing his luggage when she burst wildly into his room. "You're going to New York!" she accused him. "Sure I am," said Sam. "Why do you think we had that great farewell scene?" "Oh, darling," she sobbed, "I thought you were just going down to the beach for a swim."

Another time in Hollywood, Behrman escorted the voluble Ruth Gordon to a small dinner with Somerset Maugham and Aldous Huxley. When he returned home, he commented bitterly, "It certainly gives you a thrill to dine with two of the world's greatest writers—and hear Ruth Gordon talk."

Behrman's social habits sometimes puzzle his friends. "The minute Sam makes a date," explained one, "he's already trying to find a way to break it." "Never pick up a telephone receiver," he once counseled. "The minute you do—you're trapped." One day he bade farewell to all his friends, announced that he was off

for a visit to the fjords of Norway. A week later, however, Elmer
Rice found him dining comfortably at his favorite table in the
Plaza. "Ah, Sam," said Rice pleasantly, "I see you're forgotten, but
not gone."

Behrman, an infrequent patron of New York night spots,
popped up at the Stork Club one evening last winter, where he
noted the presence of Tallulah Bankhead, Irene Dunne, George
Jean Nathan, and of course, William Saroyan. Resolved to make
a night of it, he taxied over to "21" a little later, where the first
people he saw were Tallulah Bankhead, Irene Dunne, George
Jean Nathan, and of course, William Saroyan. "Good heavens,"
exclaimed Behrman, "there seem to be two sets of everybody!"
There's only one Sam Behrman, however.

* * *

George Jessel, whose telephone conversations with his "Mama"
have made millions laugh, has a huge income, but about forty-
one relatives seem to live on it. One day, says Jessel, his Uncle
Rafael went too far. "So," said the uncle, "I see you got on a fine
new necktie, you loafer! Me you won't even buy a grand piano!"

At a party Jessel rushed up to greet an old sweetheart, but she
was making a great play for a South American millionaire, and
gave Jessel a haughty stare. "I don't believe I got the name," she
said coldly. "No, you certainly didn't," agreed Mr. Jessel, burning,
"but baby, you certainly tried hard enough!" In 1940 he did marry
a beautiful young lady of seventeen. When the draft began he
predicted, "The Army will soon get me. My wife was born after
Pearl Harbor!"

Jessel is one of the greatest after-dinner speakers in the country
—incredibly quick with quotable repartee. A toastmaster introduced him as "an unusual specimen—you have only to put a dinner in his mouth and out comes a speech." Jessel snapped right
back with, "I want to call attention to your toastmaster, who is
also unusual. You have only to put a speech into his mouth—and
out comes your dinner." True, Joseph Choate had said the same
thing fifty years ago.

Here are three of Jessel's sure-fire after-dinner stories:

A Hollywood "wolf" noticed a beautiful girl sitting by herself in a hotel lobby. Infinitely sure of himself, he registered "Mr. So-and-so and wife," and then strolled over to make her acquaintance. Two days later they handed him a bill for six hundred dollars. "What's the idea?" he sputtered. "I've only been here two days." "That's right," said the clerk smoothly, "but your wife has been here for a month and a half." . . .

An irate lady, seeking a divorce in court, told the judge, "My husband is an out-and-out loafer who thinks of nothing day and night but horse-racing. He doesn't even remember our wedding day." "That's a lie!" shouted the outraged husband. "We were married the day Twenty Grand won the Wood Memorial." . . .

A young playwright, suddenly in the chips, bought a small sea-going yacht, and a uniform to match. Anxious to impress his old mother, he invited her for a sail, and, pointing to his cap, said, "Look, mama, now I'm a captain." She put her hand on his arm. "Sammy," she said, "by me, you're a captain. By you, you're a captain. But by captains, Sammy, you're no captain." . . .

* * *

Helen Hayes, along with Katharine Cornell, is generally considered First Lady of the American stage today. Miss Hayes made her debut back in 1908, at the age of seven. The place was the old Herald Square Theatre, opposite Macy's, and the occasion was the premiere of a musical comedy called *Old Dutch*. Lew Fields was the star, John Bunny, Vernon Castle, and Ada Lewis were in the supporting cast, and Victor Herbert was the composer of the score. The following year, Fields transferred them all to another musical named *Summer Widowers* and Helen had a scene of her own for the first time.

She entered with a little boy who had gotten a raspberry tart for a present. Helen said, "How do you know it's raspberry?" The boy said, "Take a bite and see." Helen carefully ate the entire tart and admitted, "You were right. It's raspberry." Then she wiped her hands on the little boy's sleeve. The audience loved it. Charles

Frohman sent for her and put her in a play with John Drew. Her career was launched.

Helen Hayes was playing in stock at Poli's Theatre in Washington, at the age of sixteen, when Fritz Kreisler gave a concert there. He had been disabled in the War and came to America to raise money for Austria, his homeland. We were not yet in the War, of course. President Wilson and his wife were in the Washington audience at the concert in question.

Suddenly there was a great commotion. Kreisler was late in arriving, and was taken through the front of the theatre to the stage entrance just back of the President's box. He was talking excitedly to his accompanist in German, and some secret service men thought he was a spy, come to assassinate Mr. Wilson. By the time explanations had been made all around, the concert was an hour late and Mr. Kreisler was in no shape to give his best performance.

The sight of Helen Hayes' shining young face in the wings seemed to restore his composure. When the concert was finished, he asked her if he could play something specially for her. "*Poor Butterfly*," said Helen promptly. Somebody brought him the music, and while the audience in front was still crying for encores, the great Fritz Kreisler played *Poor Butterfly* for Helen Hayes in his dressing room backstage.

* * *

Helen Hayes' first great dramatic hit in New York was in support of William Gillette in Sir James Barrie's *Dear Brutus*. She left the company after many months to tour under the management of George Tyler. Gillette was furious. "What did Tyler do for your daughter that we did not?" he asked her mother. "Well," she said, "he has given her a tremendous raise in salary and we are to have a drawing room on every train." "You should be very happy, Madam," said Gillette coldly. "You have sold Helen for a couple of Pullman tickets."

* * *

Miss Hayes met her husband, Charles MacArthur, at a cocktail party at the home of Neysa McMein. According to legend, Mac-Arthur had a bag of peanuts in his hand. He took one look at Helen and handed her the peanuts. "I wish they were emeralds," he said. (In January 1944, MacArthur, now a major in the U. S. Army, flew with a mission to India. He came upon a couple of small but perfect emeralds and sent them to his wife. The accompanying card read, "I wish they were peanuts.")

Helen Hayes' daughter Mary was not quite five when she saw her mother on the stage for the first time. MacArthur took her to a rehearsal of Maxwell Anderson's *Mary of Scotland*. Mary watched Miss Hayes in silence while she played a stormy and dramatic scene with Queen Elizabeth. Then she turned to her father. "Mama's angry," was her comment.

During the run of *Mary of Scotland*, Miss Hayes noticed that after five or six consecutive matinees, a little boy stood at the stage door waiting for her to come out. He never spoke to her, and when one afternoon she smiled and said "Hello there," he turned brick red, and ran. After the next matinee he was waiting for her again. He thrust a little box into her hand and was gone. Inside the box she found a silver medal. The inscription read, "For scholarship. Public School 42. 1933."

* * *

The Hayes-MacArthur home is situated in Nyack, New York—about fifty miles from Broadway.

Gilbert Miller was playing host to an elaborate party at the Waldorf one evening a few years ago, when Miss Hayes took him to one side.

"Charlie is a bit high," she said, "and is having too much fun to leave now. I've got an early rehearsal tomorrow, and want to slip away. Won't you see that Charlie gets to bed O.K.?"

Miller promised. When the party broke up, he dutifully bundled MacArthur, now sound asleep, into his car and drove the full fifty miles to Nyack. When he got there, he was surprised to find that the house was boarded up and padlocked. There was nothing left to do but drive back to town and deposit MacArthur on a spare couch in the Miller apartment.

The next morning Miss Hayes called in a panic. "What have you done with Charlie?" she demanded. Miller explained that he had taken him all the way to Nyack and back.

"Good heaven," said Helen Hayes. "I forgot to tell you. We're living at the Waldorf for the winter."

* * *

Isabel Leighton, the writer, once aspired to be an actress, and landed a bit in *Deburau*, which starred Lionel Atwill. She reported her new job triumphantly to the "round table" crowd at the Hotel Algonquin. "All I do is walk once across the stage," she said. "But it's a start!" "What theatre do you open at?" asked Marc Connelly. "The Belasco," answered Miss Leighton. "Too bad it isn't the Hippodrome," said Connelly. "Your part would be twice as big."

"THE YANKEE PRINCE"

IF YOU would like to preserve your illusions about George M. Cohan, the Prince of the American Theatre, I'd advise you to pass up Ward Morehouse's fascinating and carefully documented biography. In many ways it is the most unusual book about a legendary figure in theatrical history I ever have seen. I don't believe the author himself realized what a devastating portrait he was drawing. Morehouse, like the reader, evidently began his task in a roseate glow of hero worship, but the halo began to crumble as the evidence piled up. There were a lot of wonderful things about George M. Cohan; as he grew older, unfortunately, the meaner side of his nature came to the fore. He lost touch with the theatre that had done so well by him. He turned on the actors and associates who had worshipped him. He resolutely refused to understand important new playwrights and theatrical trends. Their language was "objectionable," their preoccupation with the thornier side of life "lamentable." The glamorous and exciting part of Cohan's career ended in 1919, when the actors struck for their rights, and Cohan flabbergasted them by spearheading the opposition. Up to that time he was indeed "The Yankee Doodle Kid"; from then on he began more and more to resemble the very model of a modern postmaster general.

George Michael Cohan was born in Providence, Rhode Island, on July 3, 1878. "His father Jerry," says Morehouse, "with a keen sense of the future publicity of an Independence Day birth, did a little understandable adjusting of the birth record." George's real name was "Keohane," and his ancestry was Irish through and through. The name "Cohan" (accent always on the last syllable) caused some amusing mix-ups in his later life. "George gets 'em coming and going," grumbled an envious competitor. "The Jews think he's Jewish and the Irish *know* he's Irish!" In a little hostel in Ireland Cohan once asked for his breakfast in bed. "Go tell that Jewish gentleman," said the irked proprietor to a bellboy, "that in this place, if he wants his breakfast he can come right down to the dinin' room an' get it!" "There's a mistake somewhere," said a man at the desk. "That man's name isn't Cohen—it's Co-han. His grandfather was born right here in County Cork." "The divil!" said the proprietor. "Why didn't you say so in the first place? Boy, tell the poor lad he'll have his breakfast in bed just as soon as we can fetch it to him."

George was a fresh, cocky kid from the very beginning. His first love, which he never got over, was baseball; his pet aversion the violin lessons his parents made him take. After he had become a great success he took his father one day to a modish and expensive restaurant. A violinist played a fancy solo. "See, George," said his father jokingly, "if you had paid more attention to your violin lessons, it might be you who was playing here now." "So it might," agreed George readily, "but then you wouldn't be eating here."

George and his sister Josephine soon were incorporated into their parents' act; "The Four Cohans" became a standard head-liner on the Keith and Proctor circuits. Gradually young George took over from his father the task of supplying new material for the act. In 1899 he married a dashing young actress named Ethel Levey; in 1901, his first full-length play, *The Governor's Son*, opened in New York at the Savoy Theatre on 34th Street. (That theatre is still standing. It is opposite R. H. Macy's, and has long been a second-run motion-picture house.)

In 1904 Cohan got the luckiest break of his career. He met Sam Harris, and formed with him the producing firm of Cohan and Harris, destined to sponsor a series of the most fabulous successes ever seen on Broadway. Their first whopping hit was *Little Johnny Jones*, written by George, featuring the Four Cohans in the cast. The song hit was "Give My Regards to Broadway." Cohan had only the vaguest notion of the plot for his play when he started to promote the cash to back it; he made up the details

while he sat at a luncheon table with a prospective backer. (Years later, Ben Hecht and Charles MacArthur employed the same tactics with Sam Goldwyn. In urgent need of ten thousand dollars, they rushed into Goldwyn's office, outlined a colossal melodrama to him and pocketed his check. Months later, when Goldwyn demanded a finished script, neither Hecht nor MacArthur could remember a single detail of the plot they had improvised for him.)

At any rate, *Little Johnny Jones* knocked 'em off their seats—everywhere but in George's native town, that is. The Providence critic was so severe that Cohan swore he would never play there again. And he didn't—not for six years. Cohan himself knew that he wouldn't live up to the threats and promises he made in the course of his frequent outbursts. His partner Harris caught him one day firing an actor, so enraged that he could scarcely talk. After the actor had effected his escape, Cohan turned to Harris and said, "Remind me, Sam, never to hire that such-and-such again—unless we absolutely need him."

After *Johnny Jones* Cohan enjoyed twelve years of almost uninterrupted glory. *Forty-Five Minutes from Broadway, The Talk of New York, Get-Rich-Quick Wallingford, The Little Millionaire, Seven Keys to Baldpate* followed one another in dizzying succession. George M. Cohan was the most popular figure in the American theatre. His mere appearance on a stage anywhere from Boston to Seattle was the signal for such an outburst as only a Frank Sinatra can achieve today. His proverbial generosity made him a veritable god in the eyes of young actors and actresses. One sick, down-and-out trouper sold advertising space in a book to promote funds to finance a cure in a Western sanitarium. "How much is half a page?" asked Cohan. "Fifty dollars," said the actor hopefully. Cohan wrote out a check, drawled, "Take care of yourself, kid." The check was for $10,000.

On January 31, 1914, after the final performance of *Broadway Jones* in Detroit, Cohan presented fifty percent of all of his varied interests to his mother and father. The day after America went to war in 1917, George Cohan sat down at his desk in Great Neck,

Long Island, and on two sheets of paper dashed off a song that was destined to become the greatest of his career. *Over There* was written in little over one hour. "All I wrote was a bugle call," said Cohan later. But it sold almost two million copies, eventually won him a Congressional medal. They're still looking for a song that can match it in the war that's going on today.

Over There marked the peak of George M. Cohan's career; from then on the sour notes began to mar the rhapsody. Cohan fought the actors' strike in 1919 tooth and nail; the scars that were left from that ill-advised fight never healed. He broke with Sam Harris; wrote and produced a succession of mediocre plays on his own. He scored acting triumphs in *Ah, Wilderness!* and *I'd Rather Be Right*, but his heart wasn't in his work. He quarreled with his associates, shunned the Broadway he had loved. "They don't seem to want my plays any more," he said once. "You have to give them filth these days or it's no good." In his eyes, Eugene O'Neill's chief claim to fame was that he was the son of "that grand old trouper, James O'Neill." He knew in his heart that the parade was passing him by, became infuriated when a critic called his work "corny." "Anything," he wrote, "that hasn't to do with West 52nd Street night life is 'corny' to those smart-alecks in their ready-made dinner suits. Gosh, how I hate that word!"

Ward Morehouse loved George M. Cohan very deeply; I have nothing but admiration for his having resisted the temptation to sugar-coat his biography (as was done in the recent motion picture of his life), and having dared to set down the damning facts with the laudatory ones. His book should—but probably won't—serve as a model for future life stories of American idols.

* * *

Howard Cullman, Broadway's most popular—and successful—play angel, has the annoying habit of calling his theatrical friends at nine in the morning—which is three hours, on the average, before their rising time. "Listen," expostulated Russel Crouse, "the only reason I got into this show business is because I like to sleep late." Cullman is a bearcat for efficiency. "He's a nice man," said his secretary, "but he wants everything done yesterday."

Cullman has developed a neat technique which may give executives who read these lines an idea. At eight-thirty sharp he calls his office and has his secretary read the mail to him over the phone. He dictates his answers before he hangs up. Recipients of these notes think "Jiminy cricket, but that Cullman is a ball of fire." Frequently the ball of fire has meanwhile turned over and peacefully gone back to sleep.

* * *

The latest riser of all, probably, in the playwriting fraternity, is Ferenc Molnar, Hungarian author of *Liliom* and *The Swan.* Molnar rarely stirs before one in the afternoon. He was summoned as a witness in a court action in Budapest one time, and when he saw that the case was called for nine in the morning he almost collapsed. Two servants finally got him out of bed and dressed on the day in question. As he left the house at eight-thirty, crowds of working people were passing on the way to their offices. "Good heavens," blinked Molnar in astonishment, "are *all* these people witnesses in that fool case?"

A compatriot of Molnar's in those carefree days was Alexander Inze, who later became the publisher of *Stage Magazine* in America. Inze loved the theatre from boyhood, but rarely could promote the price of a ticket. He developed the amiable habit of mingling with the audience in the lobby at the end of the first act of a play and slipping back into the theatre with them to catch the last two. Last year Gilbert Miller sent him the script of a play and asked for his opinion of it. "The latter part is fine," reported Inze, "but I don't think much of the first act." "What do you know about first acts?" chided Miller. "You never saw one in your life."

I met another debonair Budapest playwright at the once gay Donapalota Hotel there, dining with his current and very beautiful wife. "Which wife is this, my friend?" asked an unabashed companion. The playwright frowned in puzzlement, and turned to his bride. "Which one are you, darling?" he asked. "The fifth or the sixth?"

* * *

The first time that Grace Moore aired her voice professionally was for an agent of the old Aborn Opera Company. "The voice is O.K.," he opined. "Now lift your skirt, girlie, so I can see the legs." Miss Moore got the job. "Now that I look back on it," she reminisces, "I've had quite a bit of leg trouble. Managers seemed never to consider the voice as important as what there was below."

* * *

Harry Ruby, the famous song writer, hired a new cook the very day that a large dinner party was scheduled at his home. The cook spoiled the soup, the entree, and the dessert; only the meat course was even fit to be brought to the table. After the ladies had left for the powder room, a disconsolate butler appeared with liqueurs. "Tell me," Oscar Hammerstein inquired gently, "is it all right to take brandy on an empty stomach?"

* * *

Charles W. Couldock was a distinguished stage star some years ago. He was noted both for his excellence as an actor and for his personal irascibility. In one of his plays, the opening scene was between himself, another actor, and a third actor, who played Mr. Couldock's elderly father. One night the actor playing the elderly father didn't show up. The stage manager hastily put a long white beard on a super and seated him on a chair at the fireplace, telling him just to sit there and that he, the stage manager, would speak the lines from offstage through the fireplace. There was time only to tell Mr. Couldock that there was to be a different actor playing his father and to assure him that everything would be all right.

The stage manager rang up the curtain, then hurried down below the stage to reach the fireplace on the other side of the set. In his haste he ran into a beam and knocked himself unconscious. Over his head, the play progressed to the point where Couldock was asked how old his father was. Couldock answered: "I don't know exactly. I shall ask him." He went over to the bearded super and said, "Father, how old are you?" There was no answer. Couldock stared at him, ad-libbed a line about father's being a little deaf, kicked the super in the shins, swore at him under his breath, and repeated the question, "Father, how old are you?" Again the answer was complete silence.

Couldock marched down to the footlights and addressed the audience. "Ladies and gentlemen, my father is so goddam old he can't even talk."

* * *

Howard Dietz is publicity chief of Metro-Goldwyn-Mayer, as well as the author of such successful plays as *The Band Wagon*, *The Little Show,* and a half-dozen other top-notch musicals. One day Louis B. Mayer, head of MGM, complained that Dietz was giving too much time to outside activities. "Howard," he chided, "I think you're getting to your desk too late every morning." "But you seem to forget, Mr. Mayer," Dietz reminded him, "that I also leave very early every afternoon." By the time Mayer had figured it out, the crisis was over.

Howard Dietz and Arthur Schwartz once accepted a radio job that kept them turning out a new song every day for thirty-nine weeks. "Doesn't that take a lot out of you?" asked an interviewer. "Yes," said Dietz, "but it also takes a lot out of Bach, Beethoven, and Brahms."

Of the Hollywood columnist, Louella Parsons, Dietz once declared, "Lolly can spell everything but words. She has a magnificent sense of Reno and a sense of Yuma." His own title for L. B. Mayer is "czar of all the rushes." At a banquet presided over by the impeccable Lucius Beebe, replete with the richest foods and just the right rare vintages to go with them, Dietz made a sudden rush for the washroom. When he came back, still pale and shaken, he found the host regarding him with deep disapproval. "Everything is perfectly all right, Lucius," Dietz reassured him. "The white wine came up with the fish."

Chapter Two

BACK TO
THE HOLLYWOODS

THE GOLDWYN SAGA

O F ALL THE movie producers in Hollywood, the most famous is undoubtedly Samuel Goldwyn. Part of this fame he has achieved by a series of outstanding and notable productions, part by a collection of weird statements and a misuse of the English language. Some of the sayings are undoubtedly authentic; more of them are pure inventions by Hollywood wits like Howard Dietz and Jock Lawrence, who pinned remarks on Mr. Goldwyn that he probably hasn't heard to this day. Gradually he became a legend. So many people said that a book could be written about him that Alva Johnson actually undertook one. He called it *The Great Goldwyn;* it was serialized by the *Saturday Evening Post* and published by Random House.

Mr. Goldwyn demanded advance proofs. The *Post* editors got uppity and refused; Random House, all in the spirit of good, clean fun, did likewise. Lawrence, at that time Goldwyn's publicity

43

chief, phoned frantically from the Coast. "If there is one libelous word in that book," he threatened the publishers, "we're going to sue the *Post* for two million dollars, and you for one million." The book publishers declared that this was unfair discrimination; if the *Post* was going to be sued for two million, *they* wanted to be sued for two million also. Eventually, the book delighted Mr. Goldwyn so much that he distributed hundreds of copies to his friends. It developed, however, that Mr. Goldwyn's fame—like that of all picture producers and directors—was more or less limited to New York and Hollywood. Citizens at large seemed to care

The Nineteenth Century greets the Twentieth.
(left to right) Mrs. Malaprop, Mr. Goldwyn

only about the stars themselves. Countless booksellers in the South and Middle West asked the salesmen, "Who *is* this 'Great Goldwyn' anyhow?" When this fact was reported to Mr. G., he thought they were kidding him.

There follow a handful of the choice Goldwynisms. It is impossible to say how many of them actually sprang from the lips of Sam Goldwyn. For a time he was suspected of actually encouraging their manufacture and circulation. In those days, any kind of publicity was considered good publicity. Shrewd and intuitive character that he is, however, Goldwyn sensed that a new mantle of dignity and artistic consciousness was about to descend upon the cinema, and he began to disavow these tales in increasingly testy tones. Recently, upon reading a prediction on the future of Hollywood, signed by himself, in a Sunday supplement, he is said to have remarked indignantly, "This fellow has no idea of my literary style. Tell him to read the piece my last man wrote for me."

Mr. Goldwyn's most famous dicta undoubtedly are his "Gentlemen, kindly include me out," and the matchless "In two words I tell you my opinion of that picture: im-possible." In an argument over possession of a big star's services, a Paramount man suggested that the decision be left to arbitration. "O.K.," said Goldwyn reluctantly, "if it's understood that I get him."

Another time he called up L. B. Mayer, of MGM. "Louis," he said sadly, "both of us are in trouble." "How come?" asked Mayer. "It's this Clark Gable," said Goldwyn. "You got him; I want him." When he was introduced to Aldous Huxley he beamed, "I understand you are practically a genius." He counseled a friend, "Keep what I'm telling you under your belt." A cousin told him he had named his new baby William. "What did you do that for?" disapproved Goldwyn. "Every Tom, Dick, and Harry is named William." The first time he saw a sundial, and learned what it was, he murmured, "Tsk! Tsk! What won't they think of next!"

When Goldwyn's lovely wife, Frances, persuaded him to forsake movie-making long enough to sail to Hawaii for a vacation, a farewell party was whipped up in his honor at the studio. Every one of his employees was there. His press agent whispered in his ear, "They expect you to say a few words." Goldwyn cleared his throat, and the crowd fell silent. "Well, fellows," said Sam, "bon voyage!"

His secretary complained that the files had grown so cluttered that it was growing impossible to find anything. "At least," she begged, "let me destroy the letters that are ten years old or more." "O.K.," said Sam reluctantly, "but don't forget to make copies." He asked a newly signed actor where he hailed from. "Idaho," said the youngster. "Out here, young man," Goldwyn advised him, "we pronounce it Ohio."

Goldwyn loves to play games of any description, but he can't stand losing them. The money, obviously, does not trouble him, but he feels that a defeat at golf, or gin rummy, or backgammon is a slur on his ability that is too painful to bear. He took countless golf lessons without graduating from the duffer class. One day on the practice tee, he took a mighty swipe at the ball, and sent a low liner whistling down the fairway, to land *plunk* on the green two hundred and sixty yards away. Goldwyn gaped for a moment, then wheeled on the professional and demanded, "What did I do right?" On a round with Harpo Marx he was putting so abominably that at the sixth green he hurled his putter furiously into the woods. When he wasn't looking, Harpo sent his own caddy back to redeem the club. Harpo was putting like a streak that day. Several holes later Goldwyn asked him how he explained his new-found skill. "It's this new putter," Harpo told him. "It's balanced so delicately that the ball practically rolls into the hole by itself." Goldwyn tested it, approved—and bought back his own putter for ten dollars. At the end of the round, Harpo was thirty dollars ahead. "I'll match you double or nothing," said Sam grimly. He lost. That made it sixty. "One more," he demanded. He lost again. When the debt had risen to $960 Harpo begged off. "Look," he said, "I didn't come out here today to win all this money. I came out for eighteen holes of golf. Pay me the thirty dollars you lost on the game and let's call it quits." "That's very sporting of you," conceded Goldwyn. "Now I'll match you just once more: sixty or nothing."

In a bridge game, Goldwyn drew Connie Bennett as a partner against two experts. The men wanted to play for fifty cents a point, but Connie sagely declared that her limit was a penny. Goldwyn volunteered to carry her. That meant that he was play-ing for ninety-nine cents a point. Everything went reasonably well until one hand when, with both sides vulnerable, the man at Goldwyn's right bid "one heart." Goldwyn, in a voice that spoke volumes, said "I pass." The third man also passed. Connie said "one spade." "Two hearts," declared the first bidder. "I pass," said Goldwyn a little more loudly. Connie went to two spades; the man next to her bid three hearts. "I pass," Goldwyn virtually shouted. Eventually Miss Bennett bid four spades, was doubled, and went down four tricks—eleven hundred points. Goldwyn was apoplectic. As the last card was played, he leaped to his feet, pounded on the table, and screamed at his partner: "Damn it, couldn't you HEAR me keeping quiet?"

Many years ago, George Oppenheimer assured Goldwyn, then his employer, that *The Wizard of Oz* would make a fine motion picture, and finally persuaded him to read the book. It is a juvenile, consisting of about a hundred and fifty pages of very big type. The next morning Goldwyn was enthusiastic. "I sat up till two reading it," he said as he disappeared into his office. A day later he summoned George. "You're ruining my whole social life with that book," he declared. "I was up till past midnight again with it." "Well," said George eagerly, "what do you think?" "I'm not sure yet," Goldwyn answered. "I'm only half through with it so far." He eventually bought the story, kept it on the shelf for years, and then sold it at a small profit to MGM, whose not too imaginative version of it netted millions and made a star of Judy Garland.

A lesser effort on the Goldwyn schedule was made in his absence. The night he returned, the director brought it to his house to run it through for him on his private machine. Goldwyn sat through the picture glumly, and declared at its conclusion, "It's terrible. I myself don't know what it's all about, and if I don't know what it's about, what do you think the moving picture audience will make of it?" "Maybe you don't understand it," said the mortified director, "but I'll bet your twelve-year-old son would." "We'll prove it," cried Sam, and called his boy down from his studies while the picture was run off again. "Well, son, did you understand it?" said Goldwyn confidently, but his jaw dropped when the answer came, "Of course, I understood it. It's simple as A B C!" The director's triumph was short-lived. Goldwyn wheeled on him angrily and demanded, "What do you think I'm doing in this business? Making pictures for twelve-year-olds?"

Goldwyn's nerve sometimes reaches awe-inspiring proportions. Dining at the house of a famous playwright, he declared that in all of his hectic Hollywood career, not one person ever had had occasion to sue him. His host felt obliged to remind him that two of the five gentlemen present (one being himself) were suing him at that very moment. "Present company," said Sam blandly, "is excepted." He has created more stars than any other producer because he is willing to risk millions on a brand-new personality. One of his recent pictures, for instance, called *Up in Arms*, featured Danny Kaye, a stage favorite in the key cities but virtually unknown to movie audiences. Goldwyn gambled over two million dollars on the production, and cashed in handsomely, because Kaye was a sensational hit.

One time he stubbed his toe with a foreign beauty named Anna Sten. Goldwyn starred her in a version of Zola's *Nana* and lost a fortune on the venture. Some time previously he had signed a new director and assured him, "I don't want 'yes men' around me. I want you to 'no' me once in a while—even if it costs you your job." This intrepid soul took him at his word, told him the script of *Nana* was terrible and Miss Sten was miscast, and refused to have anything to do with the project. Goldwyn fired him. For years thereafter, if anybody suggested that this director be used on another picture, Goldwyn would shake his head vigorously, and declare, "No, *sir!* That man was connected with my greatest failure."

Goldwyn wants top-flight men working for him and will pay any price to get them. He is responsible for the presence of some of the world's greatest authors in Hollywood. He hired Louis Bromfield at a huge salary, greeted him upon his arrival with, "It's good to have you with us, Mr. Bloomberg." One of his earliest importations was Maurice Maeterlinck. "I know you don't understand picture technique," Goldwyn assured him. "You don't have to. Just go home and write your greatest book over in the form of a scenario. I don't care how long it takes you." Some weeks later Maeterlinck came back with a finished script. "Now

we'll see something," beamed Goldwyn, and took it into his sanctum sanctorum. Two minutes later he rushed out tearing his hair.
"My God," he screamed. "The hero is a bee!"

I hope that all of the foregoing stories have not deceived you
about Samuel Goldwyn's ability to make outstanding and profit-
able motion pictures. For years he has been a lone wolf in Hollywood, the one big producer who never had to go to a bank to pull
him out of trouble. He has blazed many a new trail in a community where innovations are far and few between, and every penny
that went into his costly experiments was his own. He is a stickler
for detail, and spares neither time nor expense to make the tiniest
prop authentic, the most fleeting shot exact. Most of the people
who scream loudest against him end up by coming back to work
for him. In his fashion, he plays the game straight; as long as he
continues to turn out such screen classics as *Wuthering Heights*,
Arrowsmith, *Stella Dallas*, *Street Scene*, and *The Little Foxes*, his
envious competitors will know only too well that there's Samuel
Goldwyn in them thar Beverly Hills.

* * *

Hollywood has lifted eyebrows over the marriage of Victor
Moore, the 67-year-old comedian, to a girl of 22. "What's wrong
with that?" queried Buddy de Sylva. "When she is 100, he will
only be 145."

* * *

This is an incident that could happen only in Hollywood. A
zealous policewoman bagged three frowsy gypsy fortune-tellers,
herded them into a squad car, and laughed merrily while they
predicted disaster for her. The sun shone brightly through the
evidence, a sizable crystal ball, and set fire to the upholstery and
her crisp new uniform.

Possibly the police lady has grounds for a sibyl suit.

* * *

Somebody asked Bob Hope what went through his mind when he got his original view of Dorothy Lamour in a sarong. "I never gave it a second thought," he averred. "I was too busy with the first one."

* * *

Van Cartmell tells the story of a housewife who asked a little grocery boy his name. "Humphrey," answered the boy, and added that the last name was Bogart. "Humphrey Bogart, eh?" said the housewife. "That's a pretty well-known name." "It darn well ought to be," the boy agreed. "I've been delivering groceries in this neighborhood for four years."

* * *

W. C. Fields is certainly the greatest juggler in the world, and some folks will swear he's the greatest comedian too. His real name is Claude William Dukenfeld, which he signs to an original scenario every now and then just for the hell of it. He was born in Philadelphia, but ran away from home when he was eleven. Some very tough years followed. "I was a big city Huck Finn," he says. Constant colds and hacking coughs gave him his husky and rasping voice, repeated punches in the nose from older and heavier aggressors swelled and reddened his proboscis to an extraordinary degree. These two characteristics have become a sort of trademark; he keeps them up to snuff with frequent libations of Irish whiskey, a liquid to which he is not allergic. A lad came to see him last year who declared he was a long-lost son. Fields was skeptical, but asked him in. "Drink?" he inquired. "Coca-Cola," said the lad. Fields ejected him with a roar of rage. "An obvious impostor," he explained. Another time he returned from four weeks of location work in a town that was bone-dry. "Can you imagine me subsisting all those days," he marveled, "on nothing but food and water?"

Fields' first professional job was a combination of juggler and drowner at an Atlantic City beer joint. When business slackened, he would dive into the briny, and be saved just as he was going down for the third time. The crowd was expected to order beer and wienies while the waiting emergency squad restored him to consciousness. One July Fourth he "drowned" seven times.

His first great hit on Broadway was scored in the Ziegfeld Follies. He did a combination juggling-and-hokum act with a trick

billiard table that simply defies description, and that would bring just as many howls of laughter today as it did then. One night Fields got a laugh where he didn't expect it. Upon investigation, he found Ed Wynn hiding under the table, mugging at the audience. Fields, whose temper was not improved by his years of hobo camps and slow freights, hauled off and conked Wynn with a billiard cue. The crowd roared appreciatively, and laughed again every time Wynn clasped his sore head and moaned in agony. Fields calmly continued with his act, and later suggested that they include the routine every night. Wynn never butted into his number again.

"When I was a tot," confessed Fields, "I swore that if I ever got in the chips, I'd help kids who were homeless waifs like I had been. For years I couldn't afford it. Then came Hollywood and riches." "Did you start a foundation as you had planned?" asked a girl interviewer eagerly. "No," said Fields, "I'm afraid I didn't. I said to myself, 'To hell with them.'"

Every time Fields goes to the theatre he writes a note to the house manager. It reads, "My wife and I will be in your theatre tomorrow evening. We will occupy seats number G-108 and 110, where my wife will lose a pair of white silk gloves."

* * *

Edgar Bergen tells about an old ventriloquist who had no Charlie McCarthy to turn his act into a headliner. In fact, he became so convinced that there was no future for the act he had been presenting for years that he decided to set up shop as a crystal-gazer in Hollywood, a mecca, he had been told, for cultists and mesmerizers of every description. Business, unfortunately, was virtually nonexistent in his new stand, and when one morning an uncertain young woman, dressed in black, appeared upon the scene, he determined that she should have the works. "Can you put me into communication with my dead husband George?" she inquired. "You bet I can," promised the ventriloquist, and the young lady thereupon had such a satisfactory conversation with George that, instead of paying the five-dollar fee requested, she insisted on paying ten. "This is mighty white of you, lady, mighty white," he said. "And to show my appreciation, the next time you converse with your dead husband George, by golly, I'll drink a glass of water at the same time."

* * *

In Hollywood, where many a benighted soul has been coasting along on a three-thousand-dollar-a-week salary on Friday night, only to find himself out on his ear on Saturday morning, names are painted on the outside of office doors in a substance that can be scraped off very easily. Mr. A's office today may be Mr. B's tomorrow, and Mr. C's a week from Tuesday.

When Dorothy Parker was first assigned her own little cubicle in a writers' studio her fame was not yet universal, and not a soul dropped in to see her for days on end. Panting for company, Miss Parker took steps one evening after the other hired help had departed. First she scratched the "Dorothy Parker" off her door. Then she replaced it with the simple legend, "Gents' Room." The next day her problem was solved.

Gene Fowler suffered from the opposite complaint: too many visitors barged into his private office to exchange quips and keep him from work. The sign *he* painted outside his door read "Horace Witherspoon, Jr.: Famous Polish Impersonator." Nobody came near him for weeks.

* * *

Cecil B. De Mille once produced a motion picture allegedly based on E. Arnot Robertson's story of the Indo-Chinese jungle, *Four Frightened People*. The star was Claudette Colbert. De Mille took the author to a preview. "How did you like it?" he asked when the lights went on again. Miss Robertson reflected a moment. "Mr. De Mille," she said slowly, "do you remember the roar of an off-stage lion that came in somewhere about reel three? Well, I do believe that you took that straight from my story."

* * *

Jesse Lasky has been toying with the idea of filming a life of James Audubon with Errol Flynn slated to play the noted ornithologist. "Audubon," said Lasky, "often pursued a specimen for weeks." "You sure picked the right man to play him," said a friend.

* * *

One of the Glamour Colony's greatest stars gave a party last year for the crème de la crème. White ties, strapless gowns, and all the emeralds and sables in town. At the height of the festivities, a well-known agent weaved in, dressed in shapeless slacks and plastered to the gills. The hostess froze and remarked acidly that she did not remember inviting him. "Not only did you not invite me, but I *declined*," he replied, and fell on his face.

* * *

Two agents sat together watching a preview of an important picture. One happened to be the agent for the male star of the piece, the other for the female lead. They sat silently while several reels were unwound and then one nudged the other in the ribs. "Look at those two hams up there," he said with some disgust, "getting eighty percent of our dough."

* * *

Another agent story concerns a flourishing coast agency named Feitlebaum & Garfinkel. One morning Feitlebaum came to Garfinkel and explained that he was sick and tired of his cumbersome and harsh-sounding name. "With your permission," he explained, "I have changed my name this morning to O'Brien." Garfinkel said nothing, but a few mornings later he came to his partner with the declaration that he too was tired of the name he had been bearing all his life. "With your permission," he said, "I have also changed my name to O'Brien." Thereupon, the old sign was taken down and a resplendent new one, reading "O'Brien & O'Brien," was put up in its place. A few mornings later the telephone rang and a voice demanded to be connected with Mr. O'Brien. "Very good, sir," said the cheery-voiced operator, "but which Mr. O'Brien do you want: Feitlebaum or Garfinkel?"

* * *

A few years ago a new edition of Thackeray's *Henry Esmond* was published in the Modern Library series. To the amazement of the editors, there arrived a letter some days later from a prominent Hollywood agency addressed to William Makepeace Thackeray, Esq. It read as follows:

"We have read your recent book *The History of Henry Esmond, Esq.* and believe it possesses material adaptable for motion pictures.

"We are recognized agents for writers at all studios and as such would like to represent you in the sale of both your own personal services and your literary products.

"In the event you have already made a commitment to some agent for the above book, we nevertheless are impressed with your potential possibilities as a screen writer and would be interested in both your services and future stories.

"We would appreciate your advising us by return mail whether or not you are represented here in Hollywood; and in the event that you are not and desire us to represent you, we would be happy to forward to you a copy of our agency agreement with writers for your information and guidance."

A busy publisher always has time to enter into the spirit of an affair of this sort, so the following note was promptly sent back:

"Thank you for your letter telling me that you believe that my recent book, *The History of Henry Esmond*, possesses material adaptable
for motion pictures. This effort is a rather crude attempt, I fear, but
I am now working on a new novel which I think will be a natural for
pictures. I am thinking of calling the new book *Vanity Fair*.

"I will be interested in hearing what you think of this title.

> Sincerely yours,
> William Makepeace Thackeray"

Three days later another letter arrived from the agency:

"Acknowledging receipt of your letter of December 28, in reply to
our previous communication, we feel that the title which you are
thinking of giving your new book, namely *Vanity Fair*, is a good one.
We would greatly appreciate receiving a manuscript on this story. Perhaps you could also send us a manuscript at this time, or if not, a copy
of the book, *The History of Henry Esmond*.

"We would like to submit this, if we are authorized to do so by
you, to the studios for their consideration."

There the matter rests.

* * *

When Gloria Swanson's mama heard that she had married a
titled gent in Paris, she hastily phoned her lawyer. "What's a
markee?" she demanded. "It's one of those things," he explained,
"that you hang in front of a theatre to keep the rain off customers." "My God!" cried the good lady. "Gloria married one of them
this afternoon!"

* * *

Major studios register new titles for contemplated productions
with the Hays office, which promptly reports any conflicts with
previous registrations. When the Fox organization recently announced its picture based on the life of President Wilson, titled,
with unusual simplicity, *Woodrow Wilson*, the Hays office dutifully reported that it had on file one title that might conflict. It
was Mark Twain's *Pudd'nhead Wilson*.

* * *

"THE BEARD"

THERE WAS a time about ten or fifteen years ago when the most famous beard in the literary world adorned the countenance of a reasonably distinguished Irish critic who could be heard pontificating practically any afternoon near the bar of whatever publisher's cocktail party chanced to be in progress. He would stroke his beard with a gentle and tentative gesture comparable to a movie star milking a cow for a publicity photograph, and emote at length on any subject from Abyssinia to Zoroaster. One unkind critic hinted that the beard concealed a pocket-size encyclopedia; another, more acidulous, withered him one day with, "What you need, my man, is a good shave. You look like an armpit."

At any rate, the fame of this critic's beard was long ago eclipsed by that of Monty Woolley, Yale professor, bon vivant, wit, and motion-picture star, whose whiskers are his trademark and have been impressed in the pavement of Grauman's Chinese Theatre alongside Charlie Chaplin's shoes and Betty Grable's legs. Woolley was one of the guests at a Cole Porter party some years ago where the composer introduced a new number he had written called "Miss Otis Regrets She's Unable to Lunch Today, Madam." The burden of this lugubrious chant concerned an urgent appointment that Miss Otis had with the public hangman, necessitating a complete curtailment of her social activities. Woolley fell passionately in love with the song and sang it constantly at every party he attended for the next year. He sang it so well, in fact, that people began to suspect he was wasting his time at Yale. He was talked into a substantial part in a musical comedy called *On Your Toes* where he held his own against such accomplished show-stealers as Ray Bolger and Louella Gear, and then really reached the heights when Kaufman and Hart had the happy inspiration to cast him as Alexander Woollcott in *The Man Who Came to Dinner*. He played the part in Hollywood, too, and will probably be there from now on.

Woolley is reported to have summoned his butler one morning (this story is also credited sometimes to J. S. Bache) and said, "I'd like to know what my household expenses really amount to out here. If you will be good enough to leave out of the bills your rake-off on food, liquor, laundry, gasoline, and God knows what else, I will be happy to add it to your salary at the end of the month." "Mr. Woolley," said the butler gravely, "you couldn't afford it."

On one of his visits to New York between pictures, Woolley gave a party for his old friends. It was a very formal affair, and Woolley didn't consider it amusing at all when Cole Porter showed up with a bearded lady from the circus as his escort. Porter listened to Woolley's remonstrances for a moment, then turned to the bearded lady and remarked, "Madam, your son has atrocious manners."

At a bond rally in Hartford, Woolley sat toying with his famous beard, next to a prominent lady author, waiting for his turn to address the assemblage. Suddenly he belched. The lady author gave him a horrified look. Woolley bridled. "And what did you expect, my good woman?" he inquired. "Chimes?"

Woolley was so pleased with this line that he insisted it be written into his next role in Hollywood.

* * *

There is a coterie in Hollywood that plays the game of hearts for very high stakes. The card to avoid in this game is the queen of spades, and when one evening Mr. Rufus Lemaire was caught with it four hands running, he accused his friends of unfair discrimination, and sticking him on purpose. The very next hand he got the queen of spades again. He jumped out of his chair, cried, "I will never enter this house again," and stamped angrily out into the night. He was back ten minutes later, however, looking rather sheepish. It was his house.

Lemaire was host at a buffet supper another evening. The servants had forgotten to pass napkins. "It's on account of the war shortages," Oscar Levant explained. "Instead of napkins, from time to time a woolly dog will pass among you."

* * *

Mankiewicz en riposte

One of the sharpest and most unsparing wits in Hollywood is that of Herman Mankiewicz, the writer. "You are a composer after my own heart," he once told Sigmund Romberg. "You write the kind of music people whistle as they go *into* the theatre." A friend burst into his house and reported the sale of an original script for five thousand dollars. Mank turned to his wife and commanded, "Dance for the gentleman." In a poker game he told Harry Ruby, "There are two ways I always can tell when you have a good hand: your face lights up, and you play it wrong." He also told Ruby, "You look like a dishonest Abe Lincoln." "It's conditioned my whole life," admits Ruby. "I'm afraid to sit in a box at theatre." Mank is also credited with summing up a producer's career as "Poland to polo in two generations." He says, however, that the phrase was coined by Irving Caesar.

Mankiewicz's own game of bridge is on the sketchy side. Playing with George Kaufman one evening, he butchered a hand inexcusably. "When did you learn this game, Mank?" asked Kaufman. "Now don't tell me it was this afternoon. I want to know what *time* this afternoon."

* * *

Triumph of tact: Miss Marlene Dietrich had her picture taken, and fumed at the result. "I can't understand it," she said. "The last time I posed for you, the photographs were heavenly." "Ah, yes," sighed the camera man, "but you must remember that I was eight years younger then."

* * *

Two of the best-known motion-picture magnates in Hollywood are Louis B. Mayer, of MGM, and his talented and headstrong son-in-law, David Selznick. The Selznicks were in New York on the day that the President suggested a $25,000 ceiling for executives' salaries. "Golly," said Mrs. Selznick, "I wish we were in California this evening so we could hear papa holler." "Just open the window," suggested her husband. "You can probably hear him from here."

Chapter Three

THE LITERARY LIFE

DOROTHY THOMPSON, most overpowering and awe-inspiring female commentator in America, was anything but that when she first met Sinclair Lewis at a dinner party in Berlin. Lewis was so enchanted that in the middle of the dinner he leaned past a couple of startled guests and asked her to marry him.

They spent their honeymoon on a trailer trip through Britain. Later Adolf Hitler personally ordered Miss Thompson bounced out of Nazi Germany, an indignity for which she has never forgiven him.

The Lewises had a tranquil married life until Miss Thompson became so engrossed in column-writing, lecturing, radio work, and general reshaping of the world that she had no time left for anything else. Somebody asked "Red" Lewis where she was one evening. "She disappeared into the NBC Studios three years ago,"

answered Red, "and nobody has seen her since." Another time he heard that she was being mentioned for a presidential nomination. "I wonder," he said wistfully, "if they'll let me write 'My Day.'"

Heywood Broun wrote that Miss Thompson was greater than Eliza. "She not only crosses the ice but she breaks it as she goes. What's more, she's her own bloodhound."

Miss Thompson is quite ready to fight for her beliefs. A female patron of a famous East Side café made a couple of cracks in favor of the Nazis in her presence; Miss Thompson marched her outside and nailed her one on the button. She attended the disgraceful Bund rally at Madison Square Garden and gave them the old Bronx cheer until they got her out—with the aid of the police. That took guts.

It's a lucky thing for a certain bookseller in Louisville, Kentucky, that Miss Thompson never heard his comment when a Houghton Mifflin salesman showed him an advance copy of her newest book. "Dorothy Thompson. Let's see now," he mused. "Wasn't she the principal character in that show called *Rain?*"

* * *

One of the colossal nuisances of the publishing industry is the annual taking of inventory. Books are scattered among a dozen warehouses, binderies, branch depositories, and the various departments of the publisher's office itself. Each title, of course, must be tabulated separately. During the course of the year, hundreds of odd copies are given away to visitors—or filched—without review slips being made out. If the individual totals come out within a hundred copies each of the indicated records, everybody is reasonably satisfied.

All this is a preamble to a tale about the final day of inventory-taking at a downtown publisher's plant. The pair who were tabulating the figures waited until Saturday to count the books in the president's private office. The president himself was out counting strokes in every bunker on the Creek Club course. On Monday morning he bustled in bright and early (ten-thirty) and was mildly astonished to find the inventory records scattered on the floor of his inner sanctum. All of the figures were in apple-pie order except the notations on the last page. This was headed "president's office." The first notation read: "One set Encyclopædia Britannica; one Roget's Thesaurus; one Fannie Hill; one unopened bottle of Scotch." A wavering cross had been drawn through these lines and a second notation added that listed the same books, but concluded with the item, "one-*half* bottle of Scotch." This, too, had been scratched out, however, with a series of blotches and hieroglyphics, and one last line recorded in barely legible penmanship. It read: "One revolving encyclopædia."

* * *

An advanced student of literature unearthed from *Spicy Western Stories* a gem that read: "She was silent a long time. He could smell the perfume wafted upward from between her proud breasts, placed so cleverly on the lobes of her ears." *The New Yorker* snapped it up, of course, and added the perfect comment: "Novel, but we wouldn't like it as a steady thing."

* * *

Some years ago, the Hotel Ambassador played host to the first International Crossword Puzzle Tournament. This was a purely spontaneous affair and the fact that the entire executive board of Simon and Schuster and the publishers of Webster's Dictionary happened to be buzzing around was purely coincidental. The winnah and undisputed champeen turned out to be a legal gentleman named William Stern, who was not quite prepared for the prize that rewarded his great effort. It was one of those walloping big dictionaries that should come equipped with their own electric hoisting machines. The chairman managed to deposit it in Mr. Stern's outstretched hands. Mr. Stern thereupon fell flat on his face, closely followed by the chairman. The defeated contestants cheered mightily.

* * *

Harold Ross, editor of *The New Yorker*, once tried to stop private telephone calls in his office and went so far as to install a public coin booth in the reception room. The next morning he found the booth torn loose from its roots, on its back in his own

Harold Ross (right)

private office. Stretched out inside it, a calla lily clutched in his hand and a wreath on his head, lay James Thurber. When Ross once complained, "Thurber's women don't have any sex appeal," Marc Connelly reminded him, "They do for Thurber's men."

Thurber's definition of humor will do until a better one comes along: "Humor is a kind of emotional chaos told about calmly and quietly in retrospect."

* * *

When Simon and Schuster published a book called *The Ten Commandments*, somebody suggested that it be one of the publications of the Armed Services paper-bound books intended for men in the services abroad. "It is much too long," opined one director. "Wait a minute," urged Philip Van Doren Stern, who was originally trained by Simon and Schuster. "How about using only five of them and calling it *A Treasury of the World's Best Commandments*?"

HEYWOOD BROUN (1888–1939)

H EYWOOD BROUN died in 1939. The multitude of friends who loved and admired him from the bottom of their hearts find it hard to believe that it's as long as that since they saw him shambling into his favorite haunts, sloppily attired, tardy for appointments, but welcomed with shouts of joy wherever he appeared. His name bobs up in conversations as frequently as though he were still alive, turning in his daily columns. And what columns the doings of these past years would have inspired in him! By a stroke of cruel irony, the space they once occupied was turned over to the outpourings of Westbrook Pegler, who represents everything Broun detested most. "The trouble with Peg," he explained once, "is that he was bitten early in life by an income tax."

Broun's classmates at Harvard included John Reed, Walter Lippmann, and Hamilton Fish—an omen, possibly, of the later conflicts between his political convictions and his sybaritic personal habits. Foreign languages were his nemesis. An irate German professor shied an inkwell at him, but missed. His habit of fulfilling assignments at the last possible moment, if at all, failed to enchant the Harvard authorities, and he was not graduated. His classmates watched in awe while he threw all of his belongings helter-skelter into a trunk, and then climbed in himself and trampled them down after the fashion of a Burgundy grape-presser.

Broun got a job with the *Tribune*, and turned in some of the greatest baseball and football stories that have ever been written. Then he was transferred to the drama department. The day of the transfer, he acted as official scorer at a Giant-Cub ball game in the afternoon, and covered Ethel Barrymore's opening in an Edna Ferber play called *Our Mrs. McChesney* in the evening. At the

ball game, he scored a close play as an error for the visiting short-stop, thereby depriving the Giant batter of a base hit in the records. That evening, he roasted Miss Barrymore's performance to a fare-thee-well. The next day the *Tribune's* managing editor received two indignant communications. One, from the Giant batsman, read, "What's the big idea of sending a lousy dramatic critic up here to be official scorer?" The other, signed by Miss Barrymore, concluded, "How dare you assign a cheap baseball reporter to cover the opening of a Barrymore play?"

Broun loved the theatre, and the majority of his reviews were gentle and encouraging. One evening, however, an actor named Geoffrey Steyne gave a performance that displeased him. Broun allowed that Mr. Steyne was the worst actor on the American stage. Mr. Steyne sued. The whole principle of dramatic criticism was at stake in this suit; if the actor won it, obviously, a dangerous precedent would have been established. The case was dismissed, and it remained only to see what Heywood would say about Mr. Steyne on the occasion of his next New York appearance. The big night finally arrived, and the next morning initiates turned eagerly to Broun's review. He did not so much as mention Geoffrey Steyne until the last sentence of his last paragraph. This read simply, "Mr. Steyne's performance was not up to his usual standard."

Heywood was a war correspondent in France in 1918. General Pershing saw him in uniform and asked him if he had fallen into a ditch. A fellow worker once dubbed him "Six Characters in Search of a Laundry." Heywood usually forgot to put laces in his shoes. When he took them off for bowling—which he loved—he disclosed socks with such enormous holes that they looked like ankle supporters. His first wife, Ruth Hale, was just as careless as Heywood. The first time I visited their home, a step in the back staircase was broken; three years later it had not been repaired. Everybody just hopped over it, while Ruth would remark placidly, "Somebody's going to break his neck on that step some day." I had come to collect an introduction for a book that Heywood had promised to deliver some two months previously. He wrote it while I waited. Then we lunched together in his kitchen. We vaulted the broken step, and found that the icebox contained a single can of peaches. Heywood punctured the lid with a beer opener, and emptied the peaches into two saucers that he salvaged from a pile of dirty dishes in the sink. We ate standing up.

When Dorothy Parker and Beatrice Kaufman visited the Broun Home Front, Mrs. K. is reported to have discovered a couple of deep brown, bedraggled old toothbrushes hanging in the bathroom. "Good heavens," she cried, "what are those things?" "Don't you recognize them?" said the ever-helpful Miss Parker. "Those are the broomsticks the witches ride on every Hallowe'en."

The last tenant of the Brouns was Ed McNamara, who plays every Irish cop role in Hollywood. "Mac," Heywood told him, "it's a shame that with a rich, resonant voice like yours, you don't ever know what the hell you're talking about!" One night Mac came home to discover his trunk on the doorstep, and a note from Heywood written on the tag. "Dear Mac," it read, "I forgot to tell you that I sold the house."

In 1921, Heywood joined the staff of the morning *World*, where he became scared to death of the editor, Herbert Bayard Swope. Years later, although they now were close friends and met night after night at various people's houses, he still held Swope—not to mention Swope's wife, Margaret—in something like awe. When Winston Churchill's son, Randolph, wangled a job on the *World* at the tender age of eighteen, and called Swope "Herbert" the day he joined the staff, Heywood practically dropped in his tracks.

Some of Heywood's quips at this time are still quoted and collected in anthologies. The depression had not yet come along to toughen our fibre and sharpen our consciousness of social inequalities; everybody drifted along in a happy haze of bathtub gin and Wall Street profits. Heywood lost more money at poker games and the race track in a single day than he had had to his name a few years previous. At a Bankhead opening, he whispered into the star's ear, "Don't look now, Tallulah, but your show's slipping!" Invited to a poker game by Ring Lardner, he reported over the telephone, "I can't come, Ring. It's my son Woodie's night out, and I've got to stay home with the nurse." He made a disparaging statement about a fight manager in Syracuse. "You wouldn't dare come up here and repeat that," taunted the Upstater. Broun answered, "I'll be up there and say it next Friday at half-past five." "And were you?" asked the man to whom Broun was telling the story. "Of course not!" he replied. At the Baer-Carnera fight, Grantland Rice remarked, "Golly, that big fellow sure can take it." "Yeah," answered Broun, "but he doesn't seem to know what to do with it." On the day that Babe Ruth smacked out two home runs in a World Series game, and contributed a couple of sparkling catches as well, Broun's account began, "The Ruth is mighty and shall prevail."

Heywood's dawning preoccupation with the class struggle manifested itself clearly in the Sacco-Vanzetti case in 1927. He regarded the execution of these two men as a flagrant miscarriage of justice and he wrote two burning and devastating columns about the case that belong with the great pieces of invective of all time. Ralph Pulitzer of the *World* asked him to write no more on this controversial subject, and Broun staged a one-man strike. Swope patched up the quarrel, but two years later, the wound still rankled, and Heywood accepted a fabulous offer from Roy Howard of the *Telegram*. This was when Broun first began to tell us, "You can't sit on the fence much longer. It's time to choose your side for keeps." Events of recent years have been his vindication. Referring to one fence-straddling commentator, Heywood remarked, "His mind is so open that the wind whistles through it. Nothing sticks. He's afraid to stay on any side if self-aggrandizement beckons to the other." Heywood knew an appeaser when he saw one—years before any of us had occasion to use the word.

The last years of Heywood's life were devoted principally to the organization and promotion of the American Newspaper Guild. His customary carelessness disappeared like magic when he embraced this cause; newspapermen will never forget what he did to improve their pay and working conditions. Heywood respected all labor unions. It was against his principles to cross a picket line. One noon, however, the waiters at his favorite hangout were out on strike, and Heywood, lost in thought, passed the pickets. "Mr. Broun," said one of the waiters reproachfully, "we're on strike." "Tell me who your favorite customer is," said Broun contritely, "and I'll write him a letter and tell him to stay away." The waiter replied, "Why, you are, Mr. Broun." Heywood stormed into the restaurant, sent out luncheon to the pickets, and effected a settlement of the strike on the spot. He didn't know until much later that the proprietors had been dying to settle for days, and awaited only some face-saving device to get them out of an embarrassing situation. At the height of the celebration, Broun cried, "My God, I'm due at a meeting of the Book-of-the-Month Club judges!" and rushed out, leaving behind, as usual, the galleys that were to be the subject of discussion that day. The other judges can't remember one occasion when Heywood arrived at a meeting on time.

Over Thanksgiving week-end in 1938, the Averell Harrimans were hosts to a gathering of sixty at their estate in Arden. The house is located at the top of a steep hill. Heywood looked down from the summit and recalled that the year the house was built, he had eluded the guards at the outer gate, and crawled up the hill, intent on getting an exclusive interview with the ailing Edward H. Harriman, of the Union Pacific. He was caught the moment he emerged from the shrubbery, however, and hustled down to the bottom again. "Today," said Heywood, ruefully considering his build, "it's all I can do to get up the hill in an automobile." That evening, Heywood was very late to dinner. "I was down in the kitchen," he explained cheerfully to Averell Harriman, "trying to persuade the butler to strike for higher wages."

This was the week-end that Broun and Swope decided to crossexamine Duff Cooper, another of the distinguished guests. We all gathered round expectantly, and Swope asked the first question, which Broun promptly answered—at considerable length. Then Broun essayed a query, which Swope answered. It gradually dawned on us that the interview was destined to be an exclusive dialogue between Swope and Broun. Their rhetoric flowed on, while Duff Cooper sat blinking in complete silence, like a tortoise with lumbago. Later he confided to a friend that we were the rudest people he had ever met.

Two years later, we all spent another Thanksgiving with the Harrimans in Arden—all, that is, but Heywood, who was dead, and Quent Reynolds, who was reporting the Blitz from London. Swope proposed a toast that night to the two who were absent. "One," he said, "is in Heaven, and the other is in Hell."

Heywood had a genius for discovering strange methods of throwing his money away. Once he ran for Congress on the Socialist ticket. Another time he edited a local newspaper called the

Connecticut Nutmeg. His greatest extravagance was a play called *Shoot the Works,* which he wrote, financed, and appeared in personally. Indirectly, this play provided him with the greatest happiness in his life. One of the girls in the chorus was named Connie Madison, and Heywood adored her at sight. They were married in 1935. She spruced him up almost beyond recognition. Heywood's friends accepted Connie without qualification the first time they met her. George Kaufman gave her a part in *Merrily We Roll Along.* She crossed the stage once, and had a single line which read, "I wouldn't dare bob my hair. My father would throw me out." Broun, in his review, remarked, "Miss Madison was adequate."

* * *

The technical term for the transposition of letters or sounds in a word, or series of words, is metathesis, but the more familiar designation is "Spoonerism." The Rev. W. A. Spooner, Warden of New College, Oxford, achieved this dubious claim to fame when he announced to his congregation: "Let us now sing the hymn 'Kinquering congs their titles take.' " Another time he caused a mild commotion in church by demanding "Is this pie occupewed?" A radio announcer created two classics of his own when he referred to New Juinea gungles instead of New Guinea jungles, and topped it with slote flulo for flute solo. Emily Wedge of Baltimore's famous Enoch Pratt Library quotes a gentleman who declared, "My wife says I have had tee many martoonis, but I am not so much under the alfluence of incohol as some pinkle theep. I mean *thinkle peep.*"

* * *

W. Somerset Maugham urged a young friend of his to try his hand at writing a book. "But I haven't anything to write about," demurred the young man. "My boy," said Maugham, "that is the most inconclusive reason for not writing that I have ever heard."

* * *

A charming but long-winded professor spent a full hour outlining a project for a major opus to Alfred Knopf. The latter listened in growing impatience and, when he was finally able to get a word in edgewise, he propelled the professor firmly to the door, and said, "Why don't you get all this down in a written outline? Then submit it to me, and we'll consider it carefully at the next editorial meeting." "Why, Mr. Knopf," said the professor reproachfully, "what are you talking about? I have been describing a project for which you gave me a contract, and a two-thousand-dollar advance, seven years ago."

* * *

Whit Burnett, the editor of *Story Magazine,* was opening a pile of manuscripts one morning when a note fluttered out of one of the manila envelopes. "Dear Editor," it read, "you will find me a combination of Hemingway, O'Neill, Faulkner, and Saroyan, with a certain something peculiarly my own added for good measure." "This lad's father," grunted Whit, "must have been an anthology."

The Burnett son and heir has been exposed to writers and writers' shop-talk exclusively since birth. The garbage man found him alone in the kitchen once and said, "Hi, sonny! Whatcha got to say for yourself?" The little boy eyed him gravely and answered, "Have you finished your novel yet?"

Burnett had a young editorial assistant who had a Harvard accent but little else to offer, and was slightly overpaid at fifteen dollars a week. At the end of a day's work, he stopped Burnett on the way out, and said, "My wife and I are throwing a little cocktail party this evening. How's for dropping in for a couple on the way home?"

Burnett accepted. To his amazement he was taken to a fourteen-room duplex with chromium furniture, a Rodin statue, and Metro-Goldwyn-Mayer drapes. It developed that the young man's wife had six or seven million dollars in her own name.

The next morning Burnett summoned his aide. "Bill," he said, "I've been worrying about you all night. A man who lives in the style that you do has no right to be working for fifteen dollars a week. As of today, old man, I'm raising you to sixteen."

Before *Story Magazine* came to America, it was edited in the island of Majorca, off the coast of Spain, by Whit Burnett and Martha Foley, and printed on the local press. The typesetter was a worthy and painstaking fellow, but unfortunately his font included no "w"s. Issues of *Story* brought out during that period have little holes scattered all through the page where the "w"s should have been. In the spirit of good, clean fun, Miss Foley once wrote a short story that did not contain a single "w." Edward O'Brien reprinted it in his anthology of the best stories of the year.

* * *

Duell, Sloan and Pearce engaged a commercial photographer to take a picture of their serious-minded young Hindu author, Krishnalal Shridharani (*My India, My America*), at the feet of the venerable Rabindranath Tagore, with whom he studied in his youth. The commercial photographer, whose knowledge of Indians seems to be confined to the Cleveland Baseball Club, submitted his bill: "24 glossy 5 x 7. SHRID WITH TARZAN." Du sent him his ten dol.

* * *

Cass Canfield of Harper's was approached one day in his editorial sanctum by a sweet-faced but determined matron who wanted very much to discuss a first novel on which she was working. "How long should a novel be?" she demanded. "That's an impossible question to answer," explained Canfield. "Some novels, like *Ethan Frome*, are only about 40,000 words long. Others, *Gone with the Wind*, for instance, may run to 300,000." "But what is the average length of the ordinary novel?" the lady persisted. "Oh, I'd say about 80,000 words," said Canfield. The lady jumped to her feet with a cry of triumph. "Thank God!" she cried. "My book is finished!"

* * *

Max Schuster received a wire reading: "How big an advance on a novel of sixty thousand words?" He wired back: "How big are the words?"

* * *

Senator Oliver St. John Gogarty, noted wit, statesman, limerick reciter, and author of *As I Was Going Down Sackville Street,* has been paying a prolonged visit to our shores, and being in general the most thoroughly Irish Irishman ever seen on a lecture platform. Mr. Gogarty's makeup, brogue, and blarney make Pat O'Brien, Jim McNamara, and Barry Fitzgerald look like character men in the Jewish Art Theatre.

Gogarty was a character in James Joyce's *Ulysses;* "Buck Mulligan," Joyce called him. They met in 1903, when Lady Gregory, patron saint of the Abbey Theatre in Dublin, ran out of "geniuses" and advertised for more of same. She was dismayed at the poverty-stricken flood of applicants and fled. Joyce wrote the following limerick:

> There was a kind lady called Gregory,
> Said, "Come to me, poets in beggary."
> But found her imprudence
> When thousands of students
> Cried, "All we are in that caTEGory!"

Gogarty sniffs at England's time-honored sport of fox-hunting as "the pursuit of the uneatable by the unspeakable."

* * *

A very, very up-to-the-minute young lady in one of Raymond Weaver's literature classes at Columbia asked him whether he had read a best-seller of the moment. When he confessed that he had not, she cried reproachfully, "Oh, you'd better hurry up; it's been out for over three months!" "Young lady," said Weaver severely, "have you read Dante's *Divine Comedy?* No? Well, you'd better hurry up; it's been out for over six hundred years."

THE WOOLLCOTT MYTH
A MINORITY REPORT

THE TEMPTATION to forget a man's faults after his death, and to overemphasize his deeds and contributions, is understandable enough. "Do not speak ill of the dead" is a maxim to which almost everybody subscribes. In the case of Alexander Woollcott, however, this glorifying process, it seems to me, is assuming the proportions of deification. His letters have been collected by loving friends (who took good care to leave out the more waspish and vitriolic variety), his family are composing elegies for sundry magazines, and now Samuel Hopkins Adams, his old fellow alumnus and sponsor from Hamilton, is writing a biography which may be expected to give the great Woollcott myth another shot in the arm.

Not even Woollcott's worst enemies—a goodly assemblage with representatives in every city and hamlet that the Master hit in the course of his wanderings—will deny that he was an extraordinary man, who made a genuine contribution to the gaiety of the nation. He was a superb story-teller, although he often padded his tales with whimsy-whamsy of the most appalling variety. He fought with no holds barred for the things he believed in, although he could become as much aroused over a defense of Minnie Maddern Fiske as over an all-out campaign against fascism. He truly loved the theatre, and his unbounded enthusiasm helped some really good plays to catch on with the public. He turned several books into best-sellers single-handed, although a summary of the titles reveals all too clearly a taste that was most erratic, if not downright over-sentimental and second-rate. (A few of his more violent enthusiasms: *Beside the Bonnie Briar Bush, The Chicken Wagon Family, Lost Horizon,* and *Goodbye,*

Mr. Chips.) One prerequisite for his idea of a masterpiece was its discovery by himself. A new play or book that was recommended by somebody else was usually doomed in advance. When he raved about something and the whole world did not echo his sentiment, Woollcott became truly convinced he had discovered a classic and embarked upon a crusade that stopped at nothing. George Macy had the temerity to appoint him a co-judge of The Readers Club with Sinclair Lewis, Clifton Fadiman, and Carl Van Doren. He never agreed with them on anything; the oftener they rejected some of his weird proposals, the harder he would thump for them at the next meeting. Because of him, they finally changed the whole procedure governing selections.

Woollcott's manners, atrocious to begin with, became progressively worse when he discovered how much people were willing to take from a great celebrity. *The Man Who Came to Dinner* crystallized and enhanced the Woollcott myth a hundredfold; it turned his insults into high comedy, and undoubtedly prevented his being socked in the jaw at least twice a week. His closest friends forgave him his rudeness, his bad sportsmanship, his failure to understand the very fundamentals of fair play. True, Harpo Marx dubbed him "just a big dreamer with a remarkable sense of double-entry bookkeeping." Noel Coward addressed him as "Little Nell of Old Dreary." Robert Benchley called him "Louisa M. Woollcott." To George Jean Nathan he was a "Seidlitz Powder in Times Square." Charlie Brackett swore that he wouldn't even talk to a man who wouldn't make a good magazine article; Heywood Broun added that an exception might be made for sycophantic souls who would play Ghost to his Hamlet—and *never* step out of character. Edna Ferber averred that he was just "a New Jersey Nero who mistook his pinafore for a toga." These, mind you, were Woollcott's friends. What some of the myriad of people he had insulted in one way or another called him may be left to the reader's imagination. Woollcott rather liked being called bad names by his friends; common salutations among the little set he bullied and bell-wethered were, "Oh, it's you, you

faun's behind," or "Who is this harpy standing here like the kiss
of death?" or "Get out, repulsive. You are beginning to disgust
me." Such shenanigans he considered the height of humor. Let
somebody outside the charmed circle take a swipe at him, however, and Woollcott reacted like so many other people who spe-
cialize in lampooning and mocking others. When his old friend
Harold Ross, editor of *The New Yorker*, ran a profile of him
by Wolcott Gibbs that told a few unpleasant truths, Woollcott
went into a monumental rage, and didn't speak to him again for
years.

Alexander Woollcott was born in 1887, in Phalanx, New Jersey,
in a settlement that had once been dedicated to community or
cooperative living. The experiment hadn't worked, and Woollcott's grandfather had taken over the property. In 1889, the
Woollcotts moved to Kansas City, where, according to Gibbs,
little Alec developed such a knack for bellowing when he was
hurt that a group of bullies formed a syndicate to exploit his talent. When they saw an adult approaching, they would throw
Alec off the veranda of his home onto his head. He bawled so
hard that the passer-by frequently gave him a nickel as hush money.
The gang then took the nickel. Woollcott swore that this story
was a malicious lie from beginning to end.

In 1897, the Woollcotts moved to Philadelphia, and Alec attended Central High School there. Classmates were Ed Wynn
and Harry Scherman, the guiding genius of the Book-of-the-
Month Club. The three lads had little in common. Woollcott
chose Hamilton College, in Clinton, New York, as his alma mater
because he had been impressed by the worldly manner of a
graduate of that institution he met one summer. He had a fine
time there, and Hamilton, along with the Seeing Eye, Mrs. Fiske,
the Marx Brothers, Laura Richards, Ruth Gordon, Rebecca West,
Sibyl Colefax, Dr. Eckstein, and a few assorted articulate mur-
derers and yegg-men, became the greatest enthusiasm of his declining years. As an undergraduate, he edited the college magazine, and starred in female roles in the dramatic club productions.

To a snowbound group in his dormitory he introduced the game of choosing for each person on the campus the one adjective which fitted him more perfectly than any other. He pointed out that, if the proper selections were made, everybody could be identified from the list of adjectives. For himself he selected "noble," but admitted later that "this was voted down in favor of another which reduced the whole episode in his memoirs to the proportions of a disagreeable incident." When he graduated, Sam Adams gave him a letter of introduction to Carl Van Anda of the *New York Times*, where, after vain efforts to attune his expanding bulk and personality to the requirements of news reporting, he was given a whack at drama reviewing as a last resort. That was in 1914. It was the beginning of Woollcott's period of glory. A new despot came into his own.

Following a brief interlude as reporter for *Stars and Stripes* in France in 1918, where he wrote stories in the manner of Ernie Pyle with an interlarding of Elsie Dinsmore, Mr. W. settled down for an indefinite run as the country's most respected drama critic, most relentless and feared gossip, and infinitely most accomplished raconteur. All three qualities made a radio career inevitable, and as "The Town Crier" Woollcott became famous, wealthy, and more ruthless and domineering than ever. His social life was unbelievably complicated. He summoned whomever he willed to his home on East 52nd Street (named "Wits' End" by Dorothy Parker); surprisingly few refused. He spent weeks at the White House, and told the Roosevelts whom to have in to dine with him. He spoke at department-store book fairs, autographing copies of his own anthologies, and insulting his audience and other authors who appeared with him. He bought an island in Vermont, charged his guests hotel rates, and banished them when they wouldn't play croquet, cribbage, or hearts according to his own special rules. He installed a big double bed in the ground-floor guest room of this island retreat. It was comfortable but creaky, and let out a tell-tale groan when anybody moved in it. Woollcott called it the "informative double." His opinions be-

came more and more didactic, his prose style more lush and un-
trammeled.

The Man Who Came to Dinner was the direct result of a typical Woollcottian sojourn at Moss Hart's new Bucks County
estate. He bullied the servants, condemned the food, invited
friends of his own from Philadelphia to Sunday dinner, and wrote
in Hart's guest book, "This is to certify that on my first visit to
Moss Hart's house I had one of the most unpleasant times I ever
spent." He also suggested that Moss write a play in which he
could star. The next day Hart was describing Woollcott's behavior
to George Kaufman. "Wouldn't it have been horrible," he rumi-
nated, "if he had broken a leg or something and been on my
hands the rest of the summer!" The collaborators looked at each
other with dawning delight in their faces and took the cover off
the typewriter.

Some months later, Woollcott filled a lecture date in Newark,
and wheedled Hart into driving him over and back. "I'll do it on
one condition," proposed Hart. "I once clerked in a bookstore in
Newark and I'd like to show them that I'm a big shot now. I want
you to let me sit on the platform with you, and be introduced to
the audience." When they entered the hall there was a single
folding chair, sure enough, to the left of the speaker's table. Hart
sat down, and began crossing and uncrossing his legs, while
Woollcott delivered his lecture without making the slightest reference to him. At its conclusion, he said, "I usually have a question period at this time but tonight we'll dispense with it. I'm
sure you'd all want to know the same thing: who is this foolish-
looking young man seated here on the platform with me?" With
this he retired, leaving Hart to get out of the hall as best he
might.

Woollcott's last years were devoted principally to playing
himself in a road company of *The Man Who Came to Dinner*.
The rigors of the trip, coupled with the heart strain induced by a
strenuous diet that lopped off over fifty pounds, weakened him to
such an extent that he was prey to the slightest ailment. When

he felt death approaching, the spluttering vindictiveness went out of his writing; he began to make peace with the world, and to write conciliatory notes to long-time enemies. He even made up with Harold Ross. This lent weight to the contention of his friends that at heart he never was quite the irascible, ill-mannered tyrant he pretended to be. He was stricken in the midst of a broadcast in New York; his last words were a bitter denunciation of weak-minded sentimentalists who were willing to make a soft peace with Germany.

While George Kaufman and Moss Hart were working on *The Man Who Came to Dinner,* Hart went to stay with Woollcott to study him once more at first hand. Hart has an insatiable curiosity for reading messages not intended for his eyes, an idiosyncrasy that did not escape Woollcott's attention. One morning Hart was busy devouring several of Mr. W.'s missives, not yet stamped and addressed, when he found one that read, "I'll ask you up here just as soon as I can get rid of that nauseating Moss Hart, who hangs on here like a leech, although he knows how I detest him." Hart was beginning to quiver with rage when he came to the post-script, which read, "Moss, my puss: I trust this will cure you of the habit of reading other people's mail!"

Woollcott was a confirmed bachelor, whose only known romances were of a literary variety, or the plain hero-worship he bestowed on great ladies of the stage. Edna Ferber, departing for Europe one summer, declared, "I want to be alone on this trip. I don't expect to talk to a man or woman—just Alec Woollcott." When he returned from a lecture in St. Paul and reported to Frank Sullivan that he had spoken to ten thousand women, Sullivan replied, "And what did you tell them? 'NO'?" Rebecca West jestingly wrote in a copy of one of her books that she sent him, "I append my married name to remind us both to keep our passion in bounds."

The paucity of his own love life did not prevent his superin-tending the amours of his little circle, or suggesting the steps to be taken in the bringing up of his four nieces. When one of them,

Nancy, was twelve, her friends whipped up a magazine and rejected her every prose and poetry contribution promptly and firmly. Alec was as indignant as Nancy. He heartily approved when she inserted a paid advertisement (cost: six cents cash) which read as follows:

Miss Nancy B. Woollcott

THE MOST CHARMING WOMAN

IN THE WORLD

Call Between 2:30 and 3

When Nancy and her sisters visited their uncle, his grand manner and famous friends awed them completely. They reported to their horrified mother that he had a portrait of himself reading on the toilet set right into the tiles of his bathroom, entitled "Laxation and Relaxation." They also were present when Harold Ross, who has a lamentable gap between his front teeth, asked Woollcott's man for some dental floss. "Never mind floss," said Woollcott airily. "Bring him a hawser!" Woollcott was very proud of these nieces until they began to criticize him. One winter he sent his friends one of his slushy, raving notes—not about a book, play, or favorite charity this time, but a brand of whiskey. He was paid handsomely for the effort. The Lord knows what he would have said had any of his friends stooped to such commercial prostitution. The nieces sent him a note reading, "Buy stocks on margin if you must, But don't trail the family name in the dust!" In a sharp note to their father, Mr. W. remarked that if he could discover which of the nieces had dared perpetrate such sacrilege, he "would break her goddam neck."

Woollcott accompanied Edna Ferber to an auction one after-noon. Suddenly she spied her mother, and made the mistake of hailing her by an uplifted hand. There was a crash of the auctioneer's hammer, and Miss Ferber discovered that she had become the owner of a particularly hideous grandfather's clock. Every time Woollcott told the story, the price of the clock was a little higher. On the George Kaufmans' fifth wedding anniversary (in 1922) he wrote them, "I have been looking around for an appropriate wooden gift, and am pleased hereby to present you with Elsie Ferguson's performance in her new play." When Gertrude Stein visited New York in 1933, she dared to dispute a statement of the great Mr. W. "I will forgive you this once," he said grandly. "You have not been here long enough yet to know that *nobody* disputes me." "Woollcott," said Miss Stein with a hearty laugh, "you are a colossal fool." The host, who happened to be myself, was delighted.

One evening I brought to a dinner party a lovely young lady whose aunt and uncle are both well-known California novelists. Woollcott was playing cribbage with Alice Duer Miller, and couldn't be bothered with rising from his seat. He inspected her coolly, however, and deigned to remark, "I know your aunt and uncle, of course. Your aunt is a splendid woman. Your uncle is an obscenity." (I borrow here a Hemingway device to indicate a four-letter word that is not used in Simon and Schuster books.) The young lady won my heart by replying, "My definition of that word, Mr. Woollcott, is a man who uses it to a lady he is meeting for the first time." I'll say for Woollcott that he threw back his head and roared with approving laughter.

My own relations with him were severed by the Random House edition of Marcel Proust. C. K. Scott-Moncrieff, the translator of the first six parts, died before he could complete his task. After long deliberation and consultation, we selected Frederick A. Blossom to translate the seventh and last of the Proust novels. Every critic approved his work but Woollcott, who launched into a tirade in *The New Yorker,* and made statements that enabled us to prove publicly that he didn't know what he was talking about. This was the sort of thing Woollcott couldn't forgive. One thing led to another, and finally I struck his name from the Random House review list. I made a perfect picture of a man cutting his nose to spite his face—because Woollcott's enthusiasms could make a book a best-seller more surely than anything else. I think it only fair to tell this story here, to indicate that this report is not exactly impartial, and that my recollections of Mr. Woollcott are not set down with what might be termed Olympian detachment.

In the early thirties, Woollcott visited Russia, where he created a great commotion because of his striking resemblance to the bloated capitalist invariably depicted in Soviet cartoons. He weighed over two hundred pounds at the time; Soviet citizens had seen nothing like him since the fall of the Czars. Their hoots of laughter did not increase his love for the Russian experiment. ("Hoot" is apt; one Moscow journalist declared that Woollcott looked exactly like an owl.)

In England, Woollcott attended a small dinner given in honor of Edward, then Prince of Wales. He was deeply flattered when the Prince called him into private consultation after the ladies had left the room, but his elation vanished when the reason became apparent. "Woollcott," said the Prince, "you've got something to do with that blasted *New Yorker* magazine, haven't you? Well, why the devil do my copies reach me so irregularly?"

Later he visited Japan, where he was made so much of that he came back home with an overflowing heart. He raved about their "neatness and love of flowers—the sweet hum of their voices and the occasional deep boom of a vast gong at a temple on a hill." He then ventured an opinion on our "future war with Japan," of which "he heard nothing from the Japanese—but in the bar of the Shanghai Club, or in the veranda café of a Pacific liner, or among our own Army and Navy officers who are stationed in the Far East and have a lot of time on their hands. I only hope," he concluded, "that if there ever is such a war and we win it, we shall remember that we won it because we are larger, richer, and more numerous, and not feel too proud about it. For I have seen just enough of Japan and the Japanese to suspect that such a victory might be only another of history's insensitive triumphs of quantity over quality." Well, more profound folk than the ingenuous Mr. Woollcott were taken in by the wily little Japs, and maybe it isn't quite fair to bring the matter up. At least, Woollcott lived to learn how wrong he had been.

All of his life, Alec Woollcott raged because people insisted on confusing his beloved Hamilton College, at Clinton, with Colgate University, at Hamilton, New York, not many miles away. When he died, he stipulated that his ashes be deposited in the Hamilton cemetery. By the irony of fate, they were shipped first to Colgate, and had to be readdressed.

* * *

The book business today is enjoying a wave of unparalleled prosperity, but one little store in downtown New York never did share in the general increase in business. In fact, it was bankrupt. One partner was sadly surveying the premises just before the final padlocking. "I can't understand it," he mused. "Here we go busted, and only yesterday I read where the President was saying that business was never better."

"Maybe," suggested his brother, "the President had a better location than ours."

* * *

An agent tried to dissuade a client from chucking a big-salaried studio job to go back East and write a novel. "Why do it?" wailed the agent. "You can't make any money that way. How much did you make from your last novel?" "Seventy-five thousand dollars," replied the writer with some pride. "See," said the agent, "what did I tell you?"

* * *

Another agent story: An author expressed the hope that he could promote a $500 advance on his new pot-boiler. "Just to show you how good I am," declared the agent, "I will get you $1500." He called several publishers and finally found one gullible soul who fell for his palaver and agreed to the terms. The agent hung up the phone, clapped his hand to his forehead, and groaned, "Oh God, why am I such a crook?"

* * *

Harry Scherman, president of the Book-of-the-Month Club, says he is getting a bit fed up with the recurrent story of the lady who looked like a fugitive from a Hokinson drawing rushing up to him at a party and exclaiming, "I have always dreamed of meeting the president of my club." One day an employee of the Club heard that Hilary Saunders, author of *Combined Operations*, was trying to find a set of jacks to take back home to his young daughter in Britain. She brought them along with a ball to the BOMC offices and was quite put out when they disappeared. A search was instituted and the jacks were eventually recovered. Harry Scherman had sneaked them into his private office; when apprehended, he was trying vainly to get past threesies.

* * *

Richard Tregaskis, author of *Guadalcanal Diary* and *Invasion Diary,* has the most enormous eating capacity of anybody in the literary business or possibly any other business, if you get right down to it. I recently had occasion to take him out to lunch and, being in an experimental mood, ordered the same dishes as Tregaskis, course for course. When the more than ample repast was concluded, I boasted, "Well, Dick, you're certainly not the man I

Richard Tregaskis caught between entrée and salad

thought you were as far as food is concerned. I ate every single thing that you did. Frankly, I am disappointed in you." "Don't be," confessed Tregaskis. "Maybe I oughtn't to tell you this, but before coming up here to have lunch with you, I had lunch with Joe Connolly."

* * *

Thomas Craven, author of *Men of Art,* has a young son who was asked by his history teacher to name the principal contribution of the Phoenicians. The youngster's answer, given without hesitation, was "Blinds."

* * *

The accountant of a publishing house whose name you would recognize is reported to have burst into the office of the head of the firm in a state of wild jubilation one day last week. "After five long years," he chortled, "I am pleased to report to you that we now are no longer in the red!" "Glory be," cried his chief. "Make up five copies of the annual report at once so that I can wave them in the face of that so-and-so bank." "But I have no black ink," said the accountant. "We haven't needed any for so long." "Go out and buy a bottle," the chief said. "I should say not," was the reply. "In that case, we'd be back in the red."

* * *

Henry L. Mencken claims that his book, *In Defense of Women*, stemmed from his discovery that every bride he met was infinitely smarter than her somewhat befuddled bridegroom. One touching testimonial that he received for this book came from the death house of a woman's prison. It read, "If I had only known how smart I was, I would not be here."

* * *

In the summer of 1929 The Viking Press imported five hundred copies each of a couple of expensive, beautifully printed and bound editions of obscure, third-rate English poets. After the market crash in the fall of the same year, "limited" editions of this sort were a drug on the market.

George Oppenheimer, now of Hollywood, then an officer of The Viking Press, was visiting a young couple he knew in Buffalo when he spied copies of the special editions on the bookshelf. He roared with laughter, and exclaimed, "How did you ever get stuck with those lemons? We couldn't *give* them away." The lady of the house turned a cold eye on him. "They were your wedding gift to us," she reminded him.

Oppenheimer recently tried his hand at a ghost movie. It didn't quite jell, and when the preview was over, the producer said sadly, "This picture will never scare anybody." "Oh, yes, it will," said Oppenheimer. "It'll scare my agent plenty." Later they asked him if he could suggest any way of cutting the film. "Try straight up the middle," he murmured—and enlisted in the Army.

Oppenheimer once was invited for a week-end to the fabulous Hearst ranch in San Simeon, and his mother made him render a prompt and detailed report of the goings-on. The morning after his arrival she received the following wire: "Two things have happened to me here already that never happened to me before. My car was stopped by a camel and I fell downstairs in my own bedroom."

* * *

Counterpoints offers this comment on literature: A German novel is a book in which two people want each other in the first chapter but do not get each other until the last chapter. A French novel is a book in which two people get each other in the first chapter and from then on to the last chapter don't want each other any more. A Russian novel, finally, is one in which two people neither want each other nor get each other, and about this 1,450 very melancholy pages are written.

* * *

A recent biography of Hans Christian Andersen appeared under the title of *The Shoemaker's Son. The New York Labor News* requested a review copy.

* * *

Elizabeth Chevalier, author of the best-selling novel, *Drivin' Woman,* wrote in a letter to Macmillan, "Have you heard the one about the novelist who met an old friend? After they had talked for two hours, the novelist said, 'Now we've talked about me long enough—let's talk about you! What did you think of my last novel?'"

* * *

The solemn, almost mournful countenance of Robert Emmet Sherwood camouflages a playful nature that found expression at an extremely early age. His bedridden grandma was wheeled out on the porch in sunny weather; the boy Robert was discovered there, manipulating a rod and string, at the end of which dangled a live beetle. Grandma was ducking as best she could, and hollering for help. Robert saw no reason why he should be punished. "All I was doing," he explained indignantly, "was tickling up Grandma." He also emptied his Noah's Ark into Grandma's new flush toilet, gumming up the works one hundred percent. "This

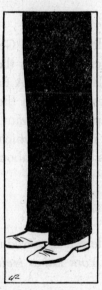

is a mighty fine watercloset," said the plumber later, "but I never told you it would pass elephants." For several weeks Robert's apoplectic grandfather kept fishing up yaks and rhinoceroses. When his grandson left for home, he delivered a bon mot which Robert used years later in his capacity of editor of *Life* (the pre-Luceite *Life*): "Robert, if I never see you again, it will be too soon." The unrepentant Robert told his parents, "I am thoroughly sick of Grandpa."

Sherwood grew up to be a great playwright, a close adviser of

President Roosevelt, the husband of a beautiful movie queen (Madeleine Hurlock), and a punster of the first water. Invited to sit in on a gambling orgy, he muttered, "Only the brave chemin de fer." When rich Spaniards sought to escape the Civil War via the international bridge leading to Hendaye, France, and were strafed unmercifully by "unidentified" warplanes, Sherwood read the reports and said, "That's what comes of putting all their Basques in one exit." At his English country home in Great Enton, he essayed a pun (unfortunately it cannot be quoted here) that caused the staid London butler to spill a platterful of mutton and gravy into the lap of an outraged guest. His wife diagnoses these moments as a throwback to the days when he edited the Harvard *Lampoon* and gave ample evidence that he was Pulitzer Prize timber by flunking Freshman English. The first time he burst across the literary firmament was with a novel called *The Virtuous Night,* which practically burst the publishers at the same time. They forgave him when the grosses on *Reunion in Vienna, Idiot's Delight, The Petrified Forest, Abe Lincoln in Illinois,* and *There Shall Be No Night* began piling up.

Robert Sherwood is a great power in the O.W.I. at the present writing. Insiders profess to recognize his touch in most of President Roosevelt's most important speeches. His tory Republican cousin asked him to bring back a souvenir from the White House. "What would you like?" asked Sherwood. "His scalp?" When the war is over, he probably will resume his practice of turning out new Pulitzer Prize plays every other year or so. His first winner, *Idiot's Delight,* gave the Goebbels propaganda machine a name for him. "You can ignore those short-wave broadcasts," hooted Goebbels. "They were written by a delighted idiot."

* * *

The librarian at Columbia University received a letter last year addressed, "Mr. L. I. Brarian. Dear Mr. Brarian."

* * *

The inmate of a St. Louis asylum borrowed three long books from the library each morning, returned them the same afternoon. The librarian tested him with the city telephone directory. Sure enough, he was back with it a few hours later. "Don't tell me you've finished that big book already," said the librarian. "I certainly have," answered the touched one. "The plot was rotten, but oh boy, *what a cast!*"

* * *

Fanny Hurst is the kind of lady who never does things by halves; when she decided to reduce, she made such a thorough job of it that some of her best friends found it difficult to recognize her. One such was the late Irvin Cobb who strolled down Fifth Avenue directly behind her for a half-dozen blocks without doffing his chapeau to her. "Well," she declared finally, "are you going to say hello to me or aren't you?" "Don't tell me you're Fanny Hurst," said the astonished Cobb. "The same Fanny Hurst," she assented coldly. "No, no," decided Cobb. "The same Hurst I will concede—but definitely *not* the same Fanny."

Mr. Cobb was also the gentleman who introduced Michael Arlen, creator of the almost-forgotten Iris March and her Green Hat, as "the only Armenian I ever met who didn't try to sell me a rug."

* * *

When Ludwig Bemelmans was meandering through Ecuador, he stopped in a dubious village café, where he was suddenly confronted by a burly, unshaven desperado who frightened him to death by plumping down into the seat next to him and demanding a double whiskey straight. Suddenly the stranger spied a tattered old copy of *Esquire* and pounced on it. He turned to a certain article, and began mumbling the words laboriously to himself. Then he was on his feet, bellowing with rage. "Those blankety-blank editors!" he roared. "They've cut out my best lines again!"

* * *

One of the most celebrated literary fracases in history had as its principals Ernest Hemingway and Max Eastman. Their highly publicized combat took place a little more than a decade ago. Hemingway had just written *Death in the Afternoon*. Mr. Eastman referred to him in a magazine article as the leading exponent of the "false-hair-on-the-chest" school of writing, not suspecting that he would bump squarely into the gentleman in the Scribner

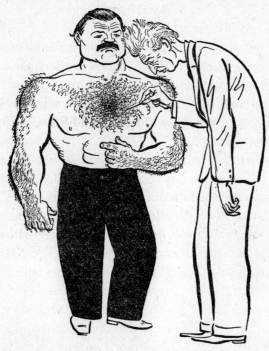

offices a few days after the piece appeared. Mr. Hemingway rose to his feet. Mr. Eastman did not know what the look in his eye portended, but he had a rough idea. There are four authentic eye-witness accounts of what happened next, all of them completely different. Eastman scored a technical victory by getting his version into print first. He contacted a *World-Telegram* reporter faster than a GI answers mess call. His story did not impress anybody who had watched Hemingway work out in a gymnasium. Such cognoscenti figured that if Ernest had ever landed one punch on the willowy Max's epiglottis, there would have been no enjoyment of laughter for the Eastman family for the next six months.

A clause in Hemingway's contract with Scribner's provides that the publishers may not change a single word in his manuscripts. Scribner's brilliant editor, Maxwell Perkins, was reading the type-written script of *Death in the Afternoon* when he encountered an old, four-lettered Anglo-Saxon word beginning with "f." He rushed frantically to the office of the elderly Charles Scribner, and read the offending passage to that dignified but flustered gen-tleman. "Remember," said Perkins, "that we're forbidden by con-tract to change a word." "Dear, dear," said Mr. Scribner, "we will have to discuss this fully when I return from lunch." Absent-mindedly he jotted down the word on a pad headed "What to Do Today."

It is rumored further that while Mr. Scribner was lunching, his secretary glanced at his pad, gasped, and exclaimed, "Holy smoke, is a secretary expected to remind her boss of *everything?*"

Cuban fishermen along the docks in Havana have grown used to the presence of the burly American who fishes with them in amiable silence and performs more important duties on the side that they know nothing about. "Señor Way" they call him, con-vinced that "Heming" is his first name, and there is evident affec-tion in their voices when they speak of him. "Señor Way," one of them went so far as to declare to a visiting correspondent, "is a great American—as great as the other two most famous men in your history." "Which two do you mean?" the correspondent asked idly. "Señor George Washington and Señor Tom Collins," was the prompt reply.

* * *

Herbert Mayes, the editor of *Good Housekeeping Magazine,* is planning a mystery cook book. Every recipe will have one impor-tant ingredient missing.

* * *

Miss Josephine Austen, librarian at Forest Park, Illinois, declares that her profession provides a unique opportunity for souvenir-collecting. Readers use unbelievable objects for bookmarks, and frequently forget to remove them before they turn in the volumes. Miss Austen's collection includes violent love letters, nail files, playing cards, bobby pins—and most unexpected of all, a very, very thoroughly fried egg.

* * *

A recent literary dinner found Carl Van Doren in a richly reminiscent mood. He recalled a vacation time in Nassau when he and Marc Connelly stumbled over two obvious old maids, napping blissfully in the sun on Paradise Beach, a camera in the sands next to them. On an impulse, the distinguished gentlemen snatched up the camera, took it into the men's private solarium, and snapped an entire reel of photographs of luxuriating nude sun-worshippers. Then they put the camera back where they had found it. What the maiden ladies said when their films were developed—or what the kodak company said to *them* when the nature of their pictures was discovered—is something for one's imagination to toy with.

Another time, Carl and Logan Clendening found themselves on the same train, bound to fulfil lecture engagements in the same city. Another passenger was a generous and convivial soul with a full bottle of excellent bourbon. One thing, said Carl, led to another. "Did you deliver your lectures O.K.?" he was asked. "We certainly did," he replied. "But Logan delivered my lecture on literature, and I gave his on surgery."

* * *

It is rumored that W. C. Fields, the comedian, found cause to deplore the lack of an adequate bookstore near his California residence. He approached the leading intellectual of the community and gave him a high-powered sales talk on the advantages of opening such a store for the local trade. "Thirty thousand will do it, my boy," said Fields with conviction. "Surely you can raise such an insignificant sum at the drop of a hat." The young man allowed that it was a fine idea and that he would like nothing better than to open a well-stocked bookstore. "I think I can get my hands on about $20,000," he told Fields. "As for that remaining $10,000, how about your putting it up for me?" "Under ordinary circumstances," Fields assured him, "nothing would give me greater pleasure, my boy. At the moment, however, I find myself in rather a strange predicament. All of my available funds are completely tied up in ready cash."

* * *

The late Max Harzof was one of the rare book trade's great "characters." There are countless anecdotes about him. Gabriel Wells tells how he once bought an Oscar Wilde manuscript for $1,040. "Why the odd price?" he asked, after the bargain had been struck. Harzof replied with commendable candor, "I wanted to make an even thousand-dollar profit."

* * *

There is a note at the back of H. Allen Smith's *Life in a Putty Knife Factory* which reads as follows: "The liveliness and grace of the typography are directly attributable to the craftsmanship of three printers named Sam, Terence, and Giambattista, one of whom was a little drunk and none of whom appeared to be amused. The paper on which the book is printed was made out of trees. Real trees."

* * *

At the height of the last Christmas rush, a slightly befuddled matron wandered into Dutton's Bookstore. "Is this Scribner's?" she inquired of a clerk. "No, madam," was the reply, "it's Dutton's." "Oh," said the lady. "I saw the sign 'Dutton's' on the window, but I thought it might be Scribner's."

* * *

A customer approached the technical book department in Scribner's Bookstore and asked for "that Acetylene book." "Acetylene torches?" inquired the clerk. "No, Acetylene Encyclopædia Britannica," answered the customer. He turned out to be a Mr. Ben Huebsch of The Viking Press.

The manager of Scribner's, incidentally, was asked how he was handling the unprecedented rush of business these days. "We open the doors at nine," he replied, "and jump out of the way."

* * *

Vincent Starrett recalls one of the funniest incidents in the late Frank Harris' alleged autobiography, that amazing three-volume conglomeration of literary lore and sophomoric pornography that under-the-counter specialists peddle for as much as fifty dollars a set. Harris described a crucial international conference with all the wealth of detail that only a man who had not been present could supply. At the height of the confab an English munitions king let out a cry of anguish. His valuable timepiece had been hooked. The chairman—prime minister of a great European power —was properly outraged. "Gentlemen," he declared icily, "this will never do. The lights will be extinguished for five minutes. All of us will file out of this chamber in darkness. The thief, as he exits, will place the watch on the table there beside the door, where the buhl clock now stands." Thereupon, concluded Harris, the delegates filed out in silence and darkness. Five minutes later the room was relighted. Not only was the watch still missing; the buhl clock also had disappeared.

* * *

It was one of those gatherings of well-heeled, supersophisticated suburbanites with whom too many good writers have been spending too much of their time in recent years. The buffet disposed of, the guests began a furious round of parlor games, panicked lest a few precious minutes be squandered in conversation. Eventually, somebody proposed a game of charades and I must tell you the four that ended the proceedings just this side of mayhem:

1. Three matrons are gossiping idly about their children. Suddenly the Marx Brothers burst into the room, sling the bewildered ladies like sacks of meal over their shoulders and make off with them. Question: What famous novel does this represent? Answer: The Brothers Carry Mas Off.

2. A bon vivant complains that his new butler has not only forgotten to put studs in his shirt, but has laid out yellow Oxfords to be worn with his dress suit. Question: What best seller does this situation represent? Answer: How Green Was My Valet.

3. Mrs. Jones and her daughter operate a chicken farm. Mrs. Jones sends said daughter out to check on the number of eggs the chickens have laid one morning. Daughter reports in a speech of four syllables. Question: What distinguished living novelist does her answer represent? Answer: Some Are Set, Marm.

4. A man examines several packs of cigarettes; rejects, in turn, Lucky Strikes, Philip Morris, Chesterfields, Old Golds, Pall Malls. Question: What statesman does he represent? Answer: Mustafa Kemal.

* * *

The day that my publishing house decided to add the *Complete Works of Tacitus,* the Roman historian, to the Modern Library series, we chose as editor Professor Moses Hadas of Columbia University and persuaded that academic luminary to attend a conference in the Random House sanctum. We had a fine talk on the subject of Tacitus and agreed as to exactly what things were to go into the anthology. Just as he was leaving, the professor turned to me and asked with a most innocent expression: "Tell me, Mr. Cerf, exactly when did you read that encyclopedia article on Tacitus?" Caught red-handed, I admitted that I had read it exactly ten minutes before his arrival. "Neat recitation," commented Hadas. "You see, I happened to write that article."

* * *

London's Savoy Hotel is where dull British author-lecturers will stay when the war is over, instead of coming over here to prey on the women's clubs, if a friend of mine on an English journal has his way. He doesn't mean *all* lecturers, of course—just the ones who have the following easily recognizable characteristics:

1. A standard costume of striped pants, frock coat, and stiff wing collars that look as though they were choking the speaker, but unfortunately never do.

2. Acute boredom while everybody else on the program is speaking.

3. Reference to the American Revolution in such jocular manner as "a bit of a show in which you chaps gave us a jolly good hiding" —accompanied by an expression intended to denote unutterable good will and sportsmanship, but that succeeds only in suggesting Arthur Treacher in his standard Hollywood role of gentleman's gentleman who despises his employer, his employer's family, and his employer's friends.

4. Repeated use of English words like "lift," "tram," "petrol," and "alum*i*nium."

These are the babies who usually conclude by blaming any shortcomings in their speech on a snifter forced upon them by an over-hospitable host just before they ascended the podium: "I believe you Americans call it a cocktail." (The last time this gambit was pulled, the comely publicity gal chaperoning the author for three horrible days whispered into my ear, "Cocktail, my eye! One more Scotch-and-soda and the old goat would have fallen clean off the platform!")

My English friend suggests that we, in turn, restrain Mickey Rooney from portraying Eton schoolboys and let English ladies be English ladies on the screen. In short, both nations are to keep their hams across the sea.

* * *

Russel Crouse refers to his friend Frank Sullivan as his "Pillar of Jello."

DARING YOUNG MAN

WILLIAM SAROYAN's calculated whimsicality and instinctive urge to plunge into action whenever there is the remotest chance to get his name into print have annoyed some of our more conservative and puritanical critics to a point where they deny him the homage that is his just due. They will not—or cannot— recognize that beneath Saroyan's cheap-jack shenanigans there throb an abundant and original talent and an imagination and love of life that have already made a rich contribution to American literature and drama. Meanwhile, with a Pultizer Prize play and two successive choices by the Book-of-the-Month Club to his credit at the advanced age of thirty-four, Mr. Saroyan, product of the vineyards of Fresno, California, self-educated son of simple Armenian parents, has done right well for himself.

Saroyan attended a Fresno public school until he was fifteen. He began selling newspapers in his spare time at the age of eight, and became a telegraph messenger at thirteen. At harvest time, he pruned vines with Mexican and Jap laborers in his uncle's fields. He observed much and forgot nothing. He loved every minute of his work and every person he encountered in the doing of it. This is the quality that has illuminated every line he has ever written. He knew, at an early age, that he was going to be a writer. The first story that he sold was *The Daring Young Man on the Flying Trapeze*. Whit Burnett, of *Story Magazine,* accepted it in 1934. Saroyan's only surprise was that it had taken so long for the literary world to discover his talents. He made a package of all the other stories he had written and dispatched them to a publisher. Their publication was an unqualified success, and Bill has been flying through the air with the greatest of ease ever since. The day he received his six author's advance copies, he boarded the Oakland-San Francisco ferry, and descended upon reasonably startled passengers with a jubilant shout. "I'm the man who wrote this book," he cried. "Yes, sir, I'm William Saroyan himself. Don't you want to buy an autographed copy?" The books went so fast that the author suggested that the publisher send him a hundred additional copies for similar exploitation.

Rejection slips did not destroy Saroyan's ebulliency for too long a period. He changed the author's name atop a sheaf of unpublished stories to "Sirak Soyan" and submitted them to the late Edward O'Brien, high priest of the short story in Britain. "These tales," he wrote, "are different in substance from the stories of my cousin, William Saroyan, but, I believe, are rather related to his work." O'Brien announced his discovery of a new major talent to the editors of *Story* just as they were writing to tell him how they had found Saroyan. O'Brien stoutly maintained that *his* Armenian discovery was the more important; Burnett defended *his* man with equal vehemence. The argument continued for several months, until Saroyan could stand it no longer, and admitted that he and his "cousin Soyan" were one and the same. O'Brien's and Burnett's laughter did not ring out so heartily as Saroyan's.

Saroyan came East the following spring, and delighted columnists, reviewers, and lion-chasers speedily discovered that here was a young man who manufactured his own copy and distributed same with prodigal generosity. Reference to him or his work in the most obscure periodical evoked a four-page reply, banged out on his ever-ready typewriter even while he was being interviewed by somebody else. His love-life was conducted with similar reticence. I had introduced him to a pair of beautiful sisters at a cocktail party. He addressed the elder of the two (she was twenty, I believe) in front of a half-dozen of us and blandly suggested that she accompany him on a trip to Philadelphia. Her indignant refusal startled him somewhat, but he rallied bravely, and called her back. "How about your sister?" he asked.

I took Bill to the very first play he ever saw on Broadway. I think the year was 1935. It was a play about the Newark Airport called *Ceiling Zero* and it starred that superlatively good actor, the late Osgood Perkins. "So that's New York theatre," said Bill at the end of two acts. "Why, for the love of Mike, I could write a better play than that in twenty-four hours!" And, by golly, he did. His first play, *My Heart's in the Highlands,* was produced as an experiment by the Group Theatre in April 1939. It was uneven

and unpolished, but astute dramatic critics, notably George Jean Nathan, recognized that their prayer for a fresh and original talent in the theatre had been answered. His next play, *The Time of Your Life,* which was presented by the Theatre Guild on October 25, 1939, won both the Pulitzer Prize and the New York Drama Critics' Award, the first play ever to receive both honors. Saroyan created a national furore by refusing the former prize. He claimed that wealth had no right to patronize art. The resultant publicity was worth not only five times the amount of the prize to Mr.

Saroyan, but it took the high and mighty Pulitzer Committee down a number of pegs as well.

Saroyan's subsequent plays have not been successful, but he has found ample compensations in other fields. *My Name Is Aram* was a Book-of-the-Month Club selection in 1940. A year later, he sold an original script to Metro-Goldwyn-Mayer for $60,000. It was called *The Human Comedy*. He promptly distributed the bulk of this money among his relatives in California, retaining something less than ten thousand dollars for himself to finance a season of Saroyan repertory that he proposed to institute in New York at the beginning of the current theatrical year. The repertory survived for exactly one week, and accounted not only for all the money he had left, but for several thousand dollars more. This did not faze Mr. Saroyan. He promptly declared the entire New York theatrical season a wash-out, and sat down to transform his motion-picture script into a novel. The result was a book that became his second successive Book-of-the-Month selection. It was a leading best-seller for months. The picture also was a whopping success. Saroyan is back in the chips again and is also in the United States Army, at the present writing in Europe with the Signal Corps. What the Army will do to William Saroyan and vice versa is anybody's guess. The last time I saw him, Army discipline had not weighed too heavily upon his ebullient spirit. Our phone operator announced, "A man who says he is the world's greatest author is here to see you." "Send Private Saroyan in," I answered.

* * *

Allan Ullman, of the *New York Times* advertising department, was the recipient of a copy of Lin Yutang's *Wisdom of China and India*. His five-year-old son was attracted by the colorful jacket, and grabbed the book. Allan grabbed it back. "Lay off, you oaf," commanded his wife. "Stop taking Gandhi from a baby."

* * *

The late G. K. Chesterton was over six feet tall and weighed upward of 300 pounds. When he tried his hand at the drama with the unusual comedy called *Magic,* Bernard Shaw referred to it as "Fatty's First Play." "It must be wonderful," a young girl once gushed to him, "to be so famous that everyone knows who you are." "If they don't," replied Chesterton sadly, "they ask."

His voice had an irritating habit of escaping from control and breaking into falsetto. When he gave his first lecture in America, Edwin Markham, author of *The Man with the Hoe,* was in the chair. The distinction of introducing so notable a visitor evidently unhinged Markham's reason; he embarrassed the speaker of the evening by a florid eulogy that went on indefinitely. Chesterton was red with embarrassment. He heaved himself to his feet, shuffled to the centre of the platform, looked plaintively around him, and murmured, "After the whirlwind, the still, small voice."

On the same visit, he was led forth to see the nightly spectacle of Broadway ablaze with those myriad glamorous lamps, now not so bright as in pre-war days. "How beautiful!" exclaimed Chesterton. "How beautiful it would be for someone who could not read!"

* * *

Two distinguished publishers marked up one of Caesar's best linen tablecloths in the exclusive Oak Room of New York's Hotel Plaza one day in an endeavor to assemble a team of bearded literati, with the inspired notion of challenging the House of David to a ball game next season. The tentative line-up worked out as follows: Chris Morley, first base; Rex Stout, second; Ernest Boyd, third; Will Durant, short stop; Georges Duplaix, left field; Elliot Paul, centre field; Ernest Hemingway, right field. The starting battery was a foregone conclusion: Charles and Mary Beard. A kibitzer suggested Bernard Shaw for hot-dog vender; his vegetarian principles would remove all temptation to consume the stock personally.

* * *

Not many years ago ex-Governor Alfred E. Smith complained that his autobiography, *Up to Now,* was not being promoted vigorously enough. "But, Governor," remonstrated his publishers, "we planted your book in every bookstore in the country." "Bookstores," snorted the Governor, unconsciously summing up every publisher's grievance for the past five generations. "Who in hell goes to bookstores?"

* * *

A bibliophile was poking around a second-hand book shop and came across a rare old quarto that he wanted. "I'll give you fifteen dollars for it," he said. "Take it," sighed the dealer, "but I paid twenty-five for it myself." "How can you stay in business on any basis like that?" scoffed the customer. "Sssh," cautioned the dealer. "I make a wrong entry in the ledger."

* * *

How many readers remember Trader Horn? "Zambesi Jack," as he liked to call himself, cut quite a swath when he arrived here in the early thirties. His preposterous memoirs were kited to best-sellerdom by one of Simon and Schuster's most ingenious publicity campaigns. His long gray beard, his picturesque cape and sombrero, and his unbelievable capacity for liquor in any form added lustre to the legend. Zambesi autographed hundreds of copies of *Trader Horn.* When his manager protested that he was sapping his strength needlessly, he made a remark that has become famous in book circles. "It's been my experience," he declared, "that people never lend an autographed book." He swore that he once had a pet tiger who liked to sleep across the foot of his bed. One night he kicked the tiger in a moment of absent-mindedness. "Do you know that one kick broke the poor tiger's spirit? Shows how careful we must be of the other fellow's feelings." Another time he claimed that he shot a mother gorilla. Just before she died she reached out her hand to her little baby gorilla. "I tried to make amends to outraged Nature. . . . I took the baby gorilla and paid a slave girl thirty shillings to nurse it." To hear Trader Horn tell it, women fell for him just as hard when he was eighty as when he was eighteen. He credited this to a love potion a beautiful witch in Zululand brewed for him.

* * *

In London, Liddell Hart said to Bernard Shaw, "Do you realize that 'sumac' and 'sugar' are the only two words in the English language that begin with 's-u' and are pronounced *shu?*" "Sure," answered Shaw.

* * *

In Oxford, Mississippi, a young lady offered William Faulkner a crystal-clear distinction between "like" and "love": "If I like 'em I lets 'em. If I loves 'em, I helps."

* * *

In Elmira, H. K. Arthur persuaded a modest lady author to visit a nudist colony, assured her there was a story to be written about its survival. A member, noticing that she was fully dressed, inquired, "Are you one of us?" "Oh, no," the novelist assured her. "I'm only aghast."

* * *

Early in life, says Ben Hecht, his Aunt Chasha taught him that self-apologies usually make an unholy mess of things. In a theatre mix-up, Aunt Chasha lost her temper, and dressed down a couple of ushers in no uncertain terms. The fat little manager rushed up and blustered, "I am afraid, Mrs. Swernofsky, I must ask you to apologize." Aunt Chasha teed off, smacked the manager over the head with her umbrella, kicked him in the shin, and whisked the enchanted Ben into the sunshine. "Remember what I tell you," she said cheerfully. "That's the only way to apologize so they remember it."

Ben Hecht is the most fascinating story-teller I have ever met. The very extravagances that mar his written works serve only to enhance his effectiveness when his audience literally can

sit at his feet. I have seen a whole roomful of people, all fond
of talking themselves, held spellbound while he wove his fantastic
stories. About the person of his old friend Maxwell Bodenheim,
poet, novelist, Bohemian of sorts, Hecht constructed a running
history, possibly fifty percent true, that interrupted a roaring stud-
poker game for three solid hours.

When they were lads together in Chicago, explained Hecht,
they went in for a bout of amateur theatricals. Hecht wrote a one-
act play that called for Bodenheim's death in an early scene. To
save the cost of a policeman's uniform it was arranged that Bodenheim was to die at the edge of the stage with only his feet showing
when he fell. Hecht could then pull him off while one of the other
actors indicated to the audience that the police had come for the
body. Rehearsals went splendidly, but on the opening night, Bodenheim succumbed to the lure of the footlights, and after staggering
about the scene for a full minute, collapsed in the exact centre of
the stage. Hecht had to rush to the corner and give the cop on
the beat a dollar to come in and haul him off.

A misguided lecture manager in Milwaukee once offered Hecht
and Bodenheim fifty dollars apiece to stage a literary debate on
any subject that appealed to them. They took the precaution of
collecting their fees in advance, and strode onto the platform.
"The subject of this debate," announced Bodenheim, "is, 'Resolved: that any person who pays good American cash to hear a
literary debate is a blithering idiot.' I will uphold the affirmative,
Mr. Hecht the negative." "I concede," cried Hecht. Then the two
of them fled before the outraged audience could get to its feet.
They haven't played Milwaukee since.

* * *

A poet came into the Doubleday office recently and asked,
"What do you pay for blank verse?" The telephone operator had
the proper reply: "Blank checks."

MISS PARKER'S PEN

UNTIL A FEW years ago, Dorothy Parker was looked upon as one of the brightest and most scintillating wits in the country. Her bons mots were quoted from Atlantic City to Del Monte, and even if she never did say thirty percent of the things she was given credit for, the residue was sufficient to insure her place among the humorists of the ages. Then, suddenly, she stopped being funny. At the same time her output of brilliant short stories and trenchant verse dwindled into a mere trickle. Some people said it was the war. Others ascribed it to a happy marriage. "Dotty," they explained, "can only do her best work when her heart is breaking." Whatever the reason, the best Parker quips all date back to 1938 and earlier; you may judge for yourself how wonderfully they have withstood the ravages of time. (The average sally, or wisecrack, is stale and flat a week after its utterance.)

Dorothy Parker was born in a Jersey summer resort, and educated, in a manner of speaking, at a convent, which she left abruptly amidst mutual rejoicing. The first marks of her fingernails began to appear on people when she was dramatic critic of *Vanity Fair,* but her acidulous comments provoked such wrath along

Broadway that a petrified management, fearing lynching parties and tar and featherings, bade her be gone. Two other lights, just beginning to shine, went with her in protest. Their names were Robert Sherwood and Robert Benchley. Miss Parker had polished off Channing Pollock's *The House Beautiful* in a single sentence. "*The House Beautiful*," she reported, "is the play lousy." When Katharine Hepburn opened in a little thing called *The Lake*, Miss Parker's comment was, "She ran the whole gamut of emotion from A to B." Hepburn made her eat those words later. They were milk and honey, anyhow, to the literary reviews she turned out later for *The New Yorker* when she hit real midseason form. Her review of Margot Asquith's biography began "The affair between Margot Asquith and Margot Asquith is one of the prettiest love affairs in literature." The caption on her dissection of Edith Wharton's life-story read, "Edie Was a Lady." Of Lucius Beebe's *Shoot If You Must*, she commented, "This must be a gift book. That is to say, a book which you wouldn't take on any other terms." She polished off one scientific volume with the dictum, "It was written without fear and without research." A. A. Milne was not exactly her meat. "Tonstant Weader," she reported, "fwowed up." There was something about the face of Harold Ross, the editor, she explained, that made her go into her office and slam the hell out of the first book that came to hand. The office was shared with

Benchley, and was known as "The Park Bench" to favored patrons of the Algonquin Hotel. At a round table in the Algonquin dining room, Miss Parker gave birth to many of the sallies that won her fame.

Somebody asked her if she had enjoyed a cocktail party at which she was seen. "Enjoyed it!" she purred. "One more drink and I'd have been under the host!" At a society dinner she entered the dining room alongside a beautiful and catty lady-playwright. The playwright stepped aside. "Age before beauty," she said sweetly. "Pearls before swine," responded Miss Parker, just as sweetly, and sailed in to as hearty a dinner as ever she ate. Over the coffee, she asked her dinner partner, "Where on earth do these people come from? I bet when the evening is over, they'll all crawl back into the woodwork."

Miss Parker spent a summer in England. Upon her return she explained that she had devoted the better part of her time to sliding up and down barristers. A drunk on the boat developed an unrequited passion for her; Dorothy referred to him as a "rhinestone in the rough." On one occasion he assured her, "I simply can't *bear* fools." "Apparently," said Miss Parker, "your mother did not have the same difficulty." Her report on a Yale prom did not endear her to the New Haven authorities. "If all those sweet young things present," she declared, "were laid end to end, I wouldn't be at all surprised."

Miss Parker could scarcely be considered the ideal week-end guest. Her hostess at one such gathering was described as "outspoken." "Outspoken by whom?" rasped Miss Parker. That evening she wired a friend in New York, "For heaven's sake, rush me a loaf of bread, enclosing saw and file." She is unfailingly polite to people's faces—so darn sweet and gracious, in fact, that some sensitive souls cannot watch her performance without a convulsion—but her angelic smile can dissolve into an angry snarl at the turn of a back. One of her victims analyzed her as one-tenth critic, nine-tenths hypocritic. Think what you will of Miss Parker in person, there is no gainsaying the fact that her short stories and verse rank with the very best. The ever-moderate Woollcott summarized her work as "so potent a distillation of nectar and wormwood, of ambrosia and deadly nightshade, as might suggest to the rest of us that we write far too much." Somerset Maugham contented himself with, "It is as difficult to say anything about Dorothy Parker that has not been said as it is about the Venus of Milo. Helen could make a scholar famous with a kiss; she can make a fool immortal with a jibe."

Two full-length plays have been written around the complex characters of Dorothy Parker. One was *Here Today*, by George Oppenheimer; the other, *Over Twenty-One*, by Ruth Gordon. "I suppose that now if I ever wrote a play about myself," commented the heroine bitterly, "I'd be sued for plagiarism."

* * *

A beminked young matron asked a clerk in one of Brooklyn's biggest department stores one day for a copy of a birth-control book called *Rhythm*. Shown the regular dollar edition she expressed a desire for a ritzier format. When she heard that it came only in the one-dollar binding, she took it reluctantly and declared, "Well, I guess it's good enough for every day."

* * *

Evelyn Waugh's *Decline and Fall* is back in print in this country after a long lapse. This is the book of which one critic said, "It has the desperate jauntiness of an orchestra fiddling away for dear life on a sinking ship." Connoisseurs remember it lovingly for one priceless sentence that might be called the epitome of British humor: "'Meet my daughter,' said the Bishop with some disgust."

* * *

Channing Pollock, in his autobiography, *Harvest of My Years*, tells the story of a train acquaintanceship made on his first journey, when he was fourteen. His fellow passenger, a stockily built man, took an interest in his youthful views on Byron and Dickens. Finally he inquired, "Have you ever read *Sherlock Holmes?*" "Don't you think," said Pollock pontifically, "that detective stories are a waste of time?" "No, I don't," said the stranger. "You see, I write them. My name is A. Conan Doyle."

* * *

S. J. Perelman had an even more astonishing encounter one time aboard a train, to hear him tell the tale. A loquacious conductor confided to him that he had been riding on trains for so long that he had begun to smell like one. "Sure enough," adds Mr. P., "two brakemen waved their lanterns at him a short time later and tried to tempt him down a siding in Kansas City. It came as a blow when I heard the next morning that he had fallen off the train during the night. The fireman said that we had circled about for an hour trying to find him but that it had been impossible to lower a boat because we did not carry a boat."

* * *

When Quentin Reynolds completed the manuscript of one of his many best-sellers, *Only the Stars Are Neutral*, he dispatched it to his publisher from London by clipper plane. The postage bill was for $16. "What on earth was your hurry?" his publisher cabled him. "You know we are not going to publish the book for three months. Stop throwing your dough around that way." The cable office called up a few minutes later. "We sent Mr. Reynolds your message," they said. "The charge is $20.81."

Reynolds reports he has given up the practice of drinking two cups of coffee at breakfast. "I found," he says, "that they kept me tossing around all morning."

* * *

Some time ago Russel Crouse promised to write a foreword for a reprint edition of *Life with Father*. Pressed for delivery of same,

he wired, "My understanding was that this foreword was to be a
joint contribution of Lindsay and Crouse. Now you'll have to wait
until I get Lindsay in a joint."

Mr. Lindsay, meanwhile, got himself involved in a "word game"
at the home of Lewis Browne. Everybody was playing except Rus-
sell Gleason, who declared firmly, "No word games for baby! I'm
anti-semantic!"

* * *

Don Marquis' favorite story had to do with revenge of a subtle
kind back in the Blue Ridge range in the rootin', tootin', feudin'
country. An ornery sprout of the McGregor family plugged a
member of the Larrabee family in the back one day. The victim
never knew what had hit him. One old Larrabee buck pointed out
that a simple killing was too merciful for the varmint. His ingenious suggestion, promptly passed unanimously, was that once
every day a shot be fired at McGregor that would *just miss him.*
For twenty years, this amiable pastime was put into effect. When
Marquis saw the victim, his hair was snow-white, his face and
hands twitched continuously, his glance darted madly from one
side to another. He was reaching for a bottle of soda pop when
a shot rang out. The bottle was shattered into a thousand fragments. McGregor howled like a coyote. "They'll do it every day
to him," commented a villager dispassionately, "till the poor b——
hangs hisself."

* * *

A ladies' club in New Jersey invited a femme book reviewer to
speak at its May meeting. She told the plot of a triple-A tear
jerker, and the entire assemblage broke into tears. All but one,
that is—a lady who sat dry-eyed and unmoved through the entire
recital. After the lecture, the reviewer asked her why she hadn't
cried. The lady's answer stopped her cold. "Oh, I'm not a member," she explained.

* * *

When Elliot Paul, whose antics make hard-pressed columnists chortle with delight, completed the manuscript of his best-selling book, *The Last Time I Saw Paris*, he exceeded all previous records by insisting that Random House send daily proofs to him at his farm in Connecticut via a pair of carrier pigeons that he brought home with him from the West. Everybody at the publishing office became very fond of the pigeons except Robert Haas, the vice president. He was on vacation when Mr. Paul brought the pigeons in and naturally their coop was installed in his private office.

This formality attended to, Mr. Paul summoned a taxicab at Madison Avenue and 57th Street and drove to Boston for a haircut.

Before the war, Elliot Paul maintained an apartment in Paris. One day his friends learned that he had rented desk space in the restaurant on the first landing stage of the Eiffel Tower. An incredulous reporter from the *Paris Herald* found him there, typing away contentedly on a story. "Well," said the reporter, "you certainly must be attached to the Eiffel Tower!" "Attached to it!" snorted Paul. "This is the only place in Paris where I can avoid seeing the damn thing!"

In New York Paul once bought a grand piano by telephone. He had the Knabe salesman wheel the instruments up to the phone one by one, and strike a few chords. Finally he heard one whose tone pleased him. "Send it along," he commanded. Another day he convinced a *Telegram* reporter that he had been appointed Professor of Drinking at a famous Midwestern university. "At last they realize that a gentleman must learn how to carry his liquor. I'll teach the whole student body," he asserted solemnly. There was hell to pay when the story appeared.

In Boston, he spent six months compiling figures on various types of employment in Massachusetts. The next job they gave him was connected with statistics on health and diseases in the Commonwealth. He disappeared for some weeks and then turned in the employment figures with new headings. Nobody ever complained; for all he knows, they are still part of the official records.

Paul's prize achievement was the hiring of a private office in New York where he could work undisturbed. He found just the place he wanted, paid three months' rent in advance, hired a secretary, paid her a month's salary, and arranged to start work the following Monday. Unfortunately, when Monday came around, Paul couldn't remember the address of his new office. He hasn't found it to this day.

Hollywood finally captured Elliot Paul. A big executive asked him how well he knew Europe. "I know every country there intimately," said Paul, "with the exception of Sweden, where I never have visited." A week later he was sent for by telegram. The locale of the story they wanted him for, of course, was Stockholm.

* * *

Overheard in a theatre lobby: "Saroyan isn't his real name, you know. It's a pseudonym. Saroyan is NATURE'S spelled backwards."

* * *

Professor Harold Laski is an Englishman, but he knows more about American law and American history than ninety-eight per-cent of the people who were born here. Every few years, he comes over to tell us about ourselves or to write a book about us. His recent *The American Presidency* was a Book-of-the-Month Club selection. He lectured at Harvard for a while but quit after a fight about the Boston Police strike in 1920. He is a close friend of Supreme Court Justice Frankfurter, and calls the Justice's disciples "the little hot-dogs." A facile phrase-maker, Laski is best known for: "A liberal is a man with both feet planted firmly in mid-air," "A big nation can take a lot of ruining," and "England sat on the fence so long before 1939 that the rust got into her soul."

Laski's memory rivals those of John Kieran and Herbert Swope. At his lectures he answers questions unhesitatingly with, "You will find that on the eighth line of page 134 of Bryce's *Common-wealth*," or, "Suppose you check the facts in the September 8,

1937, issue of *Time*." Several listeners who thought he was bluffing took the trouble to check some of these references. He was never wrong.

A young girl who was hearing him for the first time asked where he gave regular courses. "At the London School of Economics," his American publisher answered. "I believe he has been referred to there as 'the Wild Bull of the Campus.'" The girl said "Moo!"

* * *

A suburban bookstore ordered a copy of the *Encyclopedia of Sexual Knowledge* from a New York bookstore. Two days later the volume was returned. The notation read "Customer couldn't wait."

* * *

Harry Kurnitz, author of most of *The Thin Man* scenarios, relates that when he was a struggling young reporter in Philadelphia, the gay blades with whom he associated acquired, one by one, raccoon coats. They were a badge of distinction in those happy days of John Held flappers and bathtub gin; Kurnitz was extremely mortified that he could not afford one. Then one day he spied a coat made of wolf skin in a second-hand shop. It was barely within his means, but he bought it without a second's hesitation. "Did this end your inferiority complex?" I asked. "Could you once more dally with your fellow creatures on an even footing?" "It was superb," answered Kurnitz. "I wore it all winter, rain or shine. I had only one bit of trouble with it. It seems that every time there was a severe snowstorm, I found myself running madly after sleighs."

* * *

A rather down-at-the-heels magician went from one publisher to another trying to land a contract for his proposed autobiography. "I need the money," he confessed. "For ten years straight I have been sawing a woman in half and, with my luck, I always end up with the half that eats."

OH, SHAW!

ANY MAN who, at the age of eighty-eight, can dismiss a visitor with a chirpy "Get along with you now; I'm fully two years behind in my work as it is," is still a force to be reckoned with. That's what George Bernard Shaw told Lawyer Morris Ernst in London a few short weeks ago. Casual observers who construed some of his more ridiculous remarks of recent seasons as a sign of approaching senility neglected to take into account Shaw's increasing propensity for deliberately playing the clown, and being cute for visiting journalists and celebrity hunters. He still loves to see his picture in the papers, and will be just outrageous enough to corral the front page of a literary supplement. At heart, he remains one of the shrewdest horse-traders in the world.

Less than a year ago, Shaw pointed out that writers made a mistake in working twelve months of the year in Hollywood, regardless of how big their salaries might be. "The work you are doing," he reminded them, "becomes the sole property of your employers. When you write successful plays or novels, you may reasonably expect royalties on them every year for the rest of your lives—and the taxes aren't so big." Today, one prominent author after another is arranging to stay in Hollywood six months at most in the year, and is coming back to New York to write novels or plays—properties in which he can retain a vested right. It is amusing to note that a man going on to eighty-eight led the way.

I first met Bernard Shaw in his London apartment, facing the Thames Embankment, in the Spring of 1936. Random House was planning an anthology of hit plays produced by the Theatre Guild, and, of course, we wanted to head off the volume with Eugene O'Neill's *Strange Interlude* and Shaw's *Saint Joan*. Our written request elicited one of his customary "Absolutely no" cables, but Lawrence Langner gave me a note of introduction, and when Shaw consented over the phone to see me I knew that all was not lost.

He opened the door himself. The sight of that ruddy face and expanse of silvery whiskers in the doorway almost floored me. Miss Patch, his secretary, was away that day. We had the house to ourselves. First he showed me a photograph of himself with arm around Marion Davies. He had received it that morning, and obviously fancied himself in it. This led to a brief dissertation on William Randolph Hearst. "I cannot understand," said Shaw, "why so many Americans shudder at the thought of Hearst. Doesn't he represent everything you worship most: success, power, fortune? Why don't you elect him President?" My reaction must have been just what he was angling for, because he threw back his head and roared with laughter. Then he dropped the picture of Miss Davies. I made the mistake of reaching down to pick it up. Shaw snatched it angrily out of my hands. "I'm not as old as all that," he said sharply. "I do nicely for myself here without a soul in the house."

"And now about *Saint Joan*," he said finally. "What will you pay me?" I told him what we planned to pay for each play in the proposed anthology. "You can have *Saint Joan*," he said, "if you give me twice as much as anybody else. Without me, of course, you have no book."

He had me dead to rights on that. "I can't give you more than I do Eugene O'Neill," I protested. "*Strange Interlude* is just as important as *Saint Joan*." "Ah yes," he agreed, "but I know very well that you are Mr. O'Neill's own publisher in America, and he gets the entire payment. I must split mine with Dodd, Mead. That evens it."

I was very happy to settle things on that basis. Tea was brought up from the restaurant downstairs, and I said good-bye. He had a last thought just as I was stepping into the lift. "If a book club takes your collection," he called, "I shall have to ask double."

Sure enough, the Book-of-the-Month Club chose the *Theatre Guild Anthology* as a dividend, and Mr. Shaw cashed in very handsomely. In acknowledging the check he wrote, "I owe part of my success to the fact that I never had a partner in anything I did. If you wish to be a successful publisher, for heaven's sake, never take a partner." "I already have two," I answered, "but I'm not sure that all three of us together could cope with a city slicker like yourself."

Shaw's acknowledgment was a clipping of an apocryphal interview with Samuel Goldwyn. That gentleman was supposed to be imploring Shaw for permission to film *Pygmalion*. "I don't care if the picture loses money," he declared. "It's the contribution to art I'm thinking of." "That's the difference between us," Shaw assured him. "You think of nothing but art, and I think of nothing but money."

As a matter of fact, Shaw finally consented to a screen version of *Pygmalion*, but a Hungarian named Gabriel Pascal was the producer, not Goldwyn. The story goes that Pascal won Shaw by an approach that certainly was novel. "Not only do I want your permission to make a picture of *Pygmalion*," was his proposition, "but I want you to help me to raise twenty-five thousand pounds to finance it. The fact is, I'm broke at the moment." Mr. Shaw attended the preview, and signed autographs that one night as happily as the veriest Hollywood ham. He even consented to appear on the stage at the conclusion of the picture. Somebody in the gallery cried "boo." Shaw waved merrily, and said, "My friend, I quite agree with you, but what are we two against so many?" The picture was very successful both in England and America, largely due to a sensitive and characteristic performance by the late Leslie Howard. Shaw claimed that the picture netted him twenty-nine thousand pounds, but that it cost him fifty thousand in war taxes. "Another success like that," he grumbled, "and I am ruined."

Baiting Americans is an old pastime of Bernard Shaw's. "Why should anyone want to visit the United States?" he once said. "I do not want to see the Statue of Liberty. I am a master of comic

irony, but even *my* appetite for irony does not go as far as that."
He boasted to Hesketh Pearson (whose biography, *G.B.S.*, is superb reading): "I am always careful never to say a civil word to
the United States. I have scoffed at their inhabitants as a nation
of villagers. I have defined the one-hundred-percent American as
ninety-percent idiot. And they just adore me." It is barely possible
that Mr. Shaw has been reading the wrong newspapers.

When Cornelia Otis Skinner opened in a revival of Shaw's
Candida, he cabled, "Excellent. Greatest." Miss Skinner, overwhelmed, cabled back: "Undeserving such praise." Shaw answered, "I meant the play." Miss Skinner bristled, and replied,
"*So did I.*"

Shaw's romance with the actress, Ellen Terry, has been the subject of an infinite number of anecdotes and conjectures. When she
requested permission to publish some of the voluminous corre-

spondence he had addressed to her in the course of a lifetime, he refused indignantly, saying, "I will not play the horse to your Lady Godiva." "Ours was an ideal love affair," he explained, "because it was conducted principally by post. Ellen got tired of five husbands, but she never got tired of me."

He became a vegetarian in 1881, although H. G. Wells had hinted darkly that he drinks liver extracts on the sly. When his friends predicted that abstinence from meat-eating would be the death of him, he retorted that at least his coffin could be followed by a procession of all the animals he had never eaten. "They will look better than most pallbearers I have seen," he added. Mrs. Pat Campbell, in the heat of a particularly exasperating Shavian rehearsal, cried, "Shaw, some day you'll eat a pork chop, and then God help all womankind."

Shaw is a favorite subject of caricaturists, but he doesn't like any of them. He has a vast collection of photographs of himself, but I noticed nary a caricature in evidence when I visited him. He explained to a writer on *The Manchester Guardian*: "A photograph is eighty percent sitter, twenty percent photographer. A painting is seventy-five percent artist, and only twenty-five percent sitter. Caricatures? Bah! Child's play! Caricatures are never like me. Low's aren't like me at all. One day I went into a friend's flat and I did at last see a caricature of me that seemed to be good. It was cruel, of course, but still it was what a caricature should be. I thought I would bring Low to see it. Then it moved and I saw it was a mirror."

Mr. Shaw has unpleasant memories of his school days, and is determined that his plays be excluded from scholastic curricula. "I lay my eternal curse," he wrote, "on whosoever shall now or at any time hereafter make schoolbooks of my work and make me hated as Shakespeare is hated. My plays were not designed as instruments of torture." He does most of his reading standing up, often dressing or undressing at the same time. "I never shut a book," he told Mr. Pearson, "but put the next book on top of it long before it's finished. After some months there is a mountain of buried books, all wide open, so that my library is distinguished by the stain of dust or soot on it."

In an unusual burst of modesty, Shaw confessed: "In moments of crisis my nerves act in the most extraordinary way. I size up the situation in a flash, set my teeth, contract my muscles, take a firm grip on myself, and without a tremor, always do the wrong thing." "When I die," he says, "I want to be thoroughly used up. The harder I work, the more I live. Life is no brief candle for me. It is a sort of splendid torch, which I have got hold of for the moment. I want to make it burn as brightly as possible before handing it on to future generations."

* * *

It's difficult to keep up with the adventures of the absent-minded publisher of the *Saturday Review of Literature*, Hal Smith. His latest exploit took place at the corner of Fifth Avenue and 23rd Street. While the traffic light was red, a man planted himself directly in front of Hal's jalopy. The light turned to green, but the gent moved nary a step. Finally Hal leaned out of the car, and gently reminded him, "Say, bud, the light is green. How about getting the hell out of my way?" "Sorry, I can't oblige," replied the character. "Your car is on my foot!"

* * *

In 1887, an obscure young English doctor named Conan Doyle needed money badly, and whipped up a short story about a detective as a likely way to get it quickly. He named the detective Sherlock Holmes. Almost sixty years later, three new books about Sherlock Holmes were published in America within a few weeks of one another. A one-volume edition of his exploits was selling at the rate of thirty thousand copies a year. A group of solid, responsible citizens calling themselves "The Baker Street Irregulars" were dedicated to the task of "turning the Sherlock Holmes legend into a living being, incomparable and ageless." Anybody who dared to remark that, in the light of present detective-story standards, the Holmes-Watson sagas were pretty stuffy and obvious, ran the risk of being flayed alive by a Christopher Morley, or a Vincent Starrett, or an Elmer Davis.

Doyle himself didn't even like Sherlock Holmes. To him the creation of a great sleuth was just a stunt. He tried his darnedest to kill him off. In the last story in *The Memoirs of Sherlock Holmes*, published in 1894, Holmes met his arch-enemy, Professor Moriarty, face to face on the edge of an abyss, and Doyle made it abundantly clear that the two had perished together.

The author reckoned without his public, however. The outcry was so terrific that Sherlock Holmes simply had to be brought back to life. If the stories that followed were half-hearted and inferior, one would never guess it by the public reaction. Connoisseurs were not taken in. Several people wrote angry letters to the newspapers claiming that the new Dr. Holmes was an obvious impostor. A Cornish boatman told Doyle himself, "It is possible, sir, that when Holmes fell over that cliff he may not have killed himself, but he was never quite the same man afterwards."

Not many people know, incidentally, that Holmes was named after the American poet, Oliver Wendell Holmes, whose son could still recite most of the Sherlock Holmes stories by heart when he retired from the Supreme Court at ninety-odd.

At the first dinner of the "Baker Street Irregulars," Alexander Woollcott turned up in the cloak and fore-and-aft cap that William Gillette had worn in his great stage impersonation of the intrepid sleuth, and kept them on all through dinner, although the temperature of the room was over eighty. Another guest was a Mr. Laurence Paine of Boston, who had a fine time but discovered when he got home that an unsentimental loafer had taken advantage of the occasion to burglarize his apartment. He was afraid to tell the police where he had been.

When General Mark Clark went to North Africa to discuss details of the American invasion at Casablanca with loyal French officers, the rendezvous was very hush-hush, of course. The French officers detailed to meet the Clark party grew more and more tense as the night wore on without a hint of the prearranged signal. Suddenly the little boat which held Clark and his men glided silently into view. One French officer, a Colonel Watson (his father was English), could wait no longer. He waded waist-deep into the water, and extended a hand to the American officer in the prow of the boat.

"Watson," he identified himself.

"And I," said the American, "am Captain Holmes. I think, my dear Watson, that we have met before." The tension was broken. The vital business of the evening proceeded in an atmosphere of mutual amity and trust.

Logan Clendening tells a story about Sherlock Holmes' arrival in Heaven. The angels turned out en masse to meet him; the Lord Himself descended from his throne to bid him welcome.

"Holmes," He said, "to be perfectly frank, We have a little mystery of Our Own up here which you may be able to help Us solve. Adam and Eve seem to have disappeared. Nobody has been able to locate them for aeons. If you could possibly uncover them for Us. . . ."

Holmes darted to the fringe of the assemblage, and hauled two frightened, thoroughly surprised angels before the Lord. "Here they are," he said briefly. Adam and Eve readily admitted their identities. "We got tired of being stared at and asked for autographs by every darn new angel who came up here," they explained. "We assumed aliases and these simple disguises and got away with them for centuries until this smarty-pants ferreted us out."

"How did you do it?" marveled the Lord.

"Elementary, my dear God," said Sherlock Holmes. "They were the only two who had no navels."

* * *

Arthur Kober, author of the side-splitting *Dear Bella* stories and *Having Wonderful Time*, adores his mother. She, in turn, is so proud of him that she talks of little else. "His Bella stories must be wonderful," she says. "Even though he wrote them, it takes him twenty minutes himself to read one." At a party one day she met a lady who claimed that her son, too, was a writer.

"She says they want her boy should go to Hollywood and they would pay him twenty-five hundred dollars a week," she reported to Kober. "Honestly, I wanted to laugh in her face, but still I didn't say anything."

"Did you find out the lady's name?" asked Kober patiently.

"The name? I dunno. Kingsley-Schmingsley?"

"Why, that must have been Sidney Kingsley's mother," Kober told her. "Kingsley wrote *Dead End* and *The Patriots*. I'm sure he could go to Hollywood any time he wanted to for twenty-five hundred a week."

"Yeah?" said Mama Kober, somewhat deflated. "Well," she added brightly, "I didn't say anything."

Kober sent his mother to a hotel in the Catskills for a vacation, but she didn't like it much. "The food here is plain poison," she wrote, "and such small portions!"

When Arthur himself went to Hollywood, his lovely wife, Maggie, promised to keep an eye on Mrs. Kober. She phoned her one day and said, "How about going out with me this afternoon?" "What do you plan?" asked Mrs. Kober. "I thought we might go to see *Mrs. Miniver*," said Maggie. "O.K.," said Mama. "I don't know the lady, but any friend of yours is a friend of mine."

* * *

When Clifton Fadiman was serving as editor for Simon and Schuster, he opened one manuscript that consisted entirely of nudes of a Miss Jones. She wanted to sell the idea of a series of Yogi exercises in book form. Fadiman's one-line report was, "I see nothing in this manuscript except Miss Jones."

STEIN SONG

SCARCELY a day goes by at my office but somebody writes in to inquire about the safety and whereabouts of Gertrude Stein and her lifelong companion, Alice Toklas. Not many people even claim to understand the intricacies of Miss Stein's prose style, but millions admire her rugged and magnificent personality. When last heard from, the two ladies were safe, well, and reasonably happy at their villa in Bilignin, a bare thirty miles from the once fashionable resort of Aix-les-Bains. That was before the Germans took over unoccupied France, however. What's happened since then is anybody's guess.° When last heard from, the ladies were doing their own gardening, cooking, and housekeeping, but this worked no special hardship on them because they never could tolerate servants' getting in their way and generally ended up by doing everything themselves anyhow.

Gertrude Stein's latest opus, a novel called *Mrs. Reynolds*, was smuggled out of France by a friend of the author, and brought to New York via Sweden and Great Britain. It now reposes in a publisher's safe, pending an end of paper rationing. The lady who brought the script over had one unpleasant moment in England when an alert custom inspector mistook it for a secret document, written in an ingenious and entirely undecipherable code. Finally he conceded grudgingly that it was the manuscript of a novel, all right, but added that it was the first one he had ever seen that seemed to read the same from back to front as it did from front to back.

The last time that I saw Gertrude Stein in person was in 1936, when Jo Davidson and I flew down for a week-end at Bilignin. In accordance with her instructions, we flew to Geneva, although we

---

° Southern France was liberated just before the book went to press. First person to tell her experiences over the radio: Gertrude Stein.

discovered later that the airport at Lyons was twenty miles nearer
her home, not to mention an hour and a half air-time closer to
Paris. Gertrude had just been reading some poetry by Pablo
Picasso. "I read his poems," she told us happily, "and then I seized
him by both shoulders and shook him good and hard. 'Pablo,' I
said, 'go home and paint!'" Miss Stein was so pleased and engrossed in her characteristic monologue that we lost our way at
least ten times on the way to her home. We went through one
village three times. The last time the children waved to us as old
friends. Arrived at long last in Bilignin, Gertrude stopped the car
to greet every passerby and ask them pointblank the most intimate questions about their loves and business affairs, all of which
they answered cheerfully and in voluminous detail.

Gertrude Stein composing prose,
Toklas taking notes

Gertrude Stein really won the hearts of the American public
when she revisited the United States in 1931. It was just after the
Dillinger case had been wound up, and Gertrude said that she was
replacing Dillinger as the sensation of the moment. Reporters who
came to scoff at her ended by giving her front-page publicity.
When she made a short for the newsreels, Miriam Hopkins and

Mary Pickford helped her make up. Broadway loiterers stopped her for autographs. In Washington she stayed at the White House as a matter of course. The morning that she arrived in Hollywood, she demanded that Dashiell Hammett, Charlie Chaplin, and Dorothy Parker be produced for a dinner party that evening. They not only came, but boasted about it later.

Nobody would ever have mistaken Gertrude and Alice for devotees of Bergdorf-Goodman. They were not interested in ensembles. Both of them were champion dawdlers. At the last moment they would dress themselves in whatever garments happened to be handy and sally forth. In those days there was an employment agency for domestics located directly below the Random House offices. Gertrude arrived for luncheon one day a full hour late and announced cheerfully, "That fool elevator boy of yours dumped us out at the employment agency. He thought we were cooks."

Moss Hart once asked her if she had written any other plays besides *Four Saints in Three Acts.* "Of course I have," answered Gertrude. "Seventy-seven, to be exact!" At a party at my hotel apartment one evening she demanded a pot of boiled water long after the kitchen downstairs had closed. "Let me boil it for you, Miss Stein," volunteered a lady standing alongside her. Later Gertrude expressed her appreciation. "Who are you and what do you do?" she asked. "Oh, I write too," said the lady meekly. "My name is Edna Ferber." One of the few people who refused to be overawed by Miss Stein's astounding flow of rhetoric was Mortimer Adler, the author of *How to Read a Book* and the pretentiously titled *How to Think About War and Peace.* He and Gertrude got into a terrific argument one evening. Miss Toklas trembled on the outskirts of the battlefield, and was heard to remark, "Dear me! Gertrude is saying some things tonight that she won't understand herself for six months."

George Gershwin played the complete score of *Porgy and Bess* for the first time in public for the edification of Gertrude Stein. She sat beside him at the piano in a straight-backed chair, her arms folded, and said not a single word until he finished. Then she rose and threw her arms around him. "George, it's wonderful!" she cried. "Now I know it's right," said Gershwin. Gertrude has a booming, infectious laugh. She throws her head back like President Roosevelt, and slaps her thigh when something pleases her particularly. More often than not, it is a remark that she has made herself.

In the last letter that came from Gertrude Stein before postal communications with unoccupied France were cut off, she calmly asked for eleven books. "You should be flattered," she wrote complacently, "that I want so many of your new publications." The package was sent but, alas, it came back stamped "service suspended." Gertrude must have been very angry about that.

The usual print order for a new Gertrude Stein book is twenty-five hundred copies. The demand is constant. There rarely are fifty copies left over, but a second edition is never necessary. When *Mrs. Reynolds* is finally published, the manufacturing department will order the usual edition without so much as consulting anybody. Gertrude's last book, *Ida,* was supposed to be about the Duchess of Windsor, and I sent a copy to Government House in Nassau. "It was nice of you to send me *Ida,*" wrote the Duchess, "but I must confess that I didn't understand a word of it."

The Duchess had nothing on Miss Stein's faithful publishers.

* * *

The war has put a stop, for the time being at least, to the Book Fair craze, introduced innocently and legitimately a few years ago by a few large Midwestern department stores who went to infinite trouble and expense themselves to put on fine shows and really whipped up the community interest, but prostituted thereafter by chiseling, publicity-seeking phonies all over the country who wrote to the publishers literally demanding cash donations, autographed books, electric displays, prominent authors to make speeches and do fan dances, sixteen-cylinder Cadillacs and the front line of a *Mexican Hayride* chorus. "Play ball with us and we'll play ball with you," was their theme song. There were more ball-players in the book business than in the whole National League. One brave publisher, after much fatiguing brain work, finally evolved his now-celebrated Form Letter No. 891 to answer all Book Fair communications. "Your exceptionally modest request," it read, "would cost my firm only about $800, an admitted bagatelle that, if your current rate of business with us tripled as a result of your ball-playing, we could earn back easily in about two generations. Cordially and sincerely . . ."

In New York, *The Times* sponsored a fair to end all fairs at which practically every author in town took his turn on the platform, and thousands of dear little kiddies pilfered all the lovely catalogues that frantic publishers were trying to hold out for their elders. The official opener of everything in New York from a baseball season to a can of sardines is Mayor Fiorello LaGuardia, so it was taken for granted that the Little Flower would open the Book Fair. "At the Polo Grounds I throw out the first ball," mused the Mayor. "What do I do here?" "Throw out the first author," suggested an editor of the *Tribune*—a bon mot that has since echoed around the world and sent *The Times'* secret service on a frantic investigation to find out how a *Tribune* operative got into the opening ceremonies.

* * *

Robert Benchley was caught in a thunderstorm one afternoon, and came home soaked to the skin. "George," he called to his servant, "get me out of this wet suit and into a dry martini."

Benchley attended the opening night of a play called *The Squall*. After a dreary half-hour or so, a half-caste girl emoted, "Me Nubi. Me good girl. Me stay." Benchley rose in his seat, announced, "Me Benchley. Me bad boy. Me go," and staggered out of the theatre. In a drama called *Rope*, a murderer dumped his victim's body into a cedar chest, and served tea on top of it to the detective who had interrupted his gruesome business. Eventually, of course, the detective discovered what was inside the chest. "That's what comes of eating on an empty stomach," Benchley pointed out. All this was when he was acting as drama critic for *The New Yorker*.

Benchley, who has more friends than almost anybody else in the world, describes himself as an "unstylish stout." Some of his most hilarious pieces are preserved in volumes with the provoca-

Benchley the
drama critic

Benchley the
author

Benchley the
movie actor

Benchley the
bon vivant

Four sides of a many-sided character

tive titles of 20,000 *Leagues Under the Sea, or David Copperfield, From Bed to Worse, My Ten Years in a Quandary,* and *Inside Benchley.* He says it is so easy to make money as an actor in Hollywood that he's never going to write again. Last year a movie queen whose love-life would have filled ten volumes passed away. Benchley suggested for her epitaph: "She sleeps alone at last."

* * *

The Victory Book Committee arranged a noonday rally at the New York Public Library one day and announced that Gypsy Rose Lee and Clifton Fadiman would be the guests of honor. Two thousand people turned up. A script had been prepared for Fadiman, but Miss Lee declared that she preferred to stick to a few impromptu remarks of her own. Panicked at the last moment, however, by the seething throng before her, Miss Lee reached for a script at hand. It was Mr. Fadiman's, of course, and an enraptured audience heard her open her address with the sweeping statement, "All my life has been spent in the world of books." Two sponsors swooned.

After her Victory Book address, Miss Lee was so visibly nervous that a bystander called out, "What's the matter, Gypsy, frightened of crowds?" To which she replied testily, "How would you like to stand up here before such a mob with all your clothes on?"

* * *

Another report concerns a day on which the lady was autographing copies of her book in a Midwestern department store. A customer came in and asked to see the best Bible on the market for two dollars. Suddenly he spied the callipygian Miss Lee and, after gulping once or twice, planked down his two dollars, got his autographed book, and made for the nearest exit. "How about that Bible you wanted?" asked a clerk. "Can't use it now!" he cried cheerily. "I done spent my book money."

* * *

Another tale about Miss Lee has it that she woke up fully dressed one morning and cried, "Good heavens, I've been draped."

* * *

The Junior Literary Guild recently distributed a book about penguins. "This book," reported a conscientious young subscriber, "told me a good deal more about penguins than I like to know."

* * *

Did you ever hear about the tiger who cornered Mr. Aesop and ate him for Sunday dinner? "Well, Aesop," said the tiger pleasantly, "I suppose you'll be making up a fable about *this* now, too."

* * *

A discouraged young novelist was fingering his drink listlessly at the Players Club a few days back. "I know I'll never win the Pulitzer Prize," he declared. "Of course you won't," responded his publisher cheerily, "but wouldn't you rather have the critics say 'Why *didn't* this writer get the Pulitzer Prize' than 'Why *did* he get it'?"

At an adjoining table the narrator of an anecdote found himself stumped for a name. "What *is* the name of that ham in Holly-wood?" he appealed to Marc Connelly. "What *is* the name of that coal in Newcastle?" shot back Mr. C.

* * *

One of William Lyon Phelps' students at Yale asked him this question in the middle of a lecture on Browning: "Professor, which gives you the greater thrill: a student who knows and appreciates Browning as thoroughly as you do, or that same student weaving through an entire Harvard team for a touchdown?" "Billy" Phelps replied without hesitation, "I thrill to either performance, young man. The only difference is that when a student understands Browning, I do not smash my hat."

* * *

At a recent dinner party, the eminent John Gunther found him-self sitting next to Lily Duplaix, the orchidaceous wife of Georges Duplaix of Simon and Schuster. Mr. Gunther, with unfailing charm, set about winning Mme. Duplaix's heart, but unfortunately, when he was introduced to her, he caught her name as Lilly Daché, the famous milliner, and accordingly spent most of the dinner telling her everything that he knew or thought about ladies' hats. Mme. Duplaix listened in somewhat astonished silence, and directly after dinner sought out her host. "Your Mr. Gunther," she pro-nounced, "shouldn't drink so much."

* * *

Big reprint publishers who sponsor as many as fifty new titles in a single month obviously do not have time to read carefully the various additions to their line. Neither do the hapless wights who have to prepare the jacket copy. This sometimes leads to grim consequences. One eminent physician, for instance, nearly com-mitted mayhem when he discovered that a reprint of his tome on anatomy bore on the back of the jacket an advertisement for a rival practitioner's treatise on the same subject. It seems that the book thus shamefully advertised included a paragraph that labeled the good doctor "a palpable quack" and his opus "a worthless collection of undigested nonsense." A brand-new jacket appeased him somewhat, but there is a definite feeling abroad that his next reprint is headed elsewhere.

Another morning, a visitor insisted upon meeting the president of the reprint house and demanded a copy of a particular book on the art of letter-writing. "Oh, we let that go out of print long ago," said the publisher cheerfully. "But how about this new one on the same subject? It's got that dreary old stinker skinned a mile." "I do not need your invaluable assistance in composing letters," the caller remarked coldly. "I happen to be the author of the dreary old stinker."

* * *

Henry L. Mencken has evolved a happy formula for answering all controversial letters. He doesn't even have to read the blast to which it replies. "Dear Sir (or Madam)," he types. "You may be right."

* * *

One of our bookbinders has a clerk who reported a painful domestic incident last week. He arrived home very late for dinner and explained to his irate wife, "I had to wait for mine boss." "You mean to standing dere and tallink me you are making a pal out of dot dirty keppitalist?" she cried. "You and him is going hum togadder now?" "Who's tukking about keppitalists?" groaned the clerk. "I had to wait for de crosstown boss!"

Chapter Four

RICH MAN, POOR MAN...

Tʜᴇʀᴇ lives a millionaire in Canada named Harry Falconer Mc-Lean, whose amiable eccentricity consists in giving away money from time to time as the fancy seizes him. One day he turned up at a Toronto soldiers' hospital, and handed out hundred-dollar bills to patients and nurses to the tune of about twelve thousand dollars. Another day he enjoyed a musical comedy and sent every member of the chorus a mink coat. Several of the girls didn't have enough cash to pay the duty on the coats when they came back to the United States, and had to sell them on the Canadian side. A taxi driver got Mr. McLean to the Toronto station in record time one evening. Mr. McLean sent the driver's infant son a check for $2000. Canadian newshawks, intent upon spotlighting a benefactor of this kind, were doubly dumbfounded when they discovered their subject's nationality. Harry McLean is a Scotsman. Incidentally, he is a self-made man, and loathes publicity. He distributes largess for the sheer pleasure of giving. He is a rare and very swell egg.

Mr. McLean inevitably brings to mind another Scotsman who

hewed more closely to the proverbial line. That was Sir Harry Lauder, who was so tight that he himself made a joke of it, and was the first to relate that when he opened his purse one day to take out a dollar, four moths flew out. He attended a dinner of twenty one evening. It was of the caviar-champagne variety, and when the check came, it was a whopper. Several guests reached for the check, but Sir Harry's voice rang out, "No, no, gentlemen! This dinner is on me!" The next morning's headline, avers Sir Harry, read, "Scottish ventriloquist murdered!"

I met Harry Lauder, near the close of his remarkable career, at the Gleneagles Hotel in Scotland. He was probably the wealthiest guest at the hotel, but he occupied one of the smallest rooms. "What would I be doing with a sitting room?" he asked. "I'll do *my* sitting in the lobby." It poured steadily for a week, but Sir Harry and a few of his countrymen had come to Gleneagles to play golf, and by everything holy, they wouldn't have let a flood and a tidal wave interfere with their program. As he came into the clubhouse thoroughly drenched one afternoon, I asked grumpily, "Does it *always* rain up here?" "Oh, no," answered Lauder cheerfully. "Sometimes it snows." Rumor had it that there were dangerous snakes in the rough to the left of one of the tees. To make the story binding, the caddy master swore that Sir Harry drove three balls in succession into the patch in question, *and didn't even look for them.*

* * *

Among the countless other tales of tight-fisted Scots, I like best the story Thomas Lamont told the first time he saw Christopher Morley with a beard. Mr. Lamont's Scot had gone over to America as a boy, and amassed a great fortune. Eventually he decided to go home for a visit, and notified his three brothers to meet him at the station. When he alighted from his train, he saw nobody that he recognized for an instant, but then spied three figures who seemed vaguely familiar. They were his brothers, all right, but each of them had beards that ran clear down to their waists. "Now what would the three of you be growing them bear-r-rds for, lads?" he asked. "We had to," answered the eldest. "When ye went to Amer-r-rica, ye took the razor wi' ye."

* * *

The stories of Harry McLean's largess sent J. P. McEvoy to the files for records of other super-spendthrifts. He comes up with the story of "Coal-Oil Johnny" Steele, who ran through two million dollars in a few years. He spent $8000 for clothes in a single day. A hotel clerk in Philadelphia failed to accord him proper deference. "Coal-Oil Johnny" leased the entire hotel for a day for $10,-000—and fired the clerk. Then there was the Marquis of Hastings, who wagered his entire inheritance on a single horse race—and lost. And "Diamond Jim" Brady who had a separate, complete set of jeweled studs, rings, and cuff-links for every day of the month, and gave chorus girls a thousand dollars apiece for attending his parties.

Most spendthrifts are living examples of the old adage "easy come, easy go." Starving prospectors who strike gold or oil and become millionaires overnight, shop clerks who inherit fortunes from unknown relatives, soda jerkers who become internationally idolized movie stars—these are the people who build incongruous palaces in the desert (you'll find a half-dozen of them in Oklahoma), or have their doorknobs made out of solid gold, or give banquets at which a dozen dancing girls step out of a huge blackberry pie. The big bull market provided dozens of such newly-rich exhibitionists in the roaring twenties; many of them were jumping out of windows when the bubble burst.

One man used his fortune to better advantage. He made a huge bequest to his old alma mater for the construction and stocking of a fine, model library. The crash wiped him out just about the time the last stone was put in place. The trustees met to ponder the situation. They offered him the post of assistant librarian in the building he had made possible. He accepted.

* * *

The lady with the sable coat lived in a luxurious hotel that faced the park. Her chauffeur called for her every morning at eleven. As he helped her into the car one day, she noticed a shabbily dressed man on a bench across the street gazing up at the hotel with a rapt expression on his face. He was there again the next morning—and the next. The lady's curiosity was aroused. She told her chauffeur to wait, ignored his obvious disapproval, and crossed over to the man on the bench.

"I simply have to know," she told him, "why you keep staring at the hotel that way every morning."

The man smiled apologetically. "Lady," he said. "I'm a penniless failure. I sleep on this bench when the cops don't chase me. And I dream that some day—just once—I'm going to spend a night in that swell hotel across the way."

The lady, feeling very pleased with herself, declared, "Tonight your dream is going to come true. I'm going to pay for the best room in the house for you."

She summoned him to her breakfast table the following morning. "Well," she said, "how did you sleep?"

The man proved most disappointing. "Never again, lady," he answered. "I sleep better on the bench than I did here."

"Good heavens, why?" she asked. "Wasn't the bed soft and warm enough for you?"

"It wasn't that," he explained. "You see, down there I can dream I'm in the hotel. Here, the whole night through, I kept dreaming I was back on the park bench."

* * *

One of the elder DuPonts of Wilmington has a collection of Ming china second to none in the world. He keeps it in a little museum on his estate, and allows occasional visitors to inspect his treasures.

A young couple were there by invitation. While waiting for their host, the girl picked up a delicate vase. To her horror, it slipped from her fingers and smashed into a hundred fragments on the stone floor. Just then little Mr. DuPont came pattering up.

"Oh, Mr. DuPont," wailed the girl, "I have broken the little vase that stood in this niche. I do hope it wasn't one of the valuable pieces."

Mr. DuPont took a quick look at the broken fragments. "Fortunately, my dear," he said, with a reassuring pat, "it wasn't valuable at all. Don't trouble your pretty head about it."

Then he fainted dead away.

* * *

When Heywood Broun III was about ten, his father decided that a progressive schooling was what the boy needed, and went to inspect one of the most prominent of such institutions in New York. As he approached the head of the stairs, a class was dismissed. One after another, the moppets dashed into Mr. Broun's ample frame, shoved him angrily aside with mutters of annoyance, and continued on their way. Only the last little boy to leave the room stopped long enough to say "I beg your pardon" when he stepped on a Broun toe.

The teacher watched the proceedings with absorbed interest. "You'll have to excuse that last student," she said to Mr. Broun. "He's only been in the school for three days."

Heywood Broun, by the way, blithely ignored small-time hecklers who poked fun at his theories on education and politics. When friends asked him why he didn't hit back at his self-appointed critics, Broun said, "Why use dynamite when insect powder will do?"

* * *

Walter Clark, author of *The Ox-Bow Incident*, visited a little New England town to get background material for a new novel. Everybody was friendly and helpful to him, particularly the editor of the local gazette, who supplied fascinating biographical bits about the inhabitants.

One afternoon he was walking down the main street with the postmistress when a man he had not seen before approached from the opposite direction. Clark noticed that everybody averted his gaze when the man went by. One woman gathered her little girl into her arms and pointedly crossed the street to get out of his way. "Who is this fellow coming along here?" he asked. The post-mistress literally froze. "His name is Eustace Barron," she said coldly. "We do not talk about him in these parts." Clark noticed that Barron was well dressed, but had a hunted, furtive look on his face. He asked the editor about him, but that worthy gave him a withering look, and stalked off to the press room without a word.

Clark was intrigued. Here was some dark mystery that might make perfect material for his book. That evening he came back to the newspaper office, with a jug of applejack to assure his welcome. The old editor expanded visibly under its influence. Clark bided his time. The old man was chuckling over an anecdote he had just retailed, when Clark suddenly said, "Now you simply have got to tell me about this fellow Eustace Barron. Why this conspiracy of silence? Did he commit rape, murder, incest, or what?"

The editor compressed his lips. "Do you think I'd mind any little thing like that, son?" he said.

"Well, then, what was it?"

"You asked for it," said the editor. He carefully pulled down every shade in the room, tiptoed to the door to make sure nobody was eavesdropping, and finally whispered his secret into Clark's ear.

"Eustace Barron," he said, *"dipped into his capital!"*

* * *

The most faithful and persistent Boswell of the foibles of the idle rich is Lucius Beebe, who writes so beautifully in the *New York Herald Tribune* every Saturday morning about a world that ceased to exist fully thirty years ago. A few die-hards are left, clinging to the outer raiment and obsolete rituals of the lost tribe; Lucius reports the details of their death throes with an absorbed fascination.

Beebe long ago was nicknamed "Luscious Lucius" by a jealous competitor who envied him his silk-lined evening cape, his pearl-gray top-hat, his ability to ride atop a tallyho in an Easter Parade as though he did it every morning in the week—and, above all, the deep and very obvious enjoyment that he got out of life. When he wasn't concocting drivel for his "This New York" column in the Saturday *Herald Tribune*, Beebe turned out several absolutely first-rate books on American railroading.

It was Beebe who told the story of Valentina, unbelievably chic modiste of Fifth Avenue, who tried to sell a customer a sable coat. "But I already have a mink coat," said the lady. "Meenk! meenk!" echoed la Valentina. "Meenk is for football games!" Beebe reports that when this lady gave an Easter party she told each guest exactly what color dress to wear so that the general effect would be perfectly balanced. He also tells of Jack Miley's visit to the Pump Room in Chicago. In peace times, Miley is sports editor of the *News*. On the day in question, he was fried. The Pump Room specializes in flaming foods served on swords, spears, bayonets, and what have you. Miley watched the spectacle for a few moments and commanded, "Waiter, bring me a double order of scrambled eggs, extra soft, and listen, fellow, bring them on a *saber*."

"Cartier's," mourns Lucius, "isn't selling anywhere near the number of men's gold garters the shop usually does. Not because there is a declining demand; on the contrary, they aren't able to fill even the orders on hand because they can't get the good-quality elastic!" Isn't that terrible? When cruel war deprives people of the special wines, paté, caviar, and cuff links to which they are addicted, it's a lucky thing there's a fellow like Beebe around to record the ravages.

In private life, Lucius Beebe is the scion of a fine old New England family, so influential that when Lucius was requested to leave Yale, he was taken on at Harvard—a thing that isn't done every day in the week, I promise you. Legend persists that Lucius' precipitate exit from New Haven had to do with a ventriloquist whom he palmed off on the Yale Chaplain as a famous minister from the West. The minister was asked to deliver a sermon in the Yale Chapel, and progressed beautifully until the point where he stopped talking, cupped his hands about his lips, looked aloft, and called, "Am I right, Lord?" Down from the rafters (remember, he was a ventriloquist) came an answering "You certainly are, My Son!"

Beebe avers that he has the formula for a perfect summer garden: half mint, half marijuana! He awoke in his bed one morning with a bad hangover and rang for his man. "Send out the suit I had on last night for a cleaning," he ordered. "As I recall, an accident befell it." The valet hesitated. "Make it snappy," said Beebe. "All right," said the valet, "but do you want me to send it out as it is now—or would you like to take it off first?"

C. V. R. Thompson, the English humorist, sums up Lucius Beebe as "the only man outside of Warner Brothers' pictures who still says Zounds, Egad, and Oddsbodikins. . . . A crisis in Beebe's life is when he finds somebody wearing a wider lapel than his." Stanley Walker, on the other hand, predicts, "It is probable that in some happier time in the future when the sour-pussed young pipsqueaks of today are living off their social-security income and spending their old age writing their dreary memoirs, the journalists of America will do something handsome by Lucius Beebe, as the man who kept the faith during the dark years."

* * *

Stanton Griffis, head of Paramount Pictures, Madison Square Garden, the Brentano book chain, and Lord knows what else, is the man who signed Bob Hope for Paramount. That is like a publisher getting six Book-of-the-Month Club selections in a row. At a recent dinner, Mr. Griffis introduced Mr. Hope with these lines: "I want to present the funniest comedian in pictures, one of the screen's handsomest leading men, and the fellow who wrote this introduction for me—Bob Hope."

* * *

Speaking of dinners, E. Phillips Oppenheim says that he has one sure-fire formula for innumerable occasions on which he is called upon, without warning, for a few remarks. He clears his throat with a series of garrumphs, and declares severely, "As King Solomon remarked to the Queen of Sheba, 'Madame, I did not come here to speak!'"

* * *

There are a host of stories based on the penny-pinching habits of John D. Rockefeller. He got used to the sensation of signing away millions, but actual cash out of his pocket was something else again. His famous ten-cent tips were cause for hilarity the country over. His clothes concerned him little, if at all. One suit had a big patch on the coat, and a bright shine on the pants.

"What's wrong with this suit?" he asked crankily when a friend urged him to discard it. "Everything," said the friend. "Your father would be ashamed of you. You know how neatly he used to dress." "But," protested Rockefeller triumphantly, "I'm wearing a suit of my father's right now."

Mr. Rockefeller spent his last winters in Florida. Down there they tell a story that one day he went to the dentist to have a tooth pulled. "How much?" he asked in advance. "Three dollars," said the dentist, who didn't even know who his client was. "Hmph! Three dollars to pull a tooth!" grumbled John D. "Here's a dollar. Loosen it a little bit!"

* * *

Bob Lovett, a mainstay of the War Department, was an important banker before the hostilities began. He was entertaining Bob Benchley and Donald Ogden Stewart, among others, at his Locust Valley home one evening, when he was called to the telephone. "Why, yes!" his awestricken guests heard him say. "*Let* Austria have eight million dollars." Next day Stewart sent him a telegram which read, "You have made me the happiest little country in the world." The signature was "Austria."

* * *

A young banker picked up the telephone. His end of the conversation went as follows: "No. No. *No.* No. No No. *Yes. No.* No. No." Finally, with a last explosive "No" he hung up the phone. The vice-president of the bank overheard him and grumbled, "What d'ya mean by saying yes to that fellow?" "I had to," explained the other. "He asked me if I could hear him."

* * *

Mrs. Harrison Williams, frequently voted by modistes "the best-dressed woman in the United States," once bought a hat from a Paris milliner for a rather staggering sum, but with the assurance that the model would not be duplicated. The very night she returned to America, she was dancing at the Stork Club when another woman appeared with the identical hat on her head.

Mrs. Williams was indignant for a moment, but then realized that the other woman must have been bilked the same way that she was. When they passed close to one another on the floor, she pointed first to her hat, then to the other's, and smiled. The other lady looked straight through her. "Maybe she didn't understand," Mrs. Williams said to her partner. "Dance me over next to her again." This time her gestures were so broad that no misunderstanding was possible. She pointed to both hats, shook her head, and then smiled again. The woman cut her dead.

Mrs. Williams was pretty miffed about the whole thing until she went to the powder room and took a look into the mirror. She was wearing a different hat altogether that evening.

* * *

Beardsley Ruml, creator of the pay-as-you-go tax plan, is allergic to magazine profiles. A friend of his told a *New Yorker* reporter, "Ruml hates physical exercises. If you ever find him on a tennis court, you'll know it's because he dropped dead crossing it on the way to a scotch and soda." Two days after the article appeared, a Macy big shot accosted Ruml with a sharp, "What's this I hear about your being found dead drunk on a tennis court?"

* * *

At a dentist's office one day, Abel Green, the editor of *Variety*, heard a lady patient arguing over a bill. The gold inlay was $90. "Can't you make it $80?" begged the lady. The rest of the bill was $140. "Can't you make it $120?" she demanded. Finally she asked what time the doctor expected her on the following morning. "Eleven o'clock," said the doctor. Green answered for the surprised patient. "Can't you make it 10:30?" he asked.

A visitor from the sticks, whom Abel Green was entertaining at "21," asked if they have a regular $2 dinner there. "Sure," said Abel. "Do you want it on white or rye?"

SWEET ARE THE USES OF PUBLICITY

THE HIGH-POWERED (and higher-priced) "publicity counsel" of today represents billion-dollar businesses and self-made tycoons who want to be known as philanthropists and patrons of the arts. Basically, he is still the barker selling snake-oil remedies to the rubes at a carnival or the advance man of the old traveling one-ring circus. He is judged by the amount of free space he can wangle in the press, and the extent to which he can make a gullible public fall for his subtle, and often completely fictitious, propaganda.

One of the first press agents who turned publicity into a million-dollar business was the late Harry Reichenbach. This master of the art of exploitation has been called "the greatest single force in American advertising and publicity since Barnum." One of his earliest exploits was to salvage a little restaurant that had everything but customers. He put a simple bowl of water in the window with a sign reading, "The only living Brazilian invisible fish."

Increasing crowds gathered to observe this phenomenon. Some swore they could see the invisible fish make the water move. Reichenbach promptly hid a little electric fan in the corner to blow ripples on the water. "There it goes," the crowd would cry, and then, for no apparent reason, would go inside to eat dinner. Business boomed for weeks. Reichenbach claimed later that the proprietor simply couldn't

OLD DR. SHMOO'S ORIGINAL INDIAN SNAKE OIL GOOD FOR MAN & BEAST

stand prosperity: he tried to serve the invisible fish as a course.

It was inevitable that Reichenbach and the expanding motion-picture business should discover one another. He was engaged to publicize a gruesome affair called *The Return of Tarzan,* after a preview indicated that its chances were nil. A few days later a bearded professor registered at the Belleclaire Hotel in New York as "T. R. Zann" and had a "piano" hoisted to his room by block and tackle. In reality, the piano box contained a toothless old lion. Mr. Zann then called room service and ordered fifteen pounds of raw meat. The puzzled waiter who brought it took one look into the room, and fled. "There's a live lion up there," he screamed. Mr. Zann then led the animal through the main lobby, causing (1) three old ladies to faint dead away, (2) the management to call the police emergency squad, and (3) Mr. "T. R. Zann" and his lion to get reams of front-page publicity in every paper in town. By the time red-faced editors discovered it was all a publicity stunt for a fifth-rate movie there was nothing they could do about it. When the picture opened, the crowds fought to get in.

Reichenbach next turned his attention to a little number called *The Virgin of Stamboul.* A Turkish potentate and staff of seventy took an entire floor at a swank hostelry. The potentate was reluctant to be interviewed, but finally consented to reveal that his brother, the Sultan, had dispatched him to find the dastardly American sailor who had stolen the Number One favorite from the Sultan's harem. It's hard to believe, but only one reporter in town saw through this incredible hocus-pocus. The exception was a former publicity man himself, who was so intrigued by the build-up that he held his peace until the story broke in the papers. Then *The Virgin of Stamboul* (which, by an odd coincidence, featured the abduction of a harem pin-up girl by a Yankee gob) swept triumphantly into New York, and the "Sultan's brother" went back to his dish-washing job in an Armenian restaurant.

As the picture industry prospered, its publicity methods became less crude and obvious. Reichenbach kept pace with their progress. When the Metro Pictures Corporation was formed, it had everything but a production department. Reichenbach kept exhibitors intrigued for a full year by a whirlwind campaign that featured the slogan "Can they keep it up?" What they were keeping up nobody, including themselves, knew; but in the end, perseverance won its just reward, and the Metro Corporation blossomed into Metro-Goldwyn-Mayer.

The press agent for one Broadway show hired a huge truck to tour the city. The name of the play was emblazoned on its sides, and a loud speaker within blared its virtues. At one of the most important intersections in the city, the truck broke down—accidentally, of course. Traffic was snarled in every direction for a full half-hour while the merits of a fly-by-night musical comedy were broadcast to a stalled and helpless populace. Another press agent evolved the notion of taking a native California boy who had been unable to get a break in the movies, and shipping him to England where he became the janitor of a well-known London theatre. In the dead of night, the two changed the electric sign above the marquee, and put the boy's name in lights. With the photograph of this sign as his only evidence, the agent then convinced a big Hollywood studio that his client was one of the most popular stars in Britain, and secured a signed contract for him. The boy really had talent, and is a genuine picture star today. The same technique has been followed a dozen times since. A lot of those exotic foreign sirens you see writhing around the screen drew their first breaths in such typically oriental oases as Wichita, Kansas.

One publicity man made a Broadway chop house nationally famous by the simple expedient of scattering sawdust on the floor. Another guided a shoe emporium to fame and fortune by persuading the proprietor to boost his fixed price from $6.95 to $12.95. The shoe man was incredulous until the promoter proved his point by an actual experiment. He put two identical pairs of shoes in the show window, side by side. His sign read, "There is absolutely no difference between these shoes. One pair is priced at

$6.95; the other at $12.95. We just want to see which price you prefer." Three women out of every four who entered the shop, suspecting chicanery of one sort or another, insisted upon paying $12.95.

Harry Reichenbach's most conspicuous achievement was connected with that third-rate, innocuous painting called "September Morn." The proprietor of a Broadway art store had seen the original in Paris, and thought it had commercial possibilities. He had ordered innumerable reproductions in assorted sizes at a cost of over sixty thousand dollars. The unpredictable American public, however, paid no attention to "September Morn" and the dealer seemed stuck with his entire investment. It was at this juncture that he enlisted the services of Reichenbach. He got results within twenty-four hours.

Reichenbach put the biggest available print of "September Morn" in the dealer's window. Next he hired a dozen high-school kids and rehearsed them painstakingly in the routine he had decided upon. Then he burst into the office of Anthony Comstock, ever-ready head of the Anti-Vice Squad and self-appointed custodian of the people's morals. "Mr. Comstock," cried Reichenbach, "there's a vile picture on display in a Broadway window, and schoolchildren are ogling it this very minute!" Comstock grabbed his hat and the two made a running dive for the dealer's store. The kids saw Reichenbach coming, and, as previously arranged, began pointing at the picture, smirking, and making obscene remarks about it. Comstock charged into the store like a wounded bull and had the deliriously happy dealer clapped into jail. By the time the excitement and nation-wide publicity had died down, "September Morn" was undoubtedly the best-known painting in the United States, and more than two million reproductions of it were sold.

Reichenbach employed a similar technique to turn Elinor Glyn's atrocious *Three Weeks* into a rip-roaring best-seller. He sent anonymous letters of protest to puzzled post-office officials all over the country. Finally the Postmaster General barred the book from the mails—and the stampede was on.

The methods of the highly organized "lobbies" that infest Washington today are really little more than elaborations of the technique perfected by Reichenbach and his disciples. Sometimes their tricks are just as crude. A sudden deluge of thousands of taxpayers' letters on senatorial desks in the midst of debate on controversial measures does not just happen spontaneously. Some master publicity counsel is pulling the strings. There are informed commentators who will tell you that the "spontaneous public clamor" for Wendell Willkie at the 1940 Republican Convention had been planned step by step, and minute by minute, at a banker's residence six months ahead of time.

Astute publicity men have extricated million-dollar enterprises from many a jam. One of the funniest of them involved a magnate who "got in on the ground floor" of a new salmon-canning project. The price of his stock was right, and the salmon was delicious. Unfortunately, the color of the salmon was pure white, instead of the customary pink. It tasted just as good as the best, but the public was used to *pink* salmon, and would have no truck with any other kind. The inventory reached alarming proportions, and bankruptcy loomed. Then the high-powered "public relations counsel" was called in. By printing just one line in big type on every can of salmon in stock, he cleaned out the inventory in exactly four months, and, if rival canneries had not secured an ultimate injunction, would undoubtedly have put most of them out of business. The line that he suggested was simple. It read: *"This salmon is guaranteed not to turn pink in the can."*

* * *

There is a formidable blonde lady on the Bowery, according to Joseph Mitchell, who has achieved great local fame as cashier and proprietress of a movie "grind" house where ten cents gets you a double feature, newsreel, selected shorts, and a crack at a set of dishes. "Mazie" is the lady's name, and she keeps her house open from 8 A.M. to midnight. On cold days many a "bum" produces his dime early in the morning and sleeps peacefully until closing time. "Some days I don't know which this is, a movie theatre or a flop-house," sighs Mazie. "Pictures with shooting in them are bad for business. They wake up the customers." If one of the sleepers snores loudly enough to annoy the rest of the audience, Mazie charges down the aisle with a couple of copies of *True Romances* tightly folded as a bludgeon, and hollers, "Outa here on a stretcher, you big baboon! Every tooth in your head! Every bone in your body!" The women and children, reports Mitchell, enjoy this mightily, particularly when Mazie gets the wrong man, as she frequently does.

* * *

One day in 1929, Myra Hampton, now the wife of Paul Streger, the agent, gave birth to a baby boy. That night the Thanatopsis Poker Club, whose full membership knew and loved Myra, chipped in and bought the infant one share of United States Steel, then selling at something like two hundred and fifty dollars a share. Shortly thereafter Wall Street collapsed. At the next meeting of the club, Franklin P. Adams remarked casually, "I hear that Myra's kid has been clipped by the market."

NOT VULNERABLE

P. HAL SIMS, one of the greatest card-players of our time, waxes suddenly compassionate when his victim is writing out a check for an evening's losses. "Maybe I play this game a little better than you do," he will admit. "Let's have a round of golf in the morning, and I'll give you a chance to get it back." He neglects to add that he negotiates an eighteen-hole course in an average 74. This remarkable man is also a championship billiard player and shot, and, before he took on weight, bagged a number of tennis trophies as well.

It is as a bridge-player, however, that he won national fame. Before he tired somewhat of the game, he played ten or twelve hours a day, seven days a week. He owned a house at the New Jersey seashore, where bridge sharks came for a week-end and stayed for the summer. Reporters began dropping in to cover the impromptu tournaments. No servant ever remained more than four days. The only guest who was ever thrown out was an Italian who chanted hymns. Sims grew suspicious when the Italian's partner made fourteen successful finesses in a row. He called in an interpreter who discovered that the hymns went something like

> The King of Hearts is on the right,
> The Queen of Spades is by it."

Sims finally tired of feeding half of the nation's bridge experts and sold his house to Max Baer for use as a training camp.

Aboard a liner for England, Sims spotted a quartet of professional card sharps in the smoking lounge the first afternoon out and resolved to have some fun with them. On his way to their table, however, he was stopped by an English clergyman who proffered his hand and said, "Mr. Sims! I recognized you from your pictures! Please have a drink with me!"

Sims found the clergyman such stimulating company that he never did get over to the card sharps, either that afternoon or during the remainder of the voyage. Several weeks later, in the company of an official from Scotland Yard, he ran into the clergyman at the Savoy Grill in London, but was surprised to see him turn white and duck for the nearest exit. "I wonder what's gotten into Dr. Ogilvie," he said. "Dr. Ogilvie!" echoed his companion. "That's no doctor. He's one of the slickest card sharps in Britain." Sims then realized that he had been neatly decoyed aboard the steamer, and had left the field clear for the "doctor's" pals to lure more likely game into their little net.

The card sharps knew what they were up against when they confronted Hal Sims. He has the percentage of every game of chance figured to such a nicety that the slightest deviation finds him hot on the scent of skulduggery. He once picked an intricately marked deck of cards from a hundred regular ones in less than five minutes. He was kind enough to warn a friend not to play gin rummy with him for money. "No matter how carefully you mix the cards," he explained, "a few of them are bound to remain in the same order they turned up in for the previous hand. I remember the exact order of the cards for the last three."

Hal Sims has befriended many players who were down on their luck, although he knew that some of them were inveterate grifters. One notorious four-flusher phoned to say that if he didn't get a thousand dollars immediately, he'd be jailed as a confidence man in the morning. "A thousand is too much," said Sims, "but if you can get that banker we played with last night to put up five hundred, I'll make up the difference." "He gave it to me," the man reported happily an hour later, and Sims made out his check for the sum he had promised. The next time Sims saw the banker, he said, "It was nice of you to let our poor friend have that money he needed." "Yes," said the banker. "He told me what a fix he was in, so I let him have the thousand."

Mrs. Hal (Dorothy) Sims is quite a character in her own right. Her father was Isaac L. Rice, successful industrialist who invented

the Rice gambit in chess, and was a great patron of the game. Mrs. Sims' comment is, "They have another name for patron now." It is never warm enough for Mrs. Sims. I remember her bundled up in three sweaters during a Bucks County week-end that was so hot that the other guests spent most of the time in the swimming pool. She hustles her husband off to Havana every October and stays there until the following May. One July morning, her husband demanded his bathing suit. "It's all packed for Cuba," she reported. "What's the idea?" he asked. "We're not leaving for over three months." "I know," she said, "but I hate packing, so I hurried up and got it over with." Sims cheerfully calls her "the poorest bridge player in the world" and she just as cheerfully replies, "Well, then I can't get any worse." They have a standing rule that she is never allowed to bid "no trump"; Sims has finally convinced her that there is nothing "undignified" in stopping the bidding short of a game. Mrs. Sims is the inventor of the "sycic." She says it came to her in a flash. She picked up a hand one day with no spades in it—and bid a spade. Her partner nearly had a fit—until he discovered that her impulsive declaration had prevented their opponents from bidding—and making—a grand slam in the spade suit. That made her something of a heroine. She wrote up her experiment for a magazine and meant to call her new system "Psychological Bidding," but her sense of spelling, never too clearly defined, failed her in the clutch—and "sycic" it became. It was Dorothy Sims' great moment.

* * *

New York's Cavendish Club has been the scene of some of the most dramatic bridge contests of our time. Through its corridors flit the elite of bridgedom: "The Four Aces," Culbertson, Sims, and a host of others only slightly less talented. Even the hat-check girl keeps the members strictly classified. A guest couldn't find his coat one night, and started searching a rack on the right. "Oh, it wouldn't be there," the girl told him. "I distinctly remember hanging it with the two-cent-a-point players."

Some of the experts—Count Von Zedtwitz, for example—have
been known to ponder a full twenty minutes before playing a certain card; others, like Hubert Boscowitz, play so quickly that even
their partners are confused at times. Sir Cedric Hardwicke played
a few friendly rubbers as Boscowitz's partner. The latter had to
leave to catch a train. As he stood waiting for the elevator he
heard Hardwicke say, "I'll bet that blighter is in Chicago by this
time."

There was a lot of bidding on a hand at the Cavendish one
afternoon. Just before play started, George Kaufman requested,
"May I review the bidding—*with the original intonations?*"

One gentleman, no longer associated with the club, sent a dona-
tion to Bundles for Britain when that was the thing to do. The
committee was a little puzzled as to the disposal of four immacu-
late, stiff-bosomed dress shirts. A lady was handling one of them
rather gingerly when four aces dropped out on the floor!

* * *

The average card-player hasn't got a chance when he mingles
with ranking experts like Hal Sims, Ely Culbertson, or Oswald
Jacoby. These men not only play their cards with superlative skill,
but have learned to turn every personal peculiarity and facial expression of their opponents to their own advantage. This is perfectly legitimate, of course. When playing with one another, they
never dream of arranging their cards in order, since every one of
them automatically observes from what part of the hand each card
is taken. If a player exposes any part of his hand to an opponent
he has only himself to blame if said opponent takes advantage
of it.

There's a tale told, probably fictitious, of a bridge game where
Culbertson, seated at another expert's left, played a neat trick on
his adversary. The latter had bid up to six clubs. Culbertson had
the king of clubs and another small club in his hand. He purposely
let the opponent see the king at the left end of his hand, but hid
the small club among the cards on the other side. The opponent

thereupon bid "seven clubs" which Culbertson doubled. The first time the opponent had the lead, he confidently planked down his ace of clubs. When Culbertson plucked the little club from its hiding place, instead of the expected king, the opponent bellowed with rage, threw his cards on the table, and cried, "I refuse to play with crooks!"

* * *

When John Mulholland, one of the great prestidigitators of our time, was a youngster, he was added as an afterthought to a program at the National Arts Club, and forthwith gave a very creditable performance. When it was over, however, an old killjoy with a perverted sense of humor asked if the young magician could do the same tricks with any old pack of cards. Mulholland brazened it out, and found an unopened pack of cards, with the National Arts device on their orange backs, thrust into his hands. To the astonishment of the members, he performed some tricks with the new cards that eclipsed any he had done with his own prepared deck—more mystifying, indeed, than any he has been able to do since. It appears that when Mulholland unwrapped the deck he noticed (although he did not see fit to call it to the attention of the members) that a singular error had occurred at the factory in the assembling of that pack. It was made up of fifty-two aces of spades.

* * *

In London, a certain lord married a woman forty years his junior. Adele Astaire preserved for months the London *Times'* account of the ceremony, which ended with, "The bridegroom's gift to the bride was an antique pendant."

* * *

Clarence Darrow delivered the funeral oration at the bier of a friend who, after an unparalleled streak of bad luck, had committed suicide. "My friend," said Darrow simply, "decided, in a moment of temporary sanity, that his life was no longer worth living."

* * *

John M. Weyer, reports Leonard Lyons, gave a dinner for gourmets, and told a new maid, "Please remember to serve the fish whole, with tail and head, and a slice of lemon in the mouth." The maid appeared surprised, but said nothing. That evening she bore the fish triumphantly to the table, complete with tail and head. And in her mouth she carried a slice of lemon.

* * *

A maharajah who was entertaining Neysa McMein in India some winters ago queried a servant on the progress she was making in hunting. "The beautiful lady shoots divinely," reported the impeccable Hindu, "but Providence is merciful to the birds!"

Chapter Five

STRICTLY PROFESSIONAL

RELATIVE TO EINSTEIN

ONE SULTRY afternoon this summer, I discovered a famous figure trudging complacently ahead of me up Sixth Avenue, puffing on his pipe, and carrying a huge package in his arms. It was Professor Albert Einstein, discoverer of the theory of relativity, Nobel Prize winner, American citizen by grace of Nazi stupidity and intolerance. I followed him for a full block. Not one soul recognized him. "Aren't you surprised that nobody stops to gape at you?" I asked when I caught up with him. "If Lana Turner walked up this same block, a thousand people would turn to stare." "Lana Turner," replied the professor sagely, "has a great deal more to show than I have."

Professor Einstein, by this time, has become a familiar and accepted part of the Princeton family. When he and his wife first arrived from Germany, however, he knew little English, and was frankly dismayed by the homage paid him by a strange people who didn't understand beans about his mathematical theories, but plagued him for his autograph and demanded to know what he thought of American womanhood. On the dock, a reporter assured him that he looked just like Kringelein in *Grand Hotel*. "I never stopped there," said the professor.

The general public first heard about the Einstein theory of relativity when some savant proclaimed that only twelve men in all the world understood what he was talking about. This intrigued the American people in much the same way that *Information, Please* and other radio quiz programs do. Jokes about relativity, most of them awful, became part of every comedian's repertoire. The best of them was the conversation between Ginsberg, who demanded to know what relativity was, and Garfinkel, who brazenly attempted to explain it to him. "It's like this," says Garfinkel. "You go to the dentist to get a tooth pulled. You are in the chair only five minutes, but it hurts so much that you think you are there for an hour. Now on the other hand, you go to see your best girl that same evening. She is in your arms for a full hour, but it is so wonderful to have her there that to you it feels like only five minutes." Ginsberg nods dubiously. "I see," he says, "but tell me, Garfinkel—from dis he makes a *living?*"

Professor Einstein had been famous in Europe for years before he came to this country; his definitive paper on relativity had been published in 1915; he did not arrive in New York until 1933. He and his family, however, had always assiduously avoided the limelight. One story has it that at the first lush banquet at the Waldorf given to honor him, an orchid was placed on the plate of every lady before she sat down. Mrs. Einstein thought it was something to eat, and was stopped in the nick of time from cutting it with her knife and fork. Some weeks later the Einsteins were taken to the Mt. Wilson Observatory in California. Mrs. Einstein was particularly impressed by the giant telescope. "What on earth do they use it for?" she asked. Her host explained that one of its chief purposes was to find out the shape of the universe. "Oh," said Mrs. Einstein, "my husband does that on the back of an old envelope." As a matter of fact, Einstein has often said that he could write

everything basic that he knows about relativity within three pages.

Princeton University offered him a lifetime post in the Institute for Advanced Study. He accepted gratefully, and has lived comfortably near the campus ever since. After Mrs. Einstein died in 1936, the professor moved into his present home at 112 Mercer Street. It is furnished with Spartan simplicity. That's how he wants it. The hand-made furniture was shipped to him from Germany; he considers it very good luck that he managed to salvage what he did. Some of his rarest books and manuscripts were burned by Nazi vandals. But he saved enough for a fresh start. His couch is the nearest thing to a fakir's bed of nails that I have ever felt, but the professor sleeps like a log on it. His companion is a coal-black cat. Dr. Einstein believes that this cat's nightly forays are spent in "soliloquizing," and has named him "Hamlet." But the neighbors, who have different ideas, call him Casanova.

Perhaps you have heard of the twelve-year-old girl who fell into the habit of dropping in on the professor every day on her way home from school. Her parents were gratified, but somewhat mystified too. One evening the mother found an opportunity to ask the professor, "What do you two talk about every day?" "Oh," laughed the professor, "she brings me cookies and I do her arithmetic for her."

Einstein's simplicity and imperturbable good humor have won him the love of the entire Princeton faculty and student body. At a faculty meeting one day, he was importuned to explain his theories in a brief lecture. He said it was impossible. A brash associate volunteered to do it for him. After floundering around for twenty minutes, the dean begged him to desist. "Maybe twelve men can understand Einstein," he said, "but certainly *nobody* understands you." Einstein comforted his crestfallen friend. "In Germany once," he said, "a hundred Nazi professors collaborated on a book to prove that my theories were poppycock. Imagine! If I really was wrong, one would have been quite enough."

Professor Einstein became an American citizen in 1940. He loves everything about his adopted country, and is particularly

fascinated by American slang. He listened carefully three times
to the story of the employer who told his secretary, "There are
two words I must ask you never to use in my presence. One of
them is 'lousy,' the other is 'swell.'" "That's all right by me," said
the secretary. "What are the two words?" When he finally com-
prehended, the professor threw back his head and roared with
laughter. In a seminar one afternoon, he ran out of pipe tobacco.
None of the students had any either, but one of them taught him
to break up several cigarettes, and fill his pipe with cigarette tobacco. "Gentlemen," he said gravely, "I think we have made a
great discovery." The experiment, however, as you will know if
you have ever tried it yourself, proved a failure.

Oddly enough, Professor Einstein is not exactly a wizard at the
simplest forms of arithmetic. Income-tax blanks dismay him, too.
A clerk at the Princeton Bookstore caught him glancing at an in-

come-tax guide recently, and asked if he would like one. "Good
heavens, no," cried the professor. "It's terrible enough to have to
figure out the tax without having to read a whole book about it!"

When Professor Einstein visited Palm Springs last year, another
distinguished guest at his hotel was James "Schnozzola" Durante.
One day the manager called Jimmie and said, "Professor Einstein

has his violin with him, and is dying for somebody to accompany him at the piano for a little while. I told him you might oblige." Jimmie agreed, and there followed possibly the most incongruous duet in the history of music. "I don't play classical music so good," confessed Jimmie. "Every time I made a really terrible mistake the professor gave me a hurt look like I done it on purpose." As an afterthought, he said, "The professor made plenty of mistakes too."

Einstein was really stopped cold at a recent Princeton function by Jascha Heifetz's irrepressible sister Pauline. "Tell me, Professor," she said with deadly seriousness, "is this mathematics racket really on the level?"

* * *

M. F. Ashley Montagu's book, *Man's Most Dangerous Myth: The Fallacy of Race,* includes the story of the wife of a Worcester Cathedral Canon who listened to the first announcement of the theory of evolution with consternation. "Descended from the apes!" she exclaimed. "My dear, we will hope it is not true. But if it is, let us pray that it may not become generally known!"

* * *

Those two eminent scientists, the Doctors Piccard, are exact twins, as identical, to coin a phrase, as peas in a pod. This fact enabled them to play a harmless prank on a barber in their native Switzerland.

The stratosphere flier assured the barber that he had the toughest, most stubborn beard in captivity, and offered to bet that the best shave in the world would only last him a few hours. The barber angrily offered him another shave free if he should need it within twenty-four hours. He spent an hour giving him the closest shave possible without skinning him alive.

An hour later, the other brother arrived with a formidable beard and collected a free shave—after the bewildered barber had been given a strong restorative.

* * *

The late Cardinal Hinsley of Great Britain and the Archbishop of Canterbury attended the same dinner party and later shared a taxicab into town. "It is quite fitting that we take the cab together," smiled the Archbishop. "After all, we both serve God." "Yes, yes," agreed the Cardinal heartily. "You in your way; I in His."

Cardinal Hinsley liked to tell the story of two brothers who studied for the ministry. One was a little too flippant and whimsical to reach the heights; the other, a pompous and heavy-handed party, became a bishop in due course. "My brother," the whimsical one explained, "rose because of his gravity; I was held down by my levity."

Another story always credited to Cardinal Hinsley features a lecturer who told his audience that the world would probably end in seven billion years. "How long did you say?" came a terrified voice from the rear. "Seven billion years," the lecturer repeated firmly. "Thank God," said the voice. "I thought for a moment you had said seven *million.*"

* * *

A Bishop of Texas visited London and was taken to a fashionable soirée at which the ladies' dresses were cut very low. His hostess asked condescendingly if he had ever beheld such a sight. "Not," said the Bishop, "since I was weaned."

This same Bishop made a great hit with some English churchmen with a story that most of them probably have been using to advantage ever since. It concerned a colored preacher whose sermon emphasized free salvation, but who later complained about the paltriness of the collection. "Didn't you done say, Parson," protested a parishioner, "that salvation is free—free as the water we drink?" "Salvation *is* free, Brother," replied the minister. "It's free and water is free, but when we pipe it to you, you has to pay for the piping."

* * *

Irwin Edman, brilliant author and professor of philosophy at Columbia University, is that stock comedy character, the absent-minded pedagogue, in actuality. Beloved by his students for his wit, erudition, and uncanny ability to make the most abstruse subject sound easy, he is also the source of a whole saga of campus humor. One day he stopped a student on Riverside Drive and asked, "Pardon me, but am I walking north or south?" "North, Professor," was the answer. "Ah," said Edman, "then I've had my lunch."

Unable to enter his classroom, he summoned the janitor, complained that the door was broken. The janitor turned the key that was already in the lock, and opened the door. "That's what keys are for, Professor," he explained gently. Irwin spent an evening with a colleague and his wife, and the conversation was spirited until about two in the morning when, after several elaborate yawns had been ignored, the colleague said, "Irwin, I hate to put you out, but I have a nine o'clock class in the morning." "Good

ALMA MATER

lord," said Irwin, blushing violently, "I thought *you* were at *my* house!"

At Columbia, a warning bell sounds three minutes before the end of a classroom hour. Edman was lecturing on Santayana one afternoon when the warning bell sounded, and several students stirred in their seats. "Just a moment, gentlemen," said Edman. "That was not the final bell. I wish to cast a few more pearls."

His looks are deceiving. A stranger could be excused for thinking him an undergraduate rather than a professor of international repute. Early in his pedagogical career he met his former professor, Felix Adler, on the campus. "What are you doing now, Irwin?" asked Adler. "I'm teaching here, too," said Irwin. "How cute!" exclaimed Adler. In a Munich beer-hall, years before the war, Edman fell into conversation with a portly Bavarian who was impressed with his store of knowledge and inquired, "What do you do in America?" "I am a professor of philosophy at Columbia," was the answer. The German roared with laughter. "If that were true," he said, "we would be colleagues." There is a sequel to this story. Irwin was so indignant that he rushed back to his hotel for his credentials and a letter of introduction signed by Columbia's president, Nicholas Murray Butler. The abashed German admitted that *he* was the one who had been bluffing; he was only an instructor at the local high school.

Edman came back home from that visit on an Italian boat. "Put me at a table," he told the purser, "with some native Italians. I'd like to practise talking the language." The purser gravely led him to a tableful of eight nuns. When the voyage was completed, they asked him for his autograph. Edman likes to tell this story. In fact, he likes to tell any story. He is an accomplished raconteur, and can disguise the hoariest Joe Miller chestnut with Platonic double-talk.

The tale of the nuns reminds him of the Frenchman on the *Normandie* who was assigned to a table where a bushy-browed stranger was already in the midst of his dinner. The Frenchman bowed and said, "Bon appetit!" The stranger also bowed and said,

"Ginsberg." This happened every night for four nights. On the last night of the voyage, the stranger came to the table and said, "Bon appetit!" The Frenchman got up, bowed himself, and said, "Ginsberg."

* * *

A magazine called *The War Doctor* ran a cartoon that showed a group of physicians surrounding a patient on an operating table. From an incision in his stomach issued a stream of moths and butterflies. "By God," ran the caption, "he was right!"

* * *

The learned but unworldly head of the department devoted to the study of comparative religions at Harvard invariably asked the same question on every final examination: "Who, in chronological order, were the Kings of Israel?" Students came to count on this procedure as a sacred institution and prepared accordingly. Some crabby misanthrope tattled and, one precedent-shattering spring, the professor confounded his class by changing the question to: "Who were the major prophets and who were the minor prophets?" The class sat dumbfounded and all but one member slunk out of the room without writing a word. This sole survivor scribbled furiously and deposited his paper with the air of a conqueror. "Far be it from me," he had written, "to distinguish between these revered gentlemen, but it occurred to me that you might like to have a chronological list of the Kings of Israel."

* * *

Elihu Root liked to have aggressive and independent people working for him, but one promising young office boy sometimes went too far. There was the day, for instance, when he sauntered into the office, propped his elbows on Mr. Root's desk, and said, "Say, boss, there's a ball game at the Polo Grounds today I'm dying to see. Will you give me the afternoon off?"

"James," said the courtly Mr. Root, "that is not the way to ask a favor. Now you sit down in my chair and I'll show you how to do it properly."

The boy thought this was a delightful idea. He settled himself in his employer's chair. Mr. Root went outside. Then he entered softly, cap in hand, and said meekly, "If you don't mind, sir, there is a ball game today that I would like to see. Do you think you could spare me for the afternoon?"

In a flash the boy answered, "Certainly I can, Jimmie—and here's fifty cents to pay your way in."

Another time Mr. Root's firm had occasion to send an emissary to an important business conference in France. One of the bright young men in the office was selected for the trip, and was sent in to receive Root's final O.K. "I take it," said Root, "that you speak a fluent French."

"Hardly fluent," replied the young man. "But I've never had the slightest trouble making waiters and taxi-drivers understand me."

"Ah, yes," said Mr. Root, "but suppose that no waiters or taxi-drivers turn up for the conference?"

* * *

A distinguished scientist, says Louis Sobol, who probably saw him, was observing the heavens through the huge telescope at the Mt. Wilson Observatory. Suddenly he announced, "It's going to rain." "What makes you think so?" asked his guide. "Because," said the astronomer, still peering through the telescope, "my corns hurt."

* * *

A Harvard professor spent his vacation on a canoe trip in the Maine wilds. Shooting a series of rapids, he expressed concern at the growing fury of the swirling water, and the jagged rocks on every side. "Don't worry for a minute," the guide reassured him. "I know every rock in these rapids." Just then the canoe smacked into one of the rocks head-on and capsized. The bookman found himself floundering in the current, his equipment scattered in every direction. "You see," said the guide, trying to salvage his paddle, "there's one of the damn things now!"

That story reminds me of the guide who was showing some American tourists through Oxford. "I'd like to see Jowett's study," said one of them. "You know, the fellow who translated Plato." "Easiest thing in the world," said the guide, and led his party to a cloistered square near by. "That open window on the second floor, my friends, is Mr. Jowett's diggings. I say, would you like to see the Professor himself?" The Americans assured him that they would like nothing better. The guide thereupon picked up a sizable rock and hurled it with deadly accuracy through Jowett's open window. A moment later a face purple with rage appeared in the aperture. "Aha!" said the guide triumphantly. "That always gets him. There's the old boy himself!"

* * *

In Bernard Newman's *The New Europe*, he tells the story of a professor at a cosmopolitan university who set his class to writing a thesis on the general subject of "The Elephant." The Englishman devoted his essay to "The Elephant and How to Hunt Him." The Frenchman considered "The Strange Love Life of the Elephant." The German entitled his tract "Are Elephants Aryan—and Can They Be Eaten?" The Russian produced "The Elephant—Does It Exist?" The Pole, whose piece was as long as all the others put together, wrote on "The Elephant and the Polish Question."

* * *

In the Westchester County Court in White Plains, Joseph H. Choate once drew as opponent a local lawyer who tried to sway the jury by advocating that they "disregard the Chesterfieldian urbanity of the distinguished and expensive lawyer from Fifth Avenue." Choate quietly hazarded a guess that "his Chesterfieldian urbanity" might be preferable to his opponent's "Westchesterfieldian suburbanity."

* * *

When Judge Samuel Leibowitz was a criminal lawyer, his strata-
gems and wiles made him nationally famous. One that other lawyers like to tell about to this day was in connection with a gent
named Romano, who tried to shoot his wife, but plugged a passing
policeman instead. He retained Leibowitz. The prosecution produced five witnesses. Romano had none—nothing but a flimsy
alibi. He had been working that day in a fish store, he said.

The prosecutor sent for a basket of fish. He held up a halibut.
"What is it?" he asked Romano. "A flounder," declared Romano.
He then identified a bluefish as a perch, and a sea-bass as a trout.
There were twenty fish in the basket; the unhappy Romano
guessed wrong twenty times. The prosecutor rubbed his hands
gleefully—but then Leibowitz swung into action.

"Fraud," he claimed. "Was there in that array of fish a single
pike, a pickerel, or any other fish that can be made into gefülte
fish? There was not. My client told you that he worked in a fish
store in the heart of a Jewish neighborhood; the prosecutor very
carefully avoided showing him a single fish that would be sold
there. What a travesty on justice! My client is an Italian that
works in a Jewish fish market, and they try him on Christian fish."

The jury laughed long and loud. They also acquitted Romano.

Leibowitz is credited with telling one jury, "My client talks like
an idiot and acts like an idiot. Do not be deceived, gentlemen. He
really *is* an idiot."

* * *

The law firm of Stanchfield and Levy once won an important
action for Sir Joseph Duveen, who called to thank Stanchfield
and to find out what his bill would be. "You'll have to see Levy
on that," Stanchfield told him, and, while Sir Joseph was en route,
buzzed Levy on the inter-office system and said, "Duveen's on his
way to see you. He's tickled pink. I think he'll stand for twenty-
five thousand."

That was the fee that Levy demanded. Sir Joseph never batted
an eye. "Pounds?" he asked. "Certainly," said Levy.

* * *

Martin Littleton, the attorney, was the second of two scheduled speakers at a barristers' banquet not so long ago. The first guest orated at such length that everybody was ready to go home by the time Littleton, justifiably enraged, got the floor. "I'll confine my remarks to a single story," he declared. "One day when I was a boy, my father was throwing whole carrots to his hogs by the barrelful. A neighbor criticized this procedure. 'Don't give 'em whole carrots, you fool,' he said. 'If you'd cut them up and cook them, the hogs could digest them in half the time.' My father's simple retort was, 'What's time to a hog?'"

Mr. Littleton believes that his fellow speaker got the point.

* * *

Judge Ben Lindsey, of Denver, was another illustrious but long-winded jurist. He was passing sentence on one offender who listened glumly for twenty minutes, and then interrupted, "Say, Judge, is this a sentence or a filibuster?"

At a dinner in his honor, the Judge was not exactly flattered when the toastmaster recalled a famous jibe of Henry Clay. A long-winded chest-thumper cried, "I speak not only for today, but for posterity." "But it is unnecessary," called out Clay, "to talk until the arrival of your audience."

* * *

Morris Ernst has resurrected the story of an attorney who journeyed to California to try an important case, promising to wire his partner the moment a decision was announced. At long last the wire came and it read, "Justice has triumphed." The partner in New York wired back, "Appeal at once."

* * *

Oscar Levant tells about the minister in New York who phoned a minister in California. "Is this a station-to-station call?" queried the operator. "No," replied the reverend. "It's parson-to-parson."

IN THE MIDST OF LIFE...

I HAVE carefully cultivated the friendship of an undertaker in my neighborhood who combines a rare skill and tact in his trade with an objective and documented appreciation of its occasional unexpectedly humorous ramifications. This gentleman preserves in his back office an intriguing file of his fraternity's trade papers, *The Embalmer's Monthly* and *The Mortician's Digest,* and a scrapbook into which he has pasted countless witticisms relevant to burial ceremonials. He surely may be forgiven for trying to find an occasional ray of sunshine in a profession so generally steeped in sorrow and unhappiness! On the door of his retreat is tacked a poster I had made for him two Christmases ago: "Fun in an Undertaking Parlor."

My friend has been embalming in a professional way for twenty-five years. "My ideals got a jolt right after I started," he told me. "There was a hot fight going on in Congress and the newspapers as to whether or not the American soldiers who had been killed in France in 1917 and 1918 were to be brought back to the States. I found out that an undertakers' association was helping to finance the drive to bring back the bodies. Then I discovered that the cash for the other side was coming from a French wine-growers' group who wanted the bereaved parents to visit France. Just went to show me things aren't always what they appear on the surface."

One of the big funerals he was in on was that of Tex Rickard, the fabulous sports promoter. The body was put on public view at Madison Square Garden, and thousands shuffled by to look at it. Paul Gallico quotes one sports writer as saying, "Boy, I'll bet they've got him lashed down so he can't spin. Would he be revolving in that box if he saw this mob all coming in here on the cuff!"

My friend's favorite story concerns an elderly soul named Pincus who decided it was time to buy himself a coffin, and broached the point to his fellow lodge-member Nussbaum. "For a pal like you," conceded Nussbaum, "here is my best mahogany number, with sterling silver handles, lined in genuine satin, for three hundred dollars." Pincus retired for meditation, returned a half-hour later with fire in his eyes. "Hah, a fine pal!" he cried. "A stranger, Shlepkind, down the street, who don't know me from Adam, you understand, offers me the same number, with the same mahogany, silver handles, and satin lining, for fifty dollars less." "All right, all right," roared Nussbaum, "you buy your coffin from Shlepkind. But I tell you right now that, six months after they bury you, your behind will be sticking out through the bottom."

Another story in the scrap-book enlarges on the sorrow of the laborer Pietro as the body of his young wife was lowered into the ground. In the carriage on the way back from the cemetery, his friend tried to console him. "Sure, it's-a tough, Pietro; Rosa she was a fine girl. But pretty soon another pretty girl she come along and in six-a month, maybe, you get married again." "Six-a month!" wailed Pietro. "What I gonna do tonight?"

One that I had heard before told of the German who wandered down the bomb-scarred Unter den Linden eagerly scanning the front pages of every newspaper on sale at the various kiosks. "What are you looking for?" he was asked. "The death notices." "But the death notices aren't carried on Page One." "The death notice I'm looking for," said the German confidently, "will be on Page One all right!"

My friend swears that he is the hero of the story of the four chance acquaintances who launched a bridge game on a midsummer run of the Empire State Limited. They ordered frequent rounds of drinks, but finally the steward reported that the ice had run out. "I think I know where I can get some," volunteered my friend, and supplied the party until the train was well past Schenectady. "I'm afraid this is the last pitcherful," he said then. "If I take one more cube of ice, the body won't keep till Buffalo."

Death affects people in varying ways. Some are resigned, others hysterical. Most stoical on record is old Lord Higginbottom, who was reading the London *Times* in his club when a friend remarked, "Understand you buried your wife this morning." "Had to, old chap," drawled Lord H., without looking up. "She was dead, y'know."

There are nasty little rats who have devised all sorts of petty rackets designed to take advantage of people whose sensibilities and perceptions have been dulled temporarily by sorrow. One such operated an umbrella shop in Oxford Street, London. He would con each morning's obituary notices with an eagle eye, and promptly send the estate a bill for an expensive umbrella. He was always prepared to swear that the deceased had purchased it, but ninety-nine times out of a hundred, even that wasn't necessary; the executors paid small bills of this sort automatically. This particular buzzard was caught red-handed when he sent a bill to the estate of a man who had been a helpless paralytic, strapped to a bed, for fifteen years.

My friend has a great collection of epitaphs saved up. I liked the one Ben Franklin suggested for his own tombstone:

The Body of
B. Franklin, Printer,
(Like the Cover of an old Book,
Its Contents torn out,
And Stript of its Lettering and Gilding)
Lies here, Food for Worms.
But the Work shall not be lost;
For it will, (as he believ'd) appear once more,
In a new and more elegant Edition
Revised and corrected
By the Author.

Here are a few epitaphs dreamed up by celebrities whose whistlings in the dark aren't fooling anybody:

LIONEL BARRYMORE: "Well, I've played everything but a harp."

NUNNALLY JOHNSON: "I thought there was a funny taste about that last one."

W. C. FIELDS: "On the whole, I'd rather be in Philadelphia."

LEWIS STONE: "A gentleman farmer goes back to the soil."

PAUL WHITEMAN: "Gone to look for the lost chord."

WALLACE FORD: "At last I get top billing."

CONSTANCE BENNETT: "Do not disturb."

EDDIE CANTOR: "Here in nature's arms I nestle,
        Free at last from Georgie Jessel."

FONTAINE FOX: "I had a hunch something like this would happen."

H. G. WELLS: "I told you so, dammit!"

DEEMS TAYLOR: "Here lies Deems Taylor—under protest."

WARNER BAXTER: "Did you hear about my operation?"

HORACE BROWN (dentist): "Stranger, approach these bones with
                    gravity;
                  Doc Brown is filling his last cavity."

WILLIAM HAINES: "Here's something I want to get off my chest."

EDWARD EVERETT HORTON: "A nice part—only 'four sides'—but good
company and in for a long run."

My undertaker friend has framed on his walls a reproduction
of what, with good reason, he considers the most modest and sig-
nificant epitaph a famous man ever composed for himself. Thomas
Jefferson died on July 4, 1826—on the fiftieth anniversary of the
Declaration of Independence. For his tomb he chose this inscription:

"Here was buried Thomas Jefferson, author of the Declaration
of American Independence, of the statutes of Virginia for religious
freedom, and father of the University of Virginia."

Chapter Six

FUNNY BUSINESS

A TALE THAT may take a few of our high-powered traveling salesmen down a peg concerns the visit of a man in quest of a
bottle of catsup to Finkelstein's Grocery Store. The shelves of the
entire store were solidly lined with bags of salt—hundreds upon
hundreds of them. Mr. Finkelstein allowed as how he had a stock of
catsup, but had to go down to the cellar to fetch a bottle. The
customer went with him, and there, to his surprise, found another
huge stock of salt stacked on all sides. "Say," commented the customer, "you certainly must sell a lot of salt in this store!" "Nah,"
said Mr. Finkelstein with resignation. "I can't sell no salt at all.
But the feller who sells *me* salt! Can *he* sell salt!"

* * *

The late Arthur Kudner, advertising tycoon, had a single framed
quotation hanging in his office. It was made by the 1936 world's
champion hog caller: "You've got to have appeal as well as power
in your voice. You've got to convince the hogs you have something
for them."

* * *

In a little shop down on 14th Street, New York, an ingenious chap named Irving Klaw has built up a substantial business in movie stills. He has thousands of them in stock, dating way back to the days of Theda Bara and Valentino, but the bulk of his sales is concentrated, of course, on the pin-up girls who make with the legs and terrific torsos.

"Ann Sheridan," reports this authority, "in her clothes is just another actress. Put her in a bathing suit and I can't keep her in stock. Dorothy Lamour in a sarong is dynamite, but in her clothes she's a dead duck. You may be surprised, but the face is not very important in a pin-up picture."

Klaw gets most of his stock direct from the picture companies, who consider his sales good publicity. He sells them for ten cents each and up. A Rita Hayworth or Betty Grable in unmentionables is like two seats down front for *Oklahoma!*

* * *

Lewis Miller is the sales manager today of a sizable enterprise. In his salad days he covered New York State in a Model-T Ford and made his daily collections from customers en route. He was heading for home one evening with seven hundred dollars in his jeans when, just outside of Ossining, a man in shabby, ill-fitting clothes beckoned for a hitch. Miller stopped for him, and soon learned that his companion had just completed a ten-year stretch at Sing Sing for robbery. Suddenly he remembered the seven hundred dollars in cash in his pocket.

With what he considered a master-stroke of ingenuity, he pushed the accelerator all the way to the floor. The old Ford could still do sixty. A motorcycle cop could not be far behind; Miller would have police escort to the nearest station house.

The motorcycle cop arrived on schedule, bawled the daylights out of him, and wrote a ticket calling for his appearance in court the following Monday! In vain, Miller pleaded to be arrested on the spot. His passenger pulled his cap over his eyes and said nothing. Reluctantly, Miller started his car again. As they approached the darkest Bronx, he had already written off the seven hundred dollars in his mind.

Suddenly the passenger announced, "This is it, brother." Miller stopped the car. His moment had come. The man in shabby clothes stuck out his hand. There was no gun in it!

"Thanks for the lift," he said. "You've been very good to me. This is the least I could do for you."

He handed Miller the motorcycle cop's black leather summons book.

* * *

The village idiot bought a book describing inexpensive fabricated houses and became so fascinated with the subject that he drew his last penny out of the bank and ordered a house by mail. Some weeks later he wrote a bitter note of protest to the manufacturer: his house was a complete failure. An inspector came to investigate, and roared, "You loony, you've put up the whole thing upside down!" "Oh, that's the trouble, is it?" pondered the befuddled customer. "No wonder I kept falling off the porch!"

* * *

There is one night club in New York that has made a fortune out of insulting its patrons. It is called the Club Eighteen, and one Jack White guided its destinies until he died in 1942. Since then a group of underlings, well trained in his ego-demolishing methods, has carried on. Across the street from the unostentatious, badly ventilated, but always jammed Club Eighteen is the exclusive "21," dining spot of Hollywood celebrities and socialites. "We send them our overflow," explains the maestro of Club Eighteen, with a lordly flick of his cigar ashes.

One of the club's champion insulters spotted J. Edgar Hoover at a ringside table. He was asked to take a bow, and then introduced, successively, as "a former President of the United States," "a bum who invented the vacuum cleaner," and "a flatfoot from an outlying Flatbush precinct." Mr. Hoover took it all with high good nature. It is a tribute to the exquisite skill of the hecklers that only one victim out of twenty stalks out of the place in a dudgeon. One patron who couldn't take it was a moneyed race-horse owner who resented being spotlighted while a master of ceremonies shouted, "Hey, you bum, that horse you gave me in the second race at Hialeah yesterday—there's a reward out for him!"

A standard act at the Club Eighteen is an actor who is bathed in a sickly green spotlight and begins reciting Longfellow's "I shot an arrow into the air. It fell to earth I know not where." Suddenly he stops and ruminates sadly. "I lost more damn arrows!"

If you are interested in more details of this fantastic club, and can't stay up late enough nights to inspect it yourself, I refer you to Maurice Zolotow's piece about it in his lively *Never Whistle in a Dressing Room*. A famous star summed up his experience at the club: "After I had ordered some food, they heckled me until in self-defense I had to take the floor. I went there to be enter-tained and ended up entertaining myself. When I returned to my table one of the actors had eaten my sandwich and the waiter had finished my drink."

* * *

There is a humorist in charge of the Complaint Department of one of New York's biggest dry-goods emporiums. Tacked to his door is a sign that reads "Come in and grouse." A lady took him at his word a few weeks ago. It appears that some months before she had buried her beloved spouse and bought several packets of carnation seeds with which to decorate the grave. Then she went off to Mexico to pull herself together. Several months later, all hell broke loose in the Complaint Department. It seems that when the lady came home and visited the cemetery she found her husband's grave completely covered with rhubarb. "I don't know what she was screaming about," said the Complaint Manager. "We were perfectly willing to refund her the price of the seeds."

* * *

This "pearl necklace" story has been told at one time or another about every big department store in the country, although most narrators insist angrily that it happened "to their own cousin."

A lady and her daughter are sauntering down Fifth Avenue. In front of Tiffany's the young girl's "pearl necklace" breaks, and the pearls roll all over the street. She reclaims them, and suggests giving them to Tiffany's for stringing.

"We can't ask Tiffany's to restring things like that," protests the mother. "After all, the whole necklace cost only $12.98 at Blank's." Anyhow, they enter Tiffany's. The man at the repair desk takes one look at the loose pearls, asks to be excused for a moment, and returns with the general manager, who offers the startled lady fifty thousand dollars for the lot.

The explanation? The president of Blank's has smuggled in the strand of pearls for his wife by hiding them with a shipment of cheap imitations addressed to the store's bargain jewelry department. The special marking on the real pearls has been lost, and the strand mixed up with all the others. The honest lady brings them back to Blank's just in time to clear the saleswoman, who has been accused by the president of stealing the pearls for her own purposes.

Of course, a story like this *could* have happened in real life. Reasonable odds against it: 4000 to 1.

* * *

Most jewel thieves and smugglers are apprehended sooner or later, but one clever fraud has gotten away scot-free. He came into a famous New York jewelry shop and said he was looking for a special pearl for his wife's birthday. The price made no difference, he declared; he was a Texas oil millionaire, and had credentials to prove it. He finally picked out a beautiful pearl and paid $5,000 cash for it.

A few weeks later he was back. His wife was crazy about the pearl; wanted to match it for a pair of earrings. The manager of the store said he doubted whether a duplicate could be found.

"Advertise," suggested the customer. "I'll pay up to $25,000 for a duplicate of that pearl." It developed that a lady in Chicago had just such a pearl, which she was willing to sell for $20,000. The store bought it from her—but is still waiting for the "Texas millionaire" to claim it. What he had done, of course, was to sell back the store's own pearl for four times the purchase price. Even if they find him, they'll have a hard time convicting him of any crime.

* * *

A Georgetown fortune-teller gazed into his crystal ball and told his young lady client that something very amusing was about to happen to her. Then he burst into uproarious laughter. The young lady rose and smacked his face. "Why did you do that?" asked the astounded clairvoyant. "My mother," she said firmly, "always told me to strike a happy medium!"

* * *

William Faulkner tells about the time that a little Mississippi bank suddenly found itself insolvent. A Negro depositor was just about to withdraw some cash when the frightened teller got the bad news and gulped, "I am sorry, we won't be able to give you the money you want. Our bank has gone broke."

The Negro was a philosopher. "I'se heard of lots of banks failing," he lamented, "but dis am de fust time one has gone bust right in my face."

* * *

George Perry tells of the Texas lady who aimed to sell her old plow. "What you plannin' to ask for it, Miss Edna?" asked a neighbor. "Oh, I reckon 'bout thirty or forty dollars," said Miss Edna. "But you can git a new one out of the mail-order catalogue for eight-fifty," the neighbor protested. "I'm tired of this hagglin' over pennies," decided Miss Edna. "Gimme a dollar an' take the plow!"

* * *

There was a Dr. Munyon many years ago who sold a powerful lot of patent medicine by direct mail. His slogan was "There Is Hope." His ads always carried an impressive photograph of himself, revealing a senatorial phiz with a huge mop of snow-white hair.

"How much do you spend every year in advertising?" asked a visitor. "About a quarter of a million," said Dr. Munyon. "If I show you how to save fifty thousand of it," proposed the visitor, "without losing a sale, will you give me five thousand for myself?" "I will," said Munyon. "Get a haircut," said the visitor.

* * *

John Wanamaker told of meeting a boyhood friend who had experienced nothing but hard luck in his career. He had been locked out of his meagre hotel room, and he was half starved. Deeply moved, Mr. Wanamaker fed him in his own restaurant, and urged him to order every delicacy on the menu. Then he handed him enough to pay his hotel bill, and ordered him to report for a good job the next morning.

The man never came. The hotel clerk, to whom the jubilant fellow had related the whole incident, called Mr. Wanamaker about noon. The man had died during the night—of acute indigestion.

* * *

There was a total eclipse of the sun in 1932, and a newsreel company sent two expeditions to South America to get authentic pictures of it. Bad weather prevented their getting any shots worth exhibiting. The company had to have a picture, however, and put the problem to its technical expert. "I'll manufacture a picture of an eclipse for you right in my laboratory," he promised, and he was as good as his word. There was one flaw. When the picture was run off, the word "Mazda" appeared on the face of the sun.

* * *

In front of an East Side delicatessen, a well-known art connoisseur noticed a mangy little kitten, lapping up milk from a saucer. The saucer, he realized with a start, was a rare and precious piece of pottery.

He sauntered into the store and offered two dollars for the cat. "It's not for sale," said the proprietor. "Look," said the collector, "that cat is dirty and undesirable, but I'm eccentric. I like cats that way. I'll raise my offer to five dollars." "It's a deal," said the proprietor, and pocketed the five-spot. "For that sum I'm sure you won't mind throwing in the saucer," said the connoisseur. "The kitten seems so happy drinking from it." "Nothing doing," said the proprietor firmly. "That's my lucky saucer. From that saucer, so far this week, I've sold thirty-four cats."

* * *

Major Corey Ford brought back from Iceland the story of the salesman who ran from igloo to igloo trying to sell electric fans. "Fan?" each resident would exclaim in amazement. "What do we want with a fan? It is 60 below zero here now." "Sure, I know," soothed the salesman. "But you never can tell. Tomorrow it may jump to zero."

* * *

A school that taught playwriting by mail received a script from a student whose opening curtain rose on a little old French lady knitting in her chair. Her husband entered, visibly fatigued, and placed his black instrument bag on the table. "Oh, Pierre," said the lady, "you have been away all night. Was it a difficult accouchement?" "Yes," answered the weary doctor. "But it was worth it. History was made last night. The baby's name was— Victor Hugo." The author wasn't able to keep up that pace for long.

Another script began with these lines: "Time of Act One: 7000 years ago. Act Two: One day later."

* * *

Joe Brooks delivered a check from his insurance company to the widow of a deceased client. She was apparently inconsolable, and had been weeping three days without stopping. A glance at the amount of the check—it was for fifty thousand dollars—stilled her tears. "You may not believe it," she told Brooks soulfully, "but I'd give twenty thousand of this to have him back."

* * *

On a recent radio program, Fred Allen introduced one character as his "molehill man." "Every morning," he vouchsafed by way of explanation, "this fellow arrives at his office and finds a molehill on his desk. It's his job to make a mountain of it before 5 P.M. comes around."

Allen says his next sponsor will be the manufacturer of Lumpo Soap: "It doesn't lather. It doesn't float. It contains no secret oils. It is designed solely to keep you company in the tub."

* * *

A traveler for a big publishing house couldn't wait to get to St. Louis, where his oldest friend owned a prosperous bookstore. "Sam," he said to the owner the moment they were alone, "I want you to lend me $2000." "The answer, Joe," said Sam, "is positively no." "But, Sam," protested the salesman, "in 1929, when Bond and Share broke from 189 to 50, who gave you ten thousand dollars to keep you from being wiped out?" "You did," admitted Sam. "And in 1931, when your daughter Shirley had that tropical disease, who took her down to Florida because you couldn't get away from business? Who did, Sam?" "You, my friend, you did." "And in 1933, when we were fishing together, who dove into the rapids and saved you from drowning at the risk of his own life?" "You did, Joe. It was wonderful!" "Well, then, Sam, in Heaven's name, why won't you lend me $2000 now when I need it?" "All the things you say are true," said Sam, nodding his head slowly. "But what have you done for me lately?"

Chapter Seven

POWERS OF THE PRESS

THE PHENOMENON of present-day journalism is the vogue of columnists. Political pontificaters, military analysts, Washington insiders, keyhole experts, Hollywood Boswells, and night-club rounders with sharp ears are syndicated in hundreds of papers all over the land. News space may be cut and pages of advertising omitted, but let an editor omit one signed column and the readers' wrath descends upon him forthwith. "Harriet Beecher Stowe," Charles Fisher points out, "reached a meager million of her contemporaries with *Uncle Tom's Cabin;* Winchell reaches ten million of his with a note upon Miss Rogers' nightwear. Forty thousand pre-Victorians awaited the latter numbers of *Pickwick Papers;* seven million moderns wait for 'The Washington Merry-Go-Round' each day. The columnist is the autocrat of the most prodigious breakfast table ever known. He is the voice beside the cracker-barrel amplified to trans-continental dimensions. He is the only non-political figure of record who can clear his throat each day and say, 'Now, here's what I think' with the assurance that millions will listen."

One of the pioneers and by all odds the most influential of the columnists in the land, of course, is Walter Winchell. Future histories of American journalism will have to devote an entire chapter to this amazing man. Starting as a straight gossip columnist, he developed into a force whose opinions on national affairs and characters carry incredible weight. Important enemies of the United States landed behind bars because Walter Winchell put them there. H. L. Mencken credits Winchell with adding all of these now more-or-less familiar expressions to the American language: making whoopee; shafts (for legs); veddy (for very); welded, sealed, merged, and middle-aisled for married; on the verge, phffft, and curdled for blasted romance; that way (about someone); infanticipating; debutramp; moom-pitcher; Park Rowgue (for newspaperman); and The Hardened Artery (for Broadway).

Early in Winchell's columning career, when he was employed by Bernarr MacFadden's puerile and short-lived tabloid, *The Graphic,* he printed a story about the Brothers Shubert which incensed them. The producers, said Winchell, summoned the manager of one of their most dismal failures and demanded, "Why did we ever buy that lousy play?" The manager said it just hadn't worked out. The playwright was not to blame. Every business had occasional flops. Look at the Sesquicentennial Exhibition in Philadelphia; there was a real flop! "Did he write that too?" groaned Shubert.

The producers promptly barred Winchell from all their theatres. It was a spectacular feud. "I can't go to their openings, eh?" said Winchell. "Okay. I'll wait three days and go to the closings." The Marx Brothers disguised him in false whiskers, dark glasses, and a putty nose one night and introduced him to Lee Shubert backstage as their long-lost uncle. The Shuberts finally gave up the battle. They couldn't take it any more.

* * *

There is a daily columnist in Hollywood who just dotes on printing long lists of notables seen at important picture premieres.

She missed the opening of *Going My Way,* but a supposed friend volunteered to supply her with a list of big shots in the audience. She printed his story unedited. It began with a bang. "Among those present," it read, "were Miss Lizzie Borden, Mr. Marcus Aurelius, Mr. Ethan Frome . . ." Most readers got no farther.

* * *

A newspaper in Georgia awards an annual prize to the champion liar of the year, although we understand that ex-governors are barred. This year's winner averred that "Georgia soil is so rich that when they throw corn to the chickens, they have to catch it on the fly or eat it off the stalk." Nunnally Johnson, the smartest producer on the Twentieth Century-Fox lot, if not in all Hollywood, is a Georgia product. So is Erskine Caldwell. One evening an indignant Atlantan confronted Johnson. "I ask you to bear me out, suh, that our fair state of Geo'gia has never known perverts and morons like the characters in those libelous abominations, *Tobacco Road* and *God's Little Acre!*" "Why, in the part of the state I come from," answered Nunnally softly, "we regard the people Mr. Caldwell writes about as the country club set."

* * *

Screwball journalism of the type portrayed so hilariously in the Hecht-MacArthur play *The Front Page,* and more recently in Robert J. Casey's *Such Interesting People,* is a thing of the past. Rip-snorting reporters whose motors ran strictly on alcohol, who were as likely to wind up in the local hoosegow as the city desk, but who brought in the scoops that sent circulations soaring, went out with Prohibition and Babe Ruth. They have been replaced by "boiler plates" and syndicates, and less colorful but infinitely more efficient wire services that supply hundreds of papers at a time with last-minute news, impersonal, impartial, and prosaic.

Journalism was a rollicking profession in the twenties, however, if you happened to be on the right papers. Casey happened. Most of the time he operated out of Chicago, where feature reporters, influential lawyers, and gun-toting hijackers seemed to be somewhat interchangeable. The title of **his** colorful collection of yarns stems from the time-honored observation of the yokels who meet gentlemen of the press: "Gee, it must be wonderful to be a journalist. You meet such interesting people!" Winchell once answered, "You certainly do, and every one of them is in the newspaper business."

Casey went to bat with lots of outsiders, however, not all of whom were rank. There was a queer customer in Cairo, for instance, named Captain Eddy, who talked in telephone numbers, and was listed as a phony. One day he remarked in passing that he had three of the world's greatest pearls in his possession, and was looking for more. Eager to show up the Captain at last, Casey's companion summoned the greatest pearl expert in Egypt. Captain Eddy nonchalantly tossed his three pearls on the table. The expert studied them a moment, looked at the rumpled and unshaven Captain in amazement, and said in slow, careful English: "If you would sell them, I shall give you fifty thousand pounds for them. . . . They are worth more but that is all I can afford." "No, siree," said the Captain. "I'm saving those pearls for my daughter." He stuffed them back in his pocket, and shuffled off into the night.

Casey was there or thereabouts when the episode occurred that may explain Charles Lindbergh's consuming and unrelenting hatred of the press. You may remember the time when a man named Floyd Collins got trapped by a rock in a Kentucky cave. Miners drove a shaft to the cavern where he was pinned down. They worked frantically night and day while the whole country watched breathlessly to see whether or not they would reach him in time. As a matter of fact, they did not, but that isn't the point of this story. One Chicago paper, Mr. Hearst's *Examiner*, decided to put one over on its competitors by flying pictures by plane from the shaft head to the main office. Lindbergh, as you have probably guessed, was the pilot. He was a raw-boned and inexperienced kid. When he arrived on the scene of action, he had the misfortune to encounter a Mr. Steeger of the rival *Chicago Tribune.* "Ah, yes," said Steeger, "Lindbergh of the *Examiner!* Where have you been all this time? I've been waiting for you! Get these plates back to Chicago just as fast as you can make it." Lindbergh flew back to the *Examiner* office post-haste and duly delivered a box of blank, unexposed plates. Casey probably isn't exaggerating when he suggests that the smile with which young Mr. Lindbergh favored Mr. Steeger of the *Tribune* was the last he ever gave to anybody connected with a newspaper in any capacity whatever. Lindbergh got partial revenge some years later when, at a national air meet in Cleveland, he whizzed his plane so close to a group of camera men that they dove in panic into a huge mud puddle at the edge of the field to get out of his way.

* * *

"Newsmen are simple boys at heart"

Newsmen, swears Casey, are simple boys at heart. They treasure clippings with typographical errors for months, particularly when the result verges on the pornographic. They play infantile tricks on one another. They wake up outraged strangers by 4 A.M. phone calls. In Chicago they found an unfortunate innocent named "Upjohn" in the directory, and called him in relays all night long to inquire sweetly, "Are you Upjohn?" A Boston group found a Paul Revere in the book, and yanked him from bed with a phone call to demand, "Why aren't you on a horse? The British are coming!" I myself know of a sophisticated group spearheaded by no less a personage than Harold Ross, editor of *The New Yorker*, who spent a deliriously happy afternoon calling Long Island society matrons, and saying that they spoke for a nationally-known yeast manufacturer. They offered five thousand dollars for a signed testimonial, and further played on their victim's vanity by adding: "Of course, you won't keep this vulgar money yourself. We will leave it to you to pass it on to your favorite charity." The matron would coo with pleasure and then the tormentor plunged in the harpoon. "We simply want you to say," he would murmur into the mouthpiece, "'A year ago, before I discovered Blank's yeast, my face was an unholy mess of pimples and unseemly blotches.'" . . . There usually was a violent click at the other end of the wire at this point.

* * *

In Fort Smith, Arkansas, the mayor's wife died and the old icehouse burned on the same day. The local gazette printed a two-column portrait of the deceased lady on page one with a caption that made the issue a rare collector's item: "Old Eyesore Gone at Last!" The *Chicago Journal* got a society column and a shipping report all mixed up in the press room with the following results: "Mrs. So-and-So of the Chicago Beach Hotel has had a pleasant summer visiting friends in Bar Harbor and Kennebunk. After encountering heavy weather off the Virginia Cape, she put into Hampton Roads to have her bottom scraped." A novice on the *American* once asked Casey, "How do you spell pinochle?" Casey told him. The next day his story appeared in print. "Adolph Klepperman," it began, "has reached the pinochle of success."

* * *

Casey's prize story of transposed headlines concerns the *New York Herald Tribune*, which ran big stories one day on an address by Mr. Hamilton Fish and a new formula for feeding tropical fish, issued by the Aquarium. It was George Dixon, on the night shift of the rival *Mirror*, who discovered that the headlines for the two stories had been mixed in the shuffle. He called the *Tribune* and announced himself as Mr. Fish. The managing editor himself came to the phone. "We know why you are calling, Mr. Fish," he said hurriedly. "It was a dreadful mistake." Then he launched into an elaborate explanation of how things like that sometimes could happen in the best-regulated newspaper offices. Dixon was extremely gracious, and accepted the apology.

At midnight Dixon was relieved by another bright young man named Dolan who also called up the *Tribune*. A brand-new voice, equally suave and apologetic, had gotten halfway through the same involved explanation, when the managing editor got back on the wire. "Mr. Fish," he asked, "didn't you call us about this mistake barely an hour ago?" "Oh, no," said Dolan haughtily. "That must have been Mr. Hamilton Fish. This is Mr. *Tropical* Fish."

* * *

Of particular interest to booklovers is the story of the time when a prominent denizen of the Chicago underworld, Big Tim Murphy, just back from a stretch at Leavenworth, decided that Bob Casey was just the man to ghost-write his autobiography. Big Tim had his own notions about publishing procedure. "We got to be reasonable about the price of this book," he said. "Ten bucks a bite is too much. Five is enough." Casey explained that the normal price for such a tome was two dollars, of which Tim would pull down ten percent in royalties. "Nix," decided Tim. "We'll take the five bucks and give the publisher ten percent. Don't forget there's five thousand garbage-haulers alone in my control and every one of them guys is going to buy my book or else! Then there's the electricians and gas-meter readers and street sweepers. I'll just go to their meetings and tell them where to kick in with their five bucks. The trouble with you long-haired fellows, you don't pay enough attention to the business side of book writing. Me, I see both sides. . . ." For all we know, Big Tim Murphy might have revolutionized the entire publishing industry in America. Unfortunately, he suddenly became involved in the opening of a new gambling house, and abruptly lost all interest in the pursuit of literature.

I have picked out only a few of Robert Casey's salty anecdotes to retell here. For an all-around picture of high-powered newspaper publishing in the days when rugged individualism still ran riot, you'll go a long way before you find anything better than *Such Interesting People*.

* * *

When "Bugs" Baer, ace humorist of the King Feature Syndicate, first landed a good job, his friend, Ward Greene, suggested that he acquire new raiment to match the job. "What's the difference?" said Baer. "Nobody knows me." Fifteen years later Greene caught him wearing the same old rags. "What's the difference?" repeated Bugs. "*Everybody* knows me!"

* * *

Charles Michelson, long-time press agent of the Democratic Party, remembers a "roly-poly little Englishman" who acted as war correspondent in Havana in 1898. "He invited his fellow reporters up to his room for a session of poker," recalls Michelson. "As the cards were being dealt, he ordered a bottle of champagne —and one glass. His American guests blinked, but conformed, and so they sat through the evening, every man with his own bottle and glass!" The English correspondent's name was Winston Churchill.

* * *

In the golden days when Victor Lawson was the proprietor of the *Chicago Daily News*, the staff at one time included such notables as Carl Sandburg, Ben Hecht, Vincent Sheean, Rube Goldberg, and the inimitable Con Rourke. Rourke volunteered to represent the paper at the funeral of an obscure copy-reader. He had no relatives or church connections, and an amateur preacher from another paper was conscripted to conduct the services at the graveside. Unfortunately, it was raining cats and dogs, and in the middle of the ceremony the "preacher" slipped and shot under the coffin into the grave. "It was quite confusing," reported Rourke. "Half the mourners didn't see where this guy had gone and the other half were in favor of burying him with the corpse."

* * *

There was one Chicago reporter named Buddy McHugh who believed it was highly unnecessary to cover an assignment in person if he could get the information over the telephone. He didn't care who he had to say he was to get the party on the other end to divulge the wanted facts. One day he called the residence of a freshly slaughtered gangster and said, "This is Chuck Reynolds of the coroner's office." "That's funny," said the voice at the other end of the wire. "So's this." McHugh was a character in Hecht and MacArthur's hilarious *The Front Page*. He's the one who called up a lady and inquired gently, "Is it true, madam, that you were the victim of a Peeping Tom?"

Another of the many episodes in *The Front Page* that was drawn directly from life depicted the reporters of one paper trying to hide an escaped murderer long enough to score a complete scoop in the following morning's paper. The authors did exactly that when they were feature writers on the old *American*. In the play, the shivering unfortunate begs piteously for air; the managing editor lifts the top a fraction of an inch, pushes in some ozone with the palm of his hand, and assures him that he's "sitting pretty"!

* * *

A London newspaper asked a noted British novelist and an equally distinguished American poet to record their choices of the ten most beautiful words in the English language.

The British selection was: carnation, azure, peril, moon, forlorn, heart, silence, shadow, April, and apricot.

The American choice was: dawn, hush, lullaby, murmuring, tranquil, mist, luminous, chimes, golden, and melody.

* * *

When Arthur Brisbane was about to complete fifty years of journalism, Mr. Hearst, his employer, urged him to take a six-months vacation with full pay. This magnanimous offer Brisbane refused to accept, saying there were two reasons for his doing so.

"The first reason," he said, "is that if I quit writing my column for six months it might affect the circulation of your newspapers. The second reason is that it might not affect the circulation."

On several occasions, Editor Brisbane was heard telling Windsor McKay, "You're the second greatest cartoonist in the world." Harry Hershfield asked him, "Who's the first?" "I don't know," said Brisbane. "But this keeps McKay on his toes."

* * *

Before Ralph Ingersoll won a commission in the Army and wrote his thrilling *The Battle Is the Payoff*, he was editor of the newspaper *PM*. Before that he toiled briefly for Harold Ross, the unpredictable editor of *The New Yorker*. He bearded the lion in his private den one day and talked himself into an assistant editorship, although some of his elation vanished when, after he had agreed on terms and walked happily to the elevator, he heard Ross screaming, "Damn it all, I seem to hire any nut that sticks his face in here."

The advance campaign for *PM* was so brilliant and high-powered that the appearance of the actual paper was bound to be a terrific anticlimax. Everything seemed to go wrong with it at the same time. The original capital disappeared in a few short months. The circulation dropped below 90,000. A disgruntled stockholder who couldn't even get in to tell the harassed editor what he thought should be done to improve the situation was heard to exclaim, "The trouble with Ingersoll is that his failure has gone to his head."

Ingersoll hadn't failed, however. He persuaded Marshall Field to supply fresh capital and suddenly *PM* began to click.

WHERE THERE'S LIFE THERE'S SWOPE

Sir Willmott Lewis, American emissary of the London *Times*, recalls that when he first was ordered to this country, his editor warned him, "You will hear two terrific noises when you get there, but do not be frightened by either of them. They won't hurt you. One is Niagara Falls. The other is Herbert Bayard Swope." "A plausible fellow," is Swope's rejoinder—"but unsound."

Swope, an overpowering and dynamic personality, is a whole *Information, Please* board of experts concentrated into one unbelievable storehouse of facts, many of them useless. He is never less than thirty minutes late for an appointment. He once was responsible for getting a popular actress to her own husband's funeral an hour after the services had started. His manner of sweeping into a gathering of any kind is nothing less than regal. "Swoping" was a word once applied rather generally to confirmed table-hoppers and people who referred to international celebrities by their first names. He has a booming, foghorn sort of voice which frequently can be heard delivering grandiloquent statements like, "I told Franklin I didn't agree with him," or "Personally I am very angry at the United States Navy." But even his severest critics will concede that the Swope charm is irresistible, and that everybody from presidents to stable boys feels warmed and gratified at a sign of his imperial favor. If there were more Herbert Bayard Swopes around, this would be a gayer and more amusing world, although it must be conceded that certain nervous and supersensitive souls might be quite unable to live in it.

Swope comes from a family whose ancestral seat was the tiny village of Lengsfeld in Germany, in the shadow of the Wartburg, steeped in the tradition of Tannhäuser and Martin Luther. Herbert himself was born in St. Louis in 1882, ten years after his

brother Gerard. Both boys did well for themselves. Gerard became president of a little company called General Electric. Herbert rose to national prominence in 1912 by virtue of a sensational murder case. He was a star reporter on Pulitzer's *World*,
and one of the first people to hear that a gambler named Herman
Rosenthal had been bumped off outside a Broadway café called

*Mr. H. B. Swope holds an informal conversation
with Winston, Franklin and Joe*

the Metropole. Insiders knew that Rosenthal had been scheduled
to spill a sordid story of corruption in the police department to
the District Attorney the following day. Swope sensed a great
melodrama, routed the D. A. out of a sound sleep in a Turkish bath,
stuck a pen in his hand, and had him sign an indictment naming
Police Lieutenant Becker before he was fully awake. Swope then
raced back to the *World* office and splashed a headline across the
front page that he borrowed from Emile Zola: "I ACCUSE." The

District Attorney's name was Charles Whitman. Before the echoes of the case had died away, he was Governor of the State of New York.

Swope's reporting from behind the German lines in the First World War won him a Pulitzer award. When America entered the fight, he became a Lt. Commander in the Navy. In 1919, he covered the Versailles Peace Conference. His manner and attire had achieved a distinction by this time that made flunkeys rush to open doors for him at sight. Thus he got hold of a copy of the first League of Nations Covenant hours before anybody else—the journalistic scoop of a lifetime. Jealous rivals claim he had Clemenceau running errands for him. He returned home a conquering hero, and was rewarded with the title of executive editor of the *World*, a post that he filled with signal distinction for nine years. He lashed out at social injustices and subversive organizations in campaigns that rocked the entire country. He created a "page opposite editorial" that employed at one time the services of Heywood Broun, Walter Lippmann, Alexander Woollcott, Laurence Stallings, Franklin P. Adams, Frank Sullivan, and Deems Taylor. The Swope salons, held nightly in his 58th Street home, were frequented by every celebrity in town. If a ship news reporter missed a visiting notable at the pier, he knew that his man could be found the same evening at Swope's.

Since 1929, Swope has occupied himself with innumerable directorships in first-line corporations, the chairmanship of the New York Racing Commission, and a position of ex-officio adviser to cabinet ministers and chiefs of staff. Probably the job he likes best is in connection with the racing. He took me out to the Tropical Track in Miami recently (he's chairman of the board) and gave me inside information on every race. Unfortunately it was so far inside that even the horses never heard it.

Swope's favorite outdoor pastime is croquet, which gives him a chance to practise strategy on a complicated scale. In one game his partner, the late Gerald Brooks, had the temerity to make a shot without consulting Swope. "Never do that again," warned

Swope. "After this, you do exactly what I tell you, without question, and we'll win in a walk." A few turns later, Brooks' shot grazed another ball fifteen yards away. "Wonderful," exulted Swope. "Knock him into the lake!" Brooks took singular satisfaction in carrying out the order before he pointed out that it was Swope's own ball. Another morning Swope made one of his regal entrances three-quarters of an hour late, with a butler carrying his mallet and towel behind him. One man on the court was a stranger to him. "I'm Herbert Bayard Swope," he said. The stranger shook his outstretched hand gravely, and announced: "I'm Harpo Marx's chauffeur."

His family doctor once sent him to a famous specialist for a check-up, which was interrupted three times by interminable telephone conversations. Swope apologized, and explained that the first one had come from the Mayor, the second from Bernard Baruch, and the third from President Roosevelt. The specialist nodded gravely, phoned the family doctor when he had left, and said, "What did you send that man to me for? What he needs, obviously, is a psychiatrist." His frenzied concern about political, theatrical, and international complications reach their highest pitch at the precise moment he is scheduled to leave for a dinner or a show. He kept five people waiting in a car once for forty minutes. They heard him banging drawers upstairs and creating a terrific hullabaloo. When he finally appeared, he was astounded that the rest of the party was annoyed. "You knew very well," he reminded Mrs. Swope, "that I was counting our bottles of beer."

Herbert Swope's memory for names and faces is uncanny, except for a not-too-endearing habit of telling dinner partners stories that involve intimate details about their mates' previous wives and sweethearts. His own wife, a poker-faced lady full of unexpected kindnesses, is thoroughly conditioned to take almost everything he does as a matter of course, although she has been heard to declare that if she ever were to write a daily column like Mrs. Roosevelt, *hers* would be called "My *Damn* Day." One summer afternoon, a group of men stopped for a drink at his Sands Point estate on their way home from the Belmont track. Swope impulsively asked them all to stay for dinner. Mrs. Swope rang for the cook, and calmly announced, "Mae, there will be thirty-four extra for dinner this evening."

Swope always has time to dash off a line of commendation to any one of his innumerable friends who has accomplished something of note. Practically every book publisher in town has entreated him to cut down his voluminous correspondence and write a book of memoirs. What a story he could tell—although the editor might have to blue-pencil a few of the windier passages and the six-syllable words. One night a Broadway friend and his blue-eyed babe taxied Herbert Swope home from a theatrical party. Swope, as usual, carried the conversational ball. "The era of the economic royalists and predatory robber barons went out with the Hoover administration," he boomed. "I have told Franklin and I have told Wendell—I'm sure you agree with me—that if they ignore the portents and pussy-foot back to the tenets of the McKinley era, I will not be responsible for anything that happens to them." The little lady sitting next to him gazed at him in wide-eyed wonder, and said softly, "Hey, hey, Big Boy!"

* * *

A fearsome man is Colonel Robert Rutherford McCormick, publisher of the *Chicago Tribune*—especially when somebody dares to disagree with him. The Rhode Island legislature, for instance, passed a bill that displeased him. Out into the *Tribune* lobby strode the Colonel, and snipped one star from the American flag that waved there.

Colonel McCormick wrote a memorable letter to a subscriber in 1942, in which he claimed credit for introducing the ROTC into the schools, and persuading the Army to take up machine guns, mechanization, and automatic rifles. He also noted that he was the first ground officer ever to go up in the air to observe ar-

tillery fire, was first to advocate an alliance with Canada, fought unsuccessfully to fortify Guam, and all but persuaded the Navy not to divide its fleet into a two-ocean affair. He also told the Administration that "airplanes could destroy battleships," "got the Marines out of Shanghai," but couldn't quite "get the Army out of the Philippines." What a man! Carl Sandburg read this extraordinary claim and murmured, "And on the seventh day He rested!"

Colonel McCormick is the man who thinks Rhodes scholars are undercover British agents out to make the citizens of Chicago stand up every time the band plays *God Save the King*.

* * *

George Antheil, former high priest of modernistic music, when last heard of was conducting a syndicated column of advice to the lovelorn in Hollywood. This is the most incredible transformation since the late Harold Stearns, brilliant young Harvard intellectual of the twenties and author of a highly regarded treatise on American culture, suddenly bobbed up in Paris as "Peter Pickum" with a daily dope sheet on the horse races for the *Paris Tribune*. Antheil was first brought to America by the energetic Donald Friede, then a publishing partner of Horace Liveright and now a successful literary agent on the Coast. The first Antheil concert packed Carnegie Hall and featured a number that was rendered on twenty-six pianos and four airplane motors. When the cacophony of sound was at its highest pitch, somebody whispered into his companion's ear a meek, "Isn't this simply horrible?" A harridan in the row ahead turned angrily and snorted a W. C. Fieldsian "Quiet, please!"

At the very time that Antheil's *Ballet Mécanique* was startling Paris, and Stearns was picking the day's winners at Longchamps for the *Tribune*, Bill Shirer, Elliot Paul, Jay Allen, and Ed Taylor were fellow reporters on the same fabulous sheet. One day Elliot Paul announced that he was ready to begin work on the Great American Novel, and his confrères volunteered to give up their day off for a period of weeks so that Paul could devote his best efforts to the new book. For months thereafter Elliot only came to the office one day a week. "If this sheet was properly staffed," he grumbled one morning, "I wouldn't have to show up at all." After a long stretch of this routine, Paul, who is a consummate actor, staggered into the *Tribune* office one morning clutching at his heart and stammering that he had left the finished manuscript on a bus on the Boulevard Raspail. To this day nobody knows whether there ever was a manuscript at all; certainly the French police could find no trace of one.

When Stearns saw how gullible the staff was, he suddenly announced that somebody had given him a horse named Étoile Vert, and took frequent collections to help feed and stable him. The whole American colony was primed to back Étoile Vert in his first race and didn't discover until the very morning of the event that there had never been an Étoile Vert. Peter Pickum announced laconically that this horse had died of excitement in his stall the night before.

The staffs of both the *Paris Herald* and *Tribune* during those lush years of the twenties were populated by a score of talented authors who are today our most famous foreign correspondents and creators of some of our greatest best-sellers. Three young men seated at adjoining desks in a comparatively tiny city room were destined to write *Berlin Diary, The Strategy of Terror,* and *The Last Time I Saw Paris.* Around the corner was the office of the Paris correspondent of the *Chicago Daily News.* His name was John Gunther. Ernest Hemingway, Scott Fitzgerald, Whit Burnett, and Morley Callahan were on the Left Bank. This was the Paris that Americans remember and now will see again.

* * *

Clare Boothe Luce, the glamorous playwright and Congresswoman, tells this on herself. She and her important husband, Henry Luce (*Time, Life,* etc., etc.), were walking through the lobby of a Washington hotel, and overheard somebody comment, "There go Arsenic and Old Luce."

Mr. Luce always looks pretty serious. *Time* co-founder, the late Briton Hadden, once remarked to him in their undergraduate days at Yale, "Look out, Harry. You'll drop the college."

Chapter Eight

MUSIC HATH CHARMS...

GEORGE GERSHWIN (1898–1937)

ON AN OPPRESSIVELY hot Sunday evening in July 1937, a group of people were gathered in a remodeled Bucks County farmhouse, engaged in various desultory pastimes. A spiritless bridge game was in progress in one corner of the room; a bout of cribbage in another. The host was tinkering aimlessly with the radio dials. Some of the guests were splashing about in the pool outside, although there was no moon, and the night was pitch black. The heat had everybody down. Suddenly the clear voice of a news commentator came over the air: "The man who said he had more tunes in his head than he could put down on paper in a hundred years is dead tonight in Hollywood. George Gershwin passed away today at the age of thirty-eight."

Everybody at that party was a close personal friend of George. Two of them had collaborated with him on his brightest Broadway hits. We had seen him within the month—joshed him on his complaint of recurring headaches (he had been telling us details of his symptoms and disorders for years; nobody took them seriously) and on a front-page report that a little French picture cutie had entrusted him with a gold key to her front door. His unbelievable energy and vitality had astounded us for so long that we sat speechless at the thought that he was dead. Now seven years later, his music is played incessantly, and stories about him spring readily to mind. Because he graduated from Tin Pan Alley, it has taken all these years to convince some critics that George Gershwin was a great composer—one of the greatest we have produced in America. Because his monumental but strangely unobjectionable conceit encouraged his friends to circulate hilarious anecdotes about him, some of them did not realize until he was dead how deeply they liked and admired him. The stories that I have gathered for this piece are set down in loving memory. George laughed at all of them himself.

George Gershwin was born in Brooklyn on September 26, 1898. He was the second of four children. Ira, whose sparkling lyrics were so perfectly attuned to George's music, was the eldest. Another brother, Arthur, followed George. The youngest was their sister Frances, who married the inventor, Leopold Godowsky. The family moved as a unit, a mutual admiration society that was completely unaffected by temporary failure or dizzying success. Mrs. Gershwin was adored by everybody. "You must meet my mother," George would tell anybody who called. "She's the most wonderful mother in the world." On further reflection, he would frequently add, "and so modest about *me*." The father, Morris, was one of those restless souls who embark upon a new business career every year or so; the family was always ready to pull up stakes cheerfully at a moment's notice. George once figured that he lived in twenty-seven different houses before he finished school. Gershwin père was a lovable and loquacious soul whose accent lost none of its rich and indescribable flavor as the family fortunes rose. His son George was the apple of his eye. One day after the boys had hit the jackpot he was driving down Broadway in a roadster they had given him, when a cop flagged him for ignoring a red light. "But you can't do this to me!" he expostulated. "I'm Judge Gershwin's father!" "Oh, Judge Gershwin," said the copper, visibly impressed. "Pardon me for holding you up, sir."

When George was twelve, his mother bought a piano. The idea was for Ira to take lessons, but it didn't take long to discover that George was the one with music in his soul. At the High School of Commerce, he was pianist for the morning assembly exercises. At fifteen, he was a song plugger for the music-publishing house of Jerome Remick. One of his chores took him to Atlantic City, where he pounded out Remick melodies at the local five-and-ten. Down the Boardwalk, Harry Ruby was doing a similar job for a rival outfit. At night the boys would dine together at Child's and dream of writing songs of their own.

His first song was published in 1916. It was called "When You Want 'Em You Can't Get 'Em," and it earned him an advance of five dollars. His next few numbers began to carry lyrics by Arthur Francis. That was brother Ira making his debut as a lyricist, using the first names of his other brother and kid sister as a pseudonym. His first real clicks came in 1919, when he did his first complete score for *La La Lucille* (remember "Nobody But You": "Billie Burke—Alice Joyce—none of them were my choice"?) and wrote a couple of numbers for the opening bill of Broadway's biggest movie palace of its time, the Capitol. One of the numbers was "Swanee," and I've heard it twice on the radio this very week.

Beginning in 1920, George wrote the music for *George White's Scandals* for five consecutive years. A few of the hits of these scores were "Drifting Along with the Tide," "I'll Build a Stairway to Paradise," and "Somebody Loves Me." Most of the lyrics were contributed by Buddy De Sylva, now head man at the Paramount Studios. In those days, White was the great Ziegfeld's only serious rival. Gershwin didn't meet up with Ziegfeld himself until

1929, when he wrote the score of *Show Girl*. Working with Ziegfeld was perfect training for fighting on Guadalcanal, but that's another story. After the contract with Gershwin was signed, Ziegfeld went to Carnegie Hall to hear *An American in Paris*. At the symphonic poem's completion, Otto Kahn rose and made a brief speech in which he declared that George was well-nigh a genius. "In fact," said Kahn, "some day he will be a genius, but geniuses must suffer, and George hasn't suffered yet." Ziegfeld turned to Larry Hart, who was sitting next to him, and said, with a sly wink, "He'll suffer!"

George became internationally famous in 1924, when Paul Whiteman introduced his *Rhapsody in Blue* at a concert in Aeolian Hall. By now the family was located in a private house on West 103rd Street, where George worked imperturbably amidst a hubbub that suggested Grand Central Station on the eve of a Fourth of July week end. The *Rhapsody* was written there in exactly three weeks; George had to meet a deadline! That year saw, too, the first of seven musical comedies produced by Aarons and Freedley, with music by George and lyrics by Ira. Five of them made Broadway history. They were, in order, *Lady Be Good*, *Tip Toes*, *Oh, Kay, Funny Faces*, and *Girl Crazy*. They made stars of Fred and Adele Astaire, Gertrude Lawrence, Ethel Merman, and Ginger Rogers. "Fascinating Rhythm," "Do, Do, Do," "Sweet and Low Down," "Embraceable You," "I Got Rhythm," and a dozen other wonderful songs followed one another in dizzy succession. In addition, *Of Thee I Sing*, which Gershwin wrote with George Kaufman and Morrie Ryskind, won the Pulitzer Prize in 1932. George moved to a Riverside Drive penthouse, which became headquarters for a series of wondrous Sunday evening delicatessen suppers that featured Barney Greengrass' sturgeon and attracted the greatest wits and socialites of the town. That's when the Gershwin saga really started. George, who loved to play the piano for hours on end, and naïvely—also justifiably—took it for granted that nobody wanted to hear anything but his music, would finally suspend operations to seek refreshments. His place would be taken by a surly young man named Oscar Levant, who played George's music just as well as the composer.

Oscar likes to tell the story of the night he and George journeyed to Pittsburgh to play with the symphony orchestra there. George took it for granted that the lower berth of the compartment was his proper due. Before turning out the light, Oscar peered over the edges of the upper to see George sprawled complacently below, puffing a huge cigar. "Do you know what this picture represents?" said George pleasantly, when he spied Oscar's face. "It's the difference between talent and genius." One day, Oscar, George, Ira, and I journeyed up to Baker Field to see a Columbia-Navy football game. We were late, and I weaved in and out of the trolley poles on Sedgwick Avenue rather recklessly. "For God's sake, be careful!" cautioned George. "You've got *Gershwin* in the car!"

George loved to go to parties, and thought nothing of playing the entire score of a forthcoming musical for his friends. This practice irked his canny collaborator, George Kaufman. "If you play that score one more time before we open," Kaufman once told him, "people are going to think it's a revival." Kaufman also deplored Gershwin's genial habit of inviting everybody he met to sit in on rehearsals. Kaufman left one run-through with a deep scowl. "It's going to be a prize flop," he predicted. "What makes you say that? I thought it went beautifully," protested Gershwin. "Not at all," grumbled Kaufman. "The balcony was only half filled."

I accompanied George on some wonderful vacation trips. They were a succession of hilarious adventures and beautiful girls. He banged out the *Rhapsody* once in the parlor of the Colonial Hotel in Nassau at seven in the morning to please a girl he had met on the boat, and was indignant when the manager made him stop. "I guess he didn't know I was Gershwin," he consoled himself.

In Havana, a sixteen-piece rhumba band serenaded him en masse at four in the morning outside his room at the old Almen-

dares Hotel. Several outraged patrons left the next morning.
George was so flattered that he promised to write a rhumba of his
own. He did, too. His *Cuban Overture* was played for the first
time at the Lewisohn Stadium in August 1932. In Havana George
reached his greatest height of indignation. A lovely Cuban miss
failed to keep a luncheon date with him. Later that afternoon he
spied her on the Yacht Club terrace, and exclaimed, "Hey, do you
know that you stood me up today?" "Oh, I meant to phone and
tell you I couldn't meet you," said the contrite maiden, "but do you
know something? I simply couldn't think of your name." George
didn't recover for days.

He reserved one unpublished little waltz tune for affairs of the
heart. "You're the kind of girl who makes me feel like composing
a song," he would tell the enraptured lady of the moment, and
lead her off to his suite. We would follow on tiptoe to hear him
compose the familiar tune for her. "It will be dedicated to you,"
he would conclude soulfully.

One day, I happened to remark that the score of one of his infrequent failures, *Pardon My English,* was below par. George demurred. All of us were sun-bathing in the nude; George insisted that we all go inside while he proved his point by going through the score from opening chorus to finale. I can still see him sitting at the piano, stark naked, playing the songs and singing them, too, at the top of his voice. George belonged at a piano. I have never seen a man happier, more bursting with the sheer joy of living, than George when he was playing his songs. He would improvise and introduce subtle variations, and chuckle with childlike delight when his audience exclaimed over them.

The work that George Gershwin loved best was *Porgy and Bess.* He composed it in eleven months and orchestrated it in nine. Its initial production by the Guild in 1935, a bit too stuffy and pretentious, was only moderately successful. When it was revived seven years later, it really came into its own, and its songs seem destined to become part of America's richest musical heritage; the tragedy is that Gershwin wasn't living to see that come to pass.

George moved to Hollywood in 1936. He wrote the music for the Fred Astaire-Ginger Rogers picture, *Shall We Dance?* which included one of his best songs ("Oh, No, You Can't Take That Away From Me") and *A Damsel in Distress.* He was working on the *Goldwyn Follies* when he was stricken by a brain tumor.

The last years of George's life were almost equally divided between composing and painting. George took his painting very seriously, and indeed had a genuine talent for it. At a memorable dinner one evening he said, "A man told me today that I need never write another note; I could make a fortune with my palette and brush." "Isn't it amazing," said one awed lady, "that one man should possess a genius for two of the arts?" "Oh, I don't know," said George modestly. "Look at Leonardo da Vinci." At another dinner, apropos of nothing, George suddenly said, "Has anybody here seen my new cigarette case?" It was solid gold, and inscribed thereon were facsimile signatures of a score of famou~

men. It had been presented to him after a performance of his
Concerto in F. The case was passed clear around the table. As
George was putting it back into his pocket, his brother Ira produced a crumpled pack of Camels. "Anybody want a cigarette?"
he inquired pleasantly.

But Ira, like everybody else who knew him well, adored George
Gershwin. After his death, Ira wrote practically nothing for years.
That he had lost none of his talent he proved, however, with the
lyrics for *Lady in the Dark*.

George Gershwin expressed his credo in these words: "My
people are American, my time is today. Music must repeat the
thought and aspirations of the times." Seven years after his death
his exciting songs are being played more frequently than they
were during his lifetime. One critic recently remarked, "George
Gershwin brought to serious consideration a new idiom in American music, and forever changed its future direction." Once every
summer twenty thousand people gather in a New York stadium
to hear a program dedicated to his memory. As the first familiar
strains of the *Rhapsody in Blue* hush the expectant audience,
it is hard to believe that the composer has been dead since 1937.
It's such a little while since he sat beside me in Cuba listening
to the same composition on the radio, and saying, "It *is* great, isn't
it? But wait until you hear the one I'm working on now."

* * *

The character of "Sporting Life" was played in the original
production of *Porgy* by a Harlem hoofer named Bubbles. He was
one of the great dancers of the day, but had only the haziest notions of discipline and rehearsals. The conductor, Alex Smallens,
had a terrible time perfecting him for the part. Once he suggested
sarcastically, "Maybe the fault is in my conducting?" Bubbles
mollified him completely when he said in all sincerity, "Mr.
Smallens, if I had the money of the way you conduct, I'd be a
millionaire!"

* * *

About thirty years ago there was a lightweight boxer in Hoboken, New Jersey, who fought under the name of Marty O'Brien, and was a member of the town's fire brigade on the side. He was a clean, likable kid, completely on the level, and among the host of friends that he made was a rising young singer named "Bing" Crosby.

Marty O'Brien got married, and in time had a son who was too frail to become a boxer like his dad, but inclined toward a musical career. He could carry a tune like nobody's business. Marty wrote to his old friend Bing. Could Bing help the kid get the musical education he craved? Bing Crosby could—and did. O'Brien's boy studied music and in due course turned professional.

The boy was Frank Sinatra—Bing Crosby's most formidable rival in the crooner ranks today.

* * *

That lovely and nostalgic tune, "Melancholy Baby," was written in 1912 and is still a sure-fire encore for any orchestra, sweet or hot. The legend goes that George Norton, who wrote the lyrics, was in a railroad station waiting for the arrival of his best girl. Word came through that the train was delayed. While the young man paced impatiently up and down the platform, the theme of "Melancholy Baby" began to take shape in his mind. Barely had he jotted down the last lines on the back of an envelope when the station master gave him sad tidings. The train he was waiting for had been wrecked; the girl was one of the victims. Neither Norton nor Ernie Burnett, who composed the melody, has written another song hit since that day.

* * *

One place where they really take their music seriously is aboard a certain British airplane carrier. Every afternoon at four, unless there's a heavy gale running or the enemy has actually engaged the ship, there is a concert on deck. The band sits on the principal plane elevator, which is depressed about two feet, so that the musicians may follow better the baton-wielding of the conductor. He stands at the edge of the deck above, his back to the audience, which is always ample, since every man who can be spared is there under official orders.

On the afternoon in question, the carrier was coursing lazily through Mediterranean waters, and the concert was in full cry. Suddenly a mechanic in the control room noticed the plane-elevator indicator, which registered the fact that it was not quite flush with the deck. Afraid that the mechanism was out of kilter, he pressed a button hard. The ship's band, in the middle of the overture from *Carmen*, suddenly disappeared from the view of the entranced audience and plunged into the bowels of the ship. The mechanic, horrified when he saw what he had done, hastily pushed another button. The elevator shot skyward. It came to the surface with a jolt that sent every musician bouncing at least three feet in the air. But ah, those imperturbable British! Not one man stopped tooting his instrument for a moment during the entire round trip. The leader never lost a beat. When the overture was concluded, the unsmiling ship's company applauded politely.

* * *

The musical fraternity has an unending fund of anecdotes which it never tires of repeating. Moriz Rosenthal, the noted pianist, is responsible for many of them. It was either he, or Godowsky, or Hofmann—authorities differ—who accompanied Mischa Elman to that never-to-be-forgotten debut of Jascha Heifetz at Carnegie Hall. A tumultuous audience roared its approval. Elman mopped his brow, and grumbled, "It's stifling in here." "Not for pianists, Mischa," was the gentle reply.

Rosenthal attended one of Paderewski's farewell performances with another distinguished pianist and composer, Abram Chasins. It was a lamentable exhibition, and Chasins murmured sadly, "The things that man has forgotten!" "What he forgets isn't so bad," said Rosenthal. "It's what he *remembers*."

* * *

One of Chasins' most successful compositions is a piano piece called *Rush Hour in Hong Kong*. "It was published only seven months ago," he told Rosenthal proudly, "and it has just gone into its seventeenth edition!" "I was never so crazy about that piece, Abe," was the answer, "but so bad I didn't think it was!" Back at Chasins' studio, he found the piano rack covered with compositions by Bach, Beethoven, and Schubert. "My, my," commented Rosenthal. "I was under the impression that you composed by ear."

* * *

Rosenthal was dragged reluctantly one afternoon to hear a third-rate string quartet go through its paces. After the recital, the second violinist rushed up to him. "Did you like it, maestro?" he asked eagerly. "Excellent, excellent," lied Rosenthal. "And our tempi, did they suit you?" persisted the violinist. "Ah," said Rosenthal, "they were simply marvelous—particularly yours." Another day, Rosenthal was listening to a friend's newest composition. He made no audible comment, but the composer noticed that he took off his hat several times, and then put it on again.

"It's too hot in the studio here," the friend suggested. "I'll open a window." "No, no," Rosenthal assured him. "It isn't that. I was just bowing to all the dear old friends I recognized in your piece."

* * *

The story goes that Mrs. Vanderbilt once demanded to know what Fritz Kreisler would charge to play at a private musicale, and was taken aback when he named a price of five thousand dollars. She agreed reluctantly, but added, "Please remember that I do not expect you to mingle with the guests." "In that case, Madam," Kreisler assured her, "my fee will be only two thousand."

Another rich dowager was taken to a recital of the famed Budapest Quartet. Introduced later to the first violinist, she gushed, "It's a shame your little orchestra hasn't got money enough to expand. I'm going to write you out a check for five thousand dollars; we'll make that band of yours as big as Tommy Dorsey's!"

* * *

Toscanini had a painful experience one evening with a soloist who began his cadenza bravely enough but soon got into difficulty. Obviously flustered, he wandered farther and farther off key. The maestro and the entire orchestra held their breaths. Just before their cue to resume playing, the soloist managed to recover the original key. Toscanini bowed and said, "Welcome home, Mr. Ginsberg."

* * *

Oscar Levant once played with an orchestra whose conductor he detested. The conductor reciprocated the feeling and delighted in pointing out errors in his playing. Levant finally lost his temper completely and convulsed the other members of the orchestra— and also terminated his own association therewith—by shouting, "If you bawl me out once more, I'll follow your beat!"

A Hollywood notable attended a Beethoven festival with Levant because he thought it would emphasize his position as a patron of the arts. He nodded uneasily through the concert, but perked up as the final number began. It was the C Minor Symphony, which has several false climaxes. At the first two, the producer half rose from his seat. At the third, he turned angrily to Levant and muttered, "The rat fooled me again!"

Levant played background music for a Parisian picture under the guidance of another brilliant producer. "It's good," said the connoisseur, "but it's not Frenchy enough." He thought a moment, and added, "I've got it, Oscar! Put in a few more French horns!"

* * *

Did you know that Cole Porter's first two song hits were those enduring Yale favorites "Bingo" and "Bulldog, Wow Wow Wow"? His first complete score was for a show called *See America First* that was produced by Elisabeth Marbury in 1916, but lasted only a fortnight. The book of that show was by Lawrence Riggs, who later became Catholic chaplain at Yale. Porter went on to write some of the greatest popular songs of our time; "Night and Day," "Begin the Beguine," "I Get a Kick Out of You," "Just One of Those Things," are only a few of them.

Porter comes from a wealthy and socially prominent family, and lives in a rather grand manner that baffles some of his Broadway associates. One summer the Porters had a cottage near Long Beach. The stage manager of one of his old shows noticed that twice a week the Waldorf-Astoria sent a truck out to the Porter abode. Consumed with curiosity, he finally knocked on Porter's door and said, "My wife wants to know what it is so special that you can't get it in Long Beach and have to have it sent out twice a week by the Waldorf?" "Oh," said Porter, surprised, "I guess it's our laundry. They call for it Mondays, and get it back on Thursdays!"

Producers never could find him when they needed him in the old days when the boats were still running. One of them wailed the length of Broadway: "I waste hundreds of dollars in cables trying to locate the guy, and where do I finally find him? He is faltbooting down the Rhine! First, I am sick and tired of chasing him around the world when anybody else is no farther away than Lindy's, and second, what in hell is faltbooting?"

* * *

Nora Bayes and her husband, Jack Norworth, were once doing their act under the management of Lew Fields. Their stipend was $750 a week. Norworth thought they were worth a lot more, and wired Fields that their pay ought to be doubled. Fields' answer put Norworth's nose out of joint for weeks. "Frankly," he wrote, "your wife isn't worth $1500 a week to me in her present act."

The same act was incorporated later into the Ziegfeld Follies of 1908. Norworth felt that it needed a shot in the arm, and riding downtown on the subway one afternoon, he decided that a new song about the moon might do the trick. He wrote one that very day. "Shine On, Harvest Moon" was its name.

Two other famous songs that were introduced professionally by Nora Bayes were "Over There" and "Has Anybody Here Seen Kelly?" She was a temperamental songstress and changed accompanists with great regularity. They usually quit in a huff. Two of them later achieved some success on their own. One was Edmund Goulding, the ace Hollywood director. The other was George Gershwin.

* * *

The Russian composer Stravinsky tells the story of an exchange between Gershwin and himself. "How much will you charge me to come over and give me lessons in orchestration?" said Gershwin. "How much do you make a year?" answered Stravinsky. "$100,000," said Gershwin. There was a moment's silence, and then Stravinsky said: "How about your giving *me* lessons?"

* * *

In New York, a five-year-old girl was taken to a concert, warned that she must remain quiet in her seat. She listened respectfully to two intricate pieces, then turned to her mother and asked gravely, "Is it all right if I scream now?"

* * *

In Cleveland, a guest conductor was driven crazy at rehearsals because at least one member of the orchestra was always missing. After the last rehearsal, he tapped for attention and said, "I want to thank the first violinist publicly for being the only man in the entire orchestra who had the decency to attend every rehearsal." The first violinist hung his head. "It seemed the least I could do," he said in a deprecating tone. "You see, I don't expect to show up for the concert tonight."

And of course everybody must have heard about the night that Stokowski was conducting the Philadelphia Orchestra in the rendition of Beethoven's *Leonore* Overture No. 3, and the offstage trumpet call twice failed to sound on cue. Directly the last note of the overture had been played, the apoplectic Stokowski rushed into the wings with murder in his heart. He found the trumpeter struggling in the clutches of a burly watchman. "I tell you you can't blow that damn thing here," the watchman kept insisting. "There's a concert going on inside!"

* * *

No collection of musical anecdotes today should conclude with anyone but Frank Sinatra, now known simply as "The Voice" in worshipful radio circles, and as "Frank Not-So-Hotra" by frustrated rival croonatics. When Sinatra inaugurated his own weekly program, Ginger Rogers was the guest star for the first show, and the rehearsal provided a field day for rabid autograph hounds. One of them carried off the signatures of both Ginger and Sinatra in triumph. A moment later Ginger heard her address a friend disdainfully. "Swap you Sinatra for an ordinary Roosevelt and Churchill? What kind of a dope do you think I am?"

Chapter·Nine

THE GOOD OLD DAYS

W HEN THE Victoria Theatre occupied the present site of the
Rialto at 42nd Street and Seventh Avenue, and Willie
Hammerstein managed the vaudeville shows staged there, anybody in the public eye could get headline billing for a single week.
Hammerstein particularly favored good-looking gals who had just
beaten a murder rap. One such damsel shot a man on Friday and
opened at the Victoria the following Monday at $1000 for the
week. She tried to get a second week at the same figure. "Not until
you go out and shoot somebody else," Hammerstein told her
promptly.

* * *

There was an estimable Baron Fugger who lived in Germany
many decades before Hitler—fortunately for the baron, who had
an impeccable taste for food, drink, and pleasant living. He decided one day to make the Grand Tour of Italy and took the precaution of sending a trusted servant ahead of him on his proposed
route. It was the servant's duty to sample the wine at every hostel

226

and monastery along the way. If he approved, he chalked up the word *est* on the outer gate, and the baron then knew exactly where it was safe for him to refill his tank. One sunny morning the servant pulled up at the monastery of Montefiascone, a bare fifty miles north of Rome, and called for a carafe of the native wine. It was so wonderful that he rushed to the gate and chalked up "EST! EST! EST!" A few days later, the baron reached Montefiascone, and marveling at this sudden extravagance on the part of a customarily imperturbable connoisseur, wheezed up the hill on the double and demanded some of the wine that was responsible. One sip was all he needed. He unpacked his duds, and promptly drank himself to death. Just before he expired—in a daze of complete happiness—he made a solemn pact with the good friars. He left half of his entire estate to the monastery on condition that once each year, a barrel of Est, Est, Est would be emptied over his grave. Until the outbreak of World War Two, at least, this ceremony was religiously performed every Spring.

* * *

One of the most famous hotels in all the world was the original Waldorf-Astoria, which threw open its doors for the first time on March 13, 1893 (the Astoria part of the hotel was not completed until four years later) and was the centre of the New York hotel world until it was torn down to make way for the world's largest office structure, the Empire State Building. One of the most famous features of the old Waldorf-Astoria was Peacock Alley. It was said that if a person would simply sit there for two days, as at Shepheard's Hotel in Cairo, Egypt, he could see the rest of the world pass by. Another room that country folk flocked to see was the grill, which featured an honest-to-goodness trout stream. Young bucks were given a rod and reel and could actually fish for their dinner. Attendants unhooked their catch and bore it off to a sizzling grill near by; the bucks frequently filled in the moments of waiting by pushing each other into the stream. One of the memorable days in the history of the old Waldorf came when

Sergeant York, hero of the First World War, made his first visit to Manhattan. He was major domo-ed by a Tennessee Congressman not yet very well known, named Cordell Hull.

* * *

Marquis James, whose biographies of Sam Houston and Andrew Jackson are about the last word on the subjects, and who insists that he is a "fifth or sixth cousin of Jesse James," once worked as a reporter on the *New Orleans Item*. It was there that he uncovered the story of the lady of the underworld whose only real ambition was to be buried in New Orleans' swankiest cemetery. She ran the biggest brothel and gaming casino in the South; important politicians changed their vote at a nod of her peroxide curls; a police commissioner who tried to raid her establishment was literally driven out of town. But the Bishop was her stumbling block. Her generous donations to his church were refused. Her efforts to buy a plot in the Bishop's cemetery were sharply rebuffed.

One day she sold out her extensive interests and sailed for France, where she turned respectable with a vengeance, and married a marquis who took up three pages in the French *Who's Who*. When the New Orleans Bishop received a huge contribution from the Marquise de Fourabonne, how could he be expected to know that she was none other than the madame he had snubbed so often? He accepted her gift with a warm note of thanks, and assured her that her request to be buried after her death in his cemetery would be carried out to the letter.

Eventually she died, and her body was borne in state to the vault that had been built at her order. It occupied a plot at the edge of the cemetery. A wire fence was all that separated the vault from the tracks of the Southern Pacific Railroad.

Some time after the burial services—conducted by the Bishop himself—a new signal tower was erected by the railroad. Today, not ten feet from the body of the Marquise, there flashes a bright and powerful red light.

* * *

Some years ago, one of the bright young men who represented Standard Oil in China returned to America for a vacation, in the course of which he met and married a lovely girl from his home town.

"You'll just love Shanghai," he assured her again and again on the way out, "particularly my Number One Boy, Ling. You won't have to lift a finger. Ling runs the household beautifully. There is no detail he doesn't regulate."

In due course they arrived in Shanghai, the bride met Ling, the Number One Boy, and approved. The next morning her husband kissed her good-bye before reporting back on the job. "Sleep as long as you like, darling," he told her. "Ling will take care of everything."

A few hours later she awoke again, to find herself being shaken ever so gently by the Number One Boy. "Time to get dressed and go home now, Missy," he said.

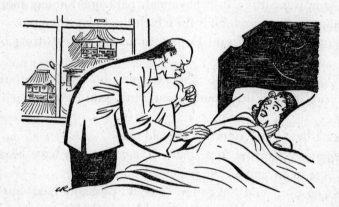

Chauncey Depew told two railroad anecdotes so frequently— and so well—that somebody suggested engraving them on his tombstone when he passed away.

One concerned a grizzled old maintenance man at Grand Central Station whose task it was to check on the shoe brakes of all the cars after the trains were made up and ready to start their runs. Depew watched him plodding from car to car one morning and called down from the platform, "How long you been doing that job, my friend?" "Forty years," was the answer. "Exactly what are you looking for under all those cars?" persisted Depew. "I'm damned if I know," said the veteran.

The other Depew standby was the farmer who had been the only witness to a disastrous head-on collision on a lonely stretch of track in Texas. Asked to tell in court what he had seen, the farmer said: "Wal, fust I seen Number 48 roarin' down the track from the West at about seventy miles an hour. Then I turned and seen Number 17 bearin' down the same track from the East just about as fast. It was easy to see they was goin' to smash right inter one another."

"What did you think while you watched all this happen?" asked the judge.

"What did I think?" repeated the farmer. "I thunk, this is one hell of a way to run a railroad!"

Depew was sitting in a Savannah park one Sunday morning, listening to the church bells for which the town is famous.

"Wonderful bells," said Depew to an old gaffer sitting beside him.

"What's that?" said the other, cupping his hand over one ear.

"I said the bells here sound wonderful," said Depew in a louder voice.

"Can't hear you," returned the old man.

Depew's voice rose to a shout. "I say that you have beautiful bells here in Savannah," he bellowed.

"It's no use," said the gaffer. "I could probably hear what you was saying if it wasn't for them goddam bells!"

* * *

Wilson Mizner was a veteran of the Alaska Gold Rush of 1897 —a burly, six-foot-four giant of a man, who dazzled Broadway for years as a dramatist, publicity expert, professional gambler, and wit. Some of his pals in the Klondike days were Tex Rickard, Jack London, Rex Beach, and Robert Service. He was a genuinely tough hombre—with a magnificent sense of humor. He is the man who coined the phrase: "Never give a sucker an even break." Cleaned out himself in a crooked roulette game, he explained without rancor, "Sure, I knew the wheel was crooked. But what could I do? It was the only one in town." He could only admire, he added, the skill and dexterity of the croupier. "That guy," he declared, "would steal a hot stove and come back later for the smoke. I know his brother, too. Blackjack dealer. He could do more with fifty-two soda crackers than most crooked dealers could do with a marked deck."

While he was in Alaska with Rickard, the latter pulled a gat and plugged a man through his sombrero. "What's the idea?" asked Mizner languidly. "You know my gal Goldie?" said the excited Tex. "Well, that rat insulted her!" "For God's sake," said Mizner, "*how?*"

A "big shot" approached a poker game that Mizner was banking. He asked to be declared in. "This game is too big for you," warned Mizner. The big shot was very much put out. "What do you take me for—a piker?" he rasped. "Cut me in here for ten thousand dollars." Mizner calmly slipped the ten one-thousand-dollar bills into his cash drawer. "Joe," he commanded, "give the gentleman a blue chip." At one time, Mizner persuaded all his fellow gamblers in New York to wear roses in their lapels as a means of identification. Times had gotten tough, and they had begun to prey upon each other.

During one of his intermittent periods of prosperity, Wilson Mizner owned a hotel in New York. A sign in the lobby read, "Guests must bury their own dead and will please not smoke opium in the elevator." He ordered a steak in his own dining room, snipped off a piece and put it in his pocket. "When I went out alone tonight," he explained, "that dame in 811 said I should choke on the first bite. This ought to fool her."

Invited to lecture before a women's club, Mizner got hold of an attendant and told her to be sure to place a pitcher of ice water and a glass on the speaker's table. "Do you want it for drinking?" she asked. "No," said Mizner, "I do a high-diving act." Another time he began tossing money about with unwonted abandon. "Where did you get it?" they asked him. "Playing a horse," he explained. "Where—in Saratoga?" "No—in vaudeville." Once he persuaded his friends for a week that he was going to marry a beautiful girl. Then he announced that the engagement was broken. "I told her about my rich uncle," he explained mournfully. "Now she's my aunt!"

Jim Tully once persuaded Mizner to try his hand at a short story. He promptly sold it to *Liberty* for a thousand dollars, but wasn't satisfied. "It took me eight hours to write that thing," he complained. Later he made an observation on the writing game that has been quoted many times since: "If you steal from one author, it's plagiarism; if you steal from many, it's research."

In the hospital for a variety of ailments, Mizner submitted to a colonic irrigation with the worst possible grace. When it was finished, he inquired of the nurse, "Now how about checking me for oil and water?"

Mizner never minced words about his numerous sins of omission and commission. "They'll find out anyhow," was his philosophy. "There's something about a closet that makes a skeleton terribly restless."

Somebody once asked Mizner what he thought of Frank Case, of the Algonquin Hotel. "He's a prince," declared Mizner. "He's the kind of guy who'd give you—" He opened his coat, looked down, and finished, "My God, this *is* his shirt!"

* * *

Oliver Herford and a famous military man were joint guests of honor at a banquet. The hostess suddenly announced, "Mr. Oliver Herford will now improvise a poem in honor of the occasion."

Herford, a modest and retiring man, shriveled in his chair. "Oh, no," he protested. "Have the general fire a cannon."

* * *

Joe E. Lewis once spent a night at Saratoga's venerable Grand Union Hotel. He swears that at three in the morning he heard his closet door creak and saw a Confederate soldier step out to demand, "Who's winning?" Naturally, Joe couldn't sleep after that. Besides, the railroad station was directly below and a switching engine kept shunting cars back and forth incessantly. Finally Joe summoned the night clerk. "Maybe you can tell me," he suggested, "what time this hotel reaches Chicago?"

Lewis went straight from Saratoga to a hospital. His first bulletin read, "I've taken a turn for the nurse."

* * *

One of the first automobiles ever seen on Fifth Avenue was built personally by Vincent Astor's father, Colonel John Jacob Astor III. It was a converted surrey, with a steam-driven engine under the seat, and probably a fringe on the top. The Colonel took it out for its first and last spin one summer day in 1900; Mrs. Astor and the eight-year-old Vincent stood outside and watched the Colonel rattle by. Suddenly the crowd started shouting. The Colonel, gratified, took a bow. Then he realized that his car was burning under him. He leaped in the nick of time.

Undaunted, the Colonel tried again several weeks later at Newport. This time he drove a steam Locomobile, and several other pioneering blue-bloods entered cars to race him. The course was an old trotting track. The contestants struck up a dizzy pace for about four laps, but then the overtaxed boilers lost their pressure, and a wag in a pony cart drove onto the track and left the whole field behind in a cloud of dust. The Colonel suffered the crowning indignity of having to push his car over the finish line.

* * *

James Thurber has had a few motoring experiences quite as frightening, in their way, as Mr. Astor's. Once he was driving with a cherished aunt on Christmas eve in Columbus, Ohio, and died a thousand anticipatory deaths while she tooted merrily through green and red traffic lights at forty miles an hour. "Why, honey," she explained later, "I thought the city had put up those lights for the Christmas festivities!" Another time he was driving himself, quite at peace with the world, when he suddenly noticed a gauge on his dashboard that registered "1650." Expecting the car to blow up any instant, he nosed it gingerly into a wayside garage, where the attendant reassured him: "That's your radio dial, Mac. You got her set at WQXR."

Thurber says his car harbors a definite grudge against him. Driving through a bleak little town out West, he mused aloud, "I'd hate to be stuck in this place." The car promptly burned out a bearing and he was stranded there for two days. Thurber hopes that engines are on their way out.

* * *

Edward R. Hewitt, in *Those Were the Days*, tells the story of the first time Mrs. Hamilton Fish took the controls of her shiny new electric runabout. She was hurtling down Third Avenue at a ten-mile-an-hour clip when a burly pedestrian stepped directly into her path. She tried to stop, but pushed the lever too far forward, thus increasing her speed. Her victim was just beginning to figure what had hit him when the flustered Mrs. Fish jammed her car into reverse, and got him again on the way back. Once

more she jammed her lever forward too far. "Hit 'im again, lady!"
cried an entranced onlooker. The pedestrian rolled out of her
way. "Twice, madam, is sufficient," he informed her.

* * *

Judge John C. Knox recalls that when he was a boy he visited a
courtroom in Greene County, Pennsylvania, presided over by a
certain U. S. Circuit Judge Wilson, with the assistance of two
associate "lay judges." The case had to do with a citizen who had
gotten snarled up with the liquor laws, an act considered not too
heinous in those parts.

The testimony was given haltingly, and then Judge Wilson asked
his lay associates what they thought the penalty ought to be.

" 'Bout ten days, I guess," said the first. "Ten days is what I
reckon too," said the second. "I think ten days myself," remarked
Judge Wilson. "And three times ten are thirty." That was the
verdict.

This was the part of Pennsylvania, you may recall, in which the
Whiskey Rebellion was staged many years ago by rugged indi-
vidualists who wanted no traffic with U. S. revenue agents. Donald Ogden Stewart burlesqued the story in Thornton Burgess'
bedtime manner. The opening lines, treasured by connoisseurs of
humor, go as follows:

"Just the *day* for a Whiskey Rebellion," said Aunt Polly and off
she ran, lipperty-lipperty-lip, to get a few shooting rifles. "Oh,
goody goody," cried little Emily. "Now we can all shoot at those
horrid Revenue Officers."

* * *

Here are a few stories about Texas from Boyce House's hilarious book, *I Give You Texas.*

There's no need to ask a man what state he's from. If he's from
Texas, he'll tell you himself; if he's not, why embarrass him? The
state is so big that El Paso natives refer to citizens of Texarkana
as "effete Easterners" and Brownsville folk regard Dallasites as
"Northern white trash." Roads leading South bear signs marked

"This way to Texas." Those who can read keep on going; the others settle in Arkansas. They're the kind who think the Alamo is pie with ice-cream. . . .

Even Texas sandstorms, continues Boyce, are something special. A farmer went to town to borrow money on his farm. The banker said, "I'll have to ride out and look over your place." "That won't be necessary," said the farmer. "Here comes the place now." On his way out, the farmer's hat blew off. He just reached up into the air and pulled down another one. . . .

A Texas rancher shot a man dead and telegraphed a slick lawyer in Fort Worth, three hundred miles away, offering a $5000 fee. The attorney wired back, "Leaving for your town on next train, bringing three eye-witnesses." . . .

Four men, one of them minus an eye, were playing poker in a West Texas saloon. Suddenly one of them yanked out a gat and intoned, "I ain't callin' no names, but the next rat I see dealin' from the bottom of the deck, I'm gonna shoot his other eye out!" . . .

Sam Houston is the hero of a thousand Texas anecdotes. At a big outdoor dinner in his honor, somebody handed him a plate of sizzling hot rice pudding. In the midst of an oration, Houston lifted a huge spoonful to his mouth, let out a roar, and then spat the rice to the ground. "You see, folks," he explained, "many a durn fool woulda swallowed that!" . . .

The court house at Stephenville has a large clock that is the pride of the town. It is illuminated at night. One citizen staggered up to a mail box, dropped a penny in the slot, glanced at the clock, and exclaimed, "Jehoshaphat, I'm nine pounds overweight." . . .

* * *

"Gate-crashing" is the intricate art of getting into places without a ticket.

The most famous gate-crasher of recent years is a character known as "One-Eyed Connelly," who boasts that he has seen seventeen consecutive World Series baseball games and twelve heavyweight championship fights without paying his way in. His methods are a closely guarded secret. Maybe he is the authentic invisible man. He once sneaked out of a model jail where he was serving a thirty-day sentence, imposed by a judge who failed to appreciate the artistry of his gate-crashing proclivities. He broke back in the next night just to show he could do it.

History records a gate-crasher back in 1841. He was a dull-witted cockney named Jones who had a passion for sneaking into Buckingham Palace, where he was picked up time and again by mortified guards. The last time they found him hiding under Queen Victoria's royal sofa.

A more legitimate blood brother of the gate-crasher is the free-pass hound, who will spend ten dollars and countless hours to get a free ticket for a fifty-cent movie. There is something about complimentary theatre passes—and to a somewhat lesser extent, free review copies of books—that tickles the vanity of the most honorable and solvent citizens. In theatrical vernacular, a free pass is known as an "Annie Oakley." Annie was a famous shot in her day, the female counterpart of Buffalo Bill, and could plug an ace of spades full of holes from a distance of a hundred yards. If you have ever noticed how many holes are punched in a free ticket, you will understand why it is called an "Annie Oakley."

* * *

When William T. Jerome was district attorney of Manhattan he made a determined effort to drive out the crooked gamblers who infested the city. One band he exposed had perfected an ingenious racket. They rode on crack trains between New York and Boston, and lured prosperous-looking victims into "a couple of rubbers of bridge."

By the time the game was over, the "fish" was usually several hundred dollars in the hole. The winner agreed to take a check, but once he had it in his hands, became suddenly conscience-stricken.

"I never thought the game would get this big," he would say. "I bet you think we're a parcel of professional gamblers. Let's call the whole thing off." He would then tear the check into shreds. Nine times out of ten the loser, vastly impressed, would insist on writing out a new one. When his vouchers came back from the bank on the first of the month, of course, *both* checks were there. The crooked gambler had palmed his original one, and torn up a blank piece of paper.

* * *

Exploring the Dangerous Trades, by Dr. Alice Hamilton, reveals the true origin of the phrase "mad as a hatter." Dr. Hamilton explains that mercury is used in the making of felt hats, and the poison resulting from its use over a period of years eventually caused the unfortunate victim's muscles to jerk violently and involuntarily. The hatter's friends drew false conclusions.

Robert Briffault, in his novel *Europa,* declares that the origin of mourning lay not in the desire of the bereaved to show sorrow over the loss of the departed, but in a desperate attempt to prevent the ghosts of said departed from haunting them in the days that followed. They figured that by dressing completely in black, they might escape the attention of presumably near-sighted ghosts entirely.

If you crave still more fascinating information, Bruce Bairns-father, creator of Old Bill and "The Better 'Ole," explains the origin of the little row of buttons on the sleeves of men's coats. It appears that His Majesty's troops in the old days didn't take very enthusiastically to the notion of wiping their noses on handkerchiefs, when a good sleeve served the same purpose. Buttons were added to the sleeve of the uniforms to introduce a keen element of hazard into this unfortunate procedure—and the custom stuck.

* * *

Edith Wharton, author of *Ethan Frome*, was what some people would call a first-rate snob. She explained that "only eight people in New York are worth dining with" and therefore had only eight chairs in her dining room. She was taken aback, however, when she learned that Mrs. William Waldorf Astor had referred to her as "that Bohemian."

* * *

James Whitcomb Riley became a poet via the unlikely route of purveyor of a cure-all patent medicine. In his early twenties he traveled all over the country with a quack doctor, and wrote poems on the backs of envelopes while the doctor was hornswoggling ruralites into buying bottles of his worthless elixir.

It was Riley who taught the doctor a routine that later became famous on the vaudeville circuits. The doctor would begin his spiel in a voice so hoarse and feeble that even the hicks in the front row couldn't hear him. Then, with a shaking hand he would pour himself a tablespoonful of his patent remedy. He would swallow it with evident relish, smack his lips, and then roar in a voice that could be heard three blocks away, "AND NOW, FOLKS . . ."

In later years, Riley liked to tell about the man with a dozen warts on his face who asked the quack if his medicine would remove them. "It can't miss," the doctor assured him. The next day, swore Riley, the man's wife followed the quack to the next town and demanded her money back. "Didn't it work?" asked the doctor in feigned amazement. "Work? Listen—Joe swallered that whole bottle of yours last night. This mornin' every one of them warts was still there—*but his face was gone!*"

* * *

Up for sale at Sotheby's famous London auction rooms recently was a letter described conservatively in the catalogue as "one of the most extraordinary" ever offered. Brief and to the point, and written by the noted English novelist Anthony Trollope to an Irish colleen in 1851, it said:

My Dearest Miss Dorothea Sankey:

My affectionate and most excellent wife is, as you are aware, still living—and I am proud to say her health is good. Nevertheless, it is always well to take time by the forelock and be prepared for all events. Should anything happen to her, will you supply her place—as soon as a proper period of decent mourning is over?

Till then, I am your devoted servant.

Trollope married a Miss Rose Heseltine in Dublin in 1844. When he wrote this letter to the mysterious Miss Sankey he was in "the dangerous forties." When he died at the age of sixty-seven, his "affectionate and most excellent wife" was still living, which left "dearest Dorothea" very definitely holding the bag—and the letter. Today it is a choice collector's item.

"THE ADVENTURES OF MARK TWAIN"

IN 1857, when Samuel Clemens was twenty-two, he became a journeyman pilot on the Mississippi, charged with keeping his packet from running aground on the numerous shoals and mud banks. This necessitated continual depth soundings, and one of the calls used to warn of shallow water and submerged rock was "mark twain." He explained later, "I was a fresh, new journalist, and needed a nom de guerre, so I confiscated the mariner's one, and have done my best to make it remain what it was in his hands —a sign and symbol and warrant that whatever is found in its company may be gambled on as being the petrified truth."

The motion-picture version of Mark Twain's life is inaccurate, sugar-coated, and far too long, but at least it made me look up his actual biography. And before I knew it, I was rereading *Tom Sawyer* and *Huckleberry Finn*. For that I am grateful. Maybe you remember the story of the tactful Englishman who first nonplussed Mark Twain by remarking, "I'd give ten thousand pounds not to have read *Huck Finn*," but then made everything perfect by adding, "so that I could have the joy again of reading it for the first time."

Mark Twain made a fortune out of his books, went bankrupt when he turned publisher himself, and then paid every cent of his debts and became rich again by virtue of new writings and fabulously successful lecture tours. His financial troubles did not increase his affection for the banking fraternity. He defined a banker as a man who "loaned you an umbrella when the sun was shining and demanded its return the moment it started to rain." He invented the story of a bank president who was proud of a glass eye that had been made for him by the greatest artist in Paris. "Twain, you need $5000," he quoted this gentleman. "I'll give it to you if you can guess which of my eyes is the glass one." "It's the left one, of course," snapped Twain. "It's the only one with a glint of human kindness in it." On another occasion, Twain sought to borrow a book from a banker who lived next door to him. "You'll have to read it here," said the neighbor. "I make it a rule never to let any book go out of my library." The next night the banker asked for the use of Twain's lawn-mower. "Sure thing," agreed Twain. "But you'll have to use it on my lawn. I make the same rules you do."

Mark Twain is credited with the classic remark, "Everybody complains about the weather, but nobody does anything about it," but Robert L. Cooke claims he can prove that Charles Dudley Warner actually coined the phrase. Twain *did* say, "If you don't like the weather in New England, just wait a few minutes." "Cauliflower," he said, "is nothing but cabbage with a college education." He told a lecture audience, "If you pick up a starving dog and make him prosperous, he will not bite you. This is the principal difference between a dog and a man." Acting as master of ceremonies at a dinner, he warned the speakers: "I once heard a preacher who was powerful good. I decided to give him every cent I had with me. But he kept at it too long. Ten minutes later I decided to keep the bills and just give him my loose change. Another ten minutes and I was darned if I'd give him anything at all. Then when he finally stopped, and the plate came around, I was so exhausted, I extracted two dollars out of sheer spite."

Mark Twain's wife, whom he adored, was a genteel and highly moral product of Eastern society. She disapproved highly of his picturesque Western vocabulary, and often persuaded him to censor some of the more outspoken passages in his manuscripts. Her intentions were the best, but her unceasing efforts to remold Twain's character probably were largely responsible for the inner tumults and confusions that assailed him in his declining years. Twain cut himself while shaving one morning, and cussed vociferously for five minutes straight. His wife heard him, and, intent upon shaming him, repeated every blasphemy he had spoken. Twain listened calmly, and told her, "You have the words, my dear, but I'm afraid you'll never get the tune." She had an appointment to meet him at the Waldorf for luncheon one day, but was very late. He left a note for her with the head waiter: "Never the Twains shall meet!" He wanted to take her to see Sarah Bernhardt, but when she heard that balcony tickets were three dollars apiece, she raised the roof. "And you're the man," she reproached him, "who told me you couldn't afford to raise our poor maids three dollars a month! You take that six dollars right out to the kitchen and give

Mark Twain and mankind

it to them!" Twain sheepishly did her bidding. The maids added four dollars of their own to the six he had given them, and went to see Sarah Bernhardt—in the orchestra.

One friend of Mark Twain (Mr. Miller Hutchison) invented both the Klaxon Horn and the Acousticon for the deaf. "Hmpfh," commented Twain. "Hutchison invented that confounded horn to deafen people so they'd have to buy his Acousticons." Another friend was the sort who would punctuate a story at least three times with, "Now stop me if you've heard this one before." Twain grew impatient one day and assured him, "I not only heard your damn story, I made it up!" Of his father he said, "When I was twenty, I thought him the stupidest man I had ever known. When I was thirty, I was amazed to learn how much the old man had learned in the past ten years."

Twain was a distinguished-looking figure in his later years. One day he was strolling in the park when a little girl pattered up to him and asked if she could walk with him. Highly flattered, Twain told her stories for an hour, then gave her a nickel and said, "Now run along home—and when you grow up you can tell your friends you once walked with Mark Twain." "Mark Twain!" echoed the little girl, bursting into tears. "I thought you were Buffalo Bill!" He received countless letters and photographs from harmless souls all over the world who insisted that they looked just like him. Twain finally composed a form letter to acknowledge such communications. It read: "I thank you very much for your letter and your photograph. In my opinion you are now more like me than any other of my numerous doubles. I may even say that you resemble me more closely than I do myself. In fact, I intend to use your picture to shave by. Yours thankfully, S. Clemens."

Speaking of Mark Twain's doubles, Fredric March's portrayal on the screen is a triumph of acting and make-up. While the picture was in production, March passed Jack Benny on the Warner Brothers lot, but didn't see him. "How do you like that?" commented Benny. "March is made up so good he doesn't even recognize me!"

* * *

Under Cover, the sensational exposé of American Fascists and Quislingites, was turned down by a dozen publishers before it was signed up by Dutton's. Every year, some manuscript that has been kicked around from pillar to post pops up as a huge best-seller.

Publishers never know just where the next success is going to come from, what obscure little writer is suddenly going to blossom into another Sinclair Lewis or Ernest Hemingway. John Galsworthy used to tell about a luncheon he had with his publisher near the beginning of his career, just before he sailed to the Far East on a P. and O. steamer. "There is no new talent coming along in London," sighed the publisher. "The writing profession is going to the dogs." "Cheer up," said Galsworthy. "Maybe I'll run across something while I'm on my trip." Several days out of England, while his boat was steaming down the West African coast, Galsworthy was approached by a diffident ship's officer, with a manuscript under his arm. "Mr. Galsworthy," he said, "may I impose upon you to read this manuscript for me? English is not my native tongue, and I have never tried to write a book before. I won't be too disappointed, therefore, if you think I've been wasting my time." Galsworthy promised the officer he would glance through the script. The officer's name was Joseph Conrad. The book was *Almayer's Folly*.

* * *

In 1918 Blasco Ibañez's *The Four Horsemen of the Apocalypse* made publishing history in America in more ways than one. Its chances in this country were rated so unlikely that an agent sold the American rights outright for $500. Years later, after the book had sold hundreds of thousands of copies and the picture version had created a new idol in the person of Rudolph Valentino, Blasco Ibañez visited the United States, and was presented with a check for $10,000 by the fortunate publisher. The perfect ending of this little idyll of honesty and good will would be a tableau of the author swooning in gratitude. As a matter of fact, he squawked to high heaven.

* * *

Some years ago *Collier's* sent Julian Street on a countrywide tour to get background material for a series of articles on out-of-the-way American towns. Wallace Morgan accompanied him to provide the illustrations. One of their stops was the old mining centre of Cripple Creek, and the local Chamber of Commerce, duly honored by their visit, turned the town inside out for their amusement. The thing that stuck in the author's mind, however, was the Cripple Creek red-light district, and when his piece duly appeared in *Collier's,* it was devoted exclusively to that section of the town. The enraged Chamber of Commerce met at once, and officially renamed the crooked lane that led through the filthiest houses in the district "Julian Street."

I wonder if the signpost is still standing.

* * *

When Victoria Lincoln, the author of *February Hill,* was a little girl of ten, the garden of her Fall River home adjoined that of the aging Lizzie Borden, central character in New England's most famous murder case. One day her mother was horrified to spy her tagging happily behind Lizzie Borden while that lady was plucking a basketful of flowers. She was rushed into the house, and warned never, never to go near Miss Borden again. "But why, Mother?" Victoria asked. The answer to her query was certainly one of the greatest pieces of understatement in the history of English speech. "You see," her mother explained, "that lady was very unkind to her mother and father!"

Certainly you have heard the little rhyme:

> Lizzie Borden took an axe
> And gave her mother forty whacks.
> And when she found what she had done,
> She gave her father forty-one.

* * *

James Buchanan Duke, of Durham, North Carolina, the country boy who revolutionized the tobacco industry of the entire world, was an enigma even to his father. "There are three things I don't pretend to understand," said that gentleman: "women, electricity, and my son Buck." As long as he lived, Duke employed when he could boys who, like himself, had been born in a small village. "A country boy," he explained, "can learn everything a city boy knows in six months. A squirt who was born into soft city life, on the other hand, couldn't learn in ten years the things every country kid knows automatically." Duke was greatly influenced by his uncle Billy, a vociferous country evangelist on the lines of Billy Sunday. Uncle Billy prayed for rain one day after a long dry spell. "And Lord," he concluded, "when you do send us rain, don't send one of those little gully-washers. Send us a regular sizzle-sozzle." Uncle Billy had to admit later that when it came to selling tobacco and cigarettes, his nephew Buck was a sizzle-sozzle of the first water.

Until the end of the Civil War, cigarette smoking was virtually unknown in America. Small quantities were imported from Turkey. About 1869, native American tobacco was used in a cigarette for the first time. By 1879, the annual output was in the neighborhood of a quarter of a billion cigarettes, all hand-rolled. It was at this point that Buck Duke stepped into the picture. He hatched the brilliant notion of including the picture of a pretty undraped actress or a popular ball-player in each package, developed the premium idea, and, most important of all, gained control of a new machine that could make cigarettes a hundred times faster than the most expert hand roller.

By the year 1908, Duke's American Tobacco Company had become a hydra-headed trust that enjoyed a monopoly not only in cigarettes, but in cigars, pipe and chewing tobacco, snuff, and even the boxes, cartons, and tin foil in which tobacco products were marketed. It also controlled the jobbers and the retail outlets (United Cigar Stores). The annual cigarette sale at this time was about nine billion. When the Government ordered a dissolution of the trust, its structure proved so intricate that only one man in the world could make head or tail of it. The world was treated to the irony of Buck Duke's being commissioned by Congress to break up his own trust!

Among the remains of the broken-up colossus was the Winston

plant of R. J. Reynolds. In 1913, this company gave the world its first "blended" cigarettes—Camels. In two years Camels captured a quarter of the country's cigarette market. American Tobacco frantically countered (1916) with Lucky Strikes, Liggett and Myers with Chesterfields. Old Gold and Philip Morris came later. Backed by frenzied advertising, these brands kited cigarette consumption to the staggering annual figure of 200 billion. Probably half of the cigarettes are smoked today by women, although Duke himself wouldn't stay in the same room with a woman who lit one.

Not content with the huge fortune he acquired in tobacco, Duke built up a billion-dollar hydro-electric company, wangled a substantial interest in the Mellon aluminum monopoly, donated a hundred million dollars to Duke University, and fathered the Doris Duke Cromwell who has figured in so many page-one newspaper stories in the past decade.

When Buck Duke first came to New York in 1884, he lived in a hall bedroom that cost him two dollars a week. He died in his marble mansion on Fifth Avenue—one of the stateliest and most ornate in town. Duke himself was sometimes a little startled by his latter-day surroundings. He liked to tell the story of the first time he rode down Fifth Avenue on a horse-drawn rubberneck wagon. The spieler called attention to the palatial new residences. "There's the Morgan place," he said. "Pierpont?" asked Duke. "No, Junius," said the announcer. "And here's the home of the Vanderbilts." "Cornelius?" suggested Duke. "Wrong again," snapped the announcer. "William Henry." A moment later he pointed to a new church. "Christ Church," he announced, and when Buck Duke said nothing, added, "Go on, kid, take a chance!"

Chapter Ten

THIS, GENTLEMEN, IS HISTORY!

W HEN FRANCIS MEYNELL, the great typographer and founder of the Nonesuch Press, visited America, he was tendered a dinner by the American Institute of Graphic Arts. Aware that students of printing as far away as Kansas City were going to journey to New York to hear his talk, Meynell spent days in feverish preparation, and marched off to the dinner with a sixteen-page typewritten manuscript in his pocket.

Unfortunately, a preliminary "cocktail party," hosted by the genial Rockwell Kent, lasted a full two hours longer than had been anticipated, owing in part to Mr. Kent's discovery of a half-dozen bottles of prime Irish whiskey, in part to the fact that most of the guests began falling on their faces. When Meynell faced the Institute audience, he swayed a bit, forgot all about the prepared speech in his pocket, and told the following story:

In the time of Nero, when sport-loving Romans crowded the Colosseum every Saturday to see a Christian tossed to the lions (on some Sundays there were double-headers), there was one special victim who had given the authorities untold trouble before he was rounded up. Nero had eleven of his most ferocious lions starved for a full week to assure a neat performance when they were turned on this Christian the following Saturday. Eighty thousand spectators turned out, not including the press. The Christian stood alone in the centre of the arena, calm and unafraid.

The first lion was released. He made a bee-line for the Christian. The crowd wetted its lips. But then an amazing thing happened. The Christian bent down and whispered something in the lion's ear. The lion's tail went between his legs, he lowered his head, and slinked out of the arena. When the same performance

was followed by six more half-starved kings of the forest, and the gallant crowd was beginning to holler for its money back, Nero, sore as a pup, summoned the Christian and curtly said, "If you will tell me what you say to those lions to make them act that way, I will grant you a full pardon." "It's very simple, Nero," explained the Christian. "I just whisper in their ears: 'Remember, you'll be expected to say a few words after dinner!'"

With this story, Mr. Meynell called it a day. He was so conscience-stricken the following morning that he had a special edition printed of the speech he really had intended to make, and sent a copy with his compliments to every person who had attended the meeting. It's quite a collectors' item today.

* * *

Edgar Saltus, author of that lush chronicle of Roman times, *The Imperial Purple,* told another tale about Nero's simple efforts to keep his Romans amused. There came a time when there were no more early Christians left in captivity to feed to the lions, and other prisoners were pressed into the service. These poor wights were given a fifty-fifty chance. They were allowed to pull a slip from a helmet. If the one they selected read "no" they were sitting pretty; if it read "yes" it was a break for the lions.

One culprit was in the jug because he had an annoying habit of stealing friends' and countrymen's wives. Indignant cuckolded husbands were determined that he be erased from the picture once and for all; they marked both of *his* slips "yes." A female gladiatrix managed to tip him off in the nick of time. "Think nothing of it," warbled the irresponsible lady-killer. "I'll meet you at the Zeusevelt Bar in twenty minutes." He reached into the helmet, picked up a slip, read it, tore it into shreds, laughed merrily, and started to walk off. "Just a minute," cried the infuriated captors. "What did your slip say?" "Never mind that," said the prisoner. "Just read the one you have left!"

* * *

Lewis Galantière is fond of regaling dinner parties with this rich quotation from Gibbon: "With the venerable proconsul [Gordian], his son was likewise declared emperor. His manners were less pure, but his character was equally amiable with that of his father. Twenty-two acknowledged concubines, and a library of sixty-two thousand volumes, attested the variety of his inclinations, and from the productions which he left behind him, it appears that the former as well as the latter were designed for use rather than ostentation."

* * *

The famous Lady Godiva was born way back in 1040. I didn't believe it until I checked the date in the Encyclopædia Britannica. She took her famous ride through the streets of Coventry, astride a white charger and clad only in her luxuriant golden tresses, as a protest against her husband's oppressive tax levies. Everybody refrained from looking at her with the possible exception of her husband (so contrite that he slashed the tax rate in half) and a tailor, henceforth known as Peeping Tom, who was promptly stricken blind. That's the legend, anyhow. A later historian named Fred Allen declared that another errant citizen considered peeping too but changed his mind when he heard the final arrangements. "Gadzooks," he exclaimed, "I've seen plenty of white horses before. What's all the shooting about?"

* * *

Henry IV, who ruled England from 1399 to 1413, was a puritanical soul. Persuaded that his subjects wore too many jeweled and golden ornaments, he decreed that such personal adornments be prohibited. Nobody paid any attention to the law until he added one amendment: prostitutes and pickpockets were exempted. The next day there wasn't a jewel or gold ornament to be seen in the city of London. His French wife soon put a stop to this nonsense; she appeared at court one day looking like a show window at Tiffany's. The law was stricken from the books.

* * *

When Sir Walter Raleigh was imprisoned in the Tower of London, he decided to while away the interminable hours by writing a history of the world. He had covered about two hundred pages of foolscap when, one morning, he was interrupted by a great noise in the prison courtyard. Two prisoners, working there, had become involved in a violent argument. Blows were struck. Inmates clung to the barred windows of their cells and yelled gibes and encouragement until the guards tore the men apart just in time to avoid mayhem.

When the prisoners were assembled for mess that noon, nobody talked about anything else. Eight prisoners gave the attentive Sir Walter their version of the fracas. No two stories were the same.

As soon as he was back in his prison apartment, Sir Walter took the manuscript of his history of the world, tore it into pieces, and threw it into the fire.

* * *

The original draft of George Washington's Farewell Address— a priceless document—is one of the treasures belonging to the New York Public Library. The privileged souls who are allowed to examine it are told also the surprising fact that this address never was actually delivered; it was just printed in a newspaper.

The original draft was prepared by James Madison in 1792, but pigeonholed when Washington was re-elected that same year. Four years later, Washington decided that two terms were enough for any man, thereby establishing a precedent that was not broken for 144 years. He pondered over Madison's original draft, reworded it to suit himself, and by arrangement with Editor David Claypoole, it was published in the *American Daily Advertiser* on September 17, 1796.

* * *

Neal McNeil of the *New York Times* tells how the most edible kind of wild rice was first introduced into America. (This delicacy is not to be confused with the coarse wild rice that was an important part of the Indians' diet in the Minnesota region centuries before.) It seems that the special grain was developed accidentally in the Pontine marshes in Italy; when the local authorities became aware of its delicious taste and nutritive value, they slapped a complete embargo on its exportation. Thomas Jefferson was our Minister to France at the time. He was taken on a tour of the Italian marsh region, and, as he ambled along, cannily plucked off heads of the grain and pocketed them. Back in America, he pondered on the best place to plant his prized grains, and settled on the marshy shoreline of the Carolinas. The wild rice flourished there, and was the original lure for the myriad of wild duck and other fowl that have migrated to those parts ever since.

A Tammany jurist who heard McNeil's story remarked, "This is just one more blessing we can credit to the Democrats." Another member of the party was the publisher, Max Schuster, who confessed that one evening he had broken a tooth on a grain of wild rice. His rueful comment at the time was, "Well, sir, I have seen wild rice in my day, but this is certainly the wildest yet."

* * *

Samuel Johnson blundered into a musicale at Mrs. Thrale's house one night; registered acute nausea when a soprano mutilated an aria. "Come now," said Mrs. Thrale, "make some allowances. You don't realize how very difficult that piece is." "Difficult, Madam," snorted Johnson. "I wish it were impossible!"

* * *

Voltaire was invited one night to participate in an orgy by a notoriously dissolute group of Parisians. He went, and gave such a satisfactory account of himself that the very next night he was asked to come again. "Ah, no, my friends," said Voltaire with a slight smile. "Once: a philosopher; twice: a pervert!"

* * *

Voltaire had a visitor who remarked that he had encountered another literary notable of that era on the way. "Ah," said Voltaire, "a very able man, a fine character." "That's very kind of you," said the visitor, "because he said that you were a villainous old wretch." "Well," said Voltaire with a smile, "perhaps we are both mistaken."

When Rousseau wrote his ode "To Posterity" he sent an advance copy to Voltaire. Voltaire read it with a frown and remarked, "This poem will never reach its destination."

* * *

Stories of the clashes in Parliament between Benjamin Disraeli and William Ewart Gladstone are legion. "Disraeli," shouted his enraged adversary once, "you will come to your end either upon the gallows or from some loathsome disease." "That depends," replied the unruffled Disraeli, "upon whether I embrace your principles or your mistress!"

Disraeli defined the difference between a misfortune and a calamity: "If Gladstone fell into the Thames, that would be a misfortune; if anybody pulled him out, that would be a calamity."

"Mr. Disraeli cannot possibly be sure of his facts," thundered Gladstone in one debate. "I only wish," was the reply, "that I could be as sure of anything as my opponent is of everything."

Disraeli's friends assured him that, despite his persistent efforts, he could never eliminate Gladstone as a factor in the government of England. "Have you ever watched a stone-cutter at work?" answered Disraeli. "He will hammer away at a rock for perhaps a hundred times without a crack showing in it. Then, at the one hundred and first blow, it will split in two. It is not alone that blow that accomplishes the result—but the hundred others that went before, as well."

* * *

Senator Barkley told the Washington Press Club that just after President Grover Cleveland allowed a tax bill to become law without his signature, Mrs. Cleveland woke up in the middle of the night and thought she heard burglars in the house.

"Not in the House, my dear," said Cleveland. "In the Senate."

* * *

In the McKinley Administration, John Hay was Secretary of State. China was represented at Washington by Minister Wu. The latter visited the State Department one day. Mr. Hay, asked about the conference, waxed jocular. "Oh," he said, "I talked until the Minister was 'hazy,' and then he talked until I was 'woozy.' Anything else, gentlemen?"

* * *

One of the most famous and most respected of the colleges that make up the great university of Oxford is Balliol. For some reason the venerable institution attracts African potentates and Indian nabobs in addition to eminent white students; its alumni include more black-skinned men, probably, than all the rest of the colleges combined. This gave rise to a story that has a very high rating in British circles.

An explorer was going about his business in darkest Africa when a hungry cannibal tribe bagged him in full flight and considered its Sunday-dinner problem solved. He weighed about two hundred on the hoof and there were murmurs of genuine satisfaction when they seasoned him with salt and lowered him into the pot. He was just beginning to simmer when the cannibal chief remembered his manners.

"Jove," he ejaculated, "you sound like an Oxford graduate. What college?"

"Balliol," gasped the half-baked explorer.

"Release this man," cried the chief. "Balliol men never eat one another!"

* * *

When General Pope was named to command the Union Army of Virginia in 1862, he issued a proclamation threatening the Southern forces with many dire catastrophes. The proclamation was headed "Headquarters in the Saddle." Stonewall Jackson is credited with the perfect retort: Why pay any attention to a general who obviously didn't know his headquarters from his hindquarters?

* * *

One day President Lincoln journeyed to the front to inspect the Union defenses; the task of piloting him fell to young Oliver Wendell Holmes. Holmes pointed out their enemy; the President stood up to look. Wearing his high plug hat, he made a magnificent target. A snarl of musketry fire came from the enemy trenches. The young officer dragged him under cover. Later Holmes remembered to his horror that he had muttered "Get down, you fool!" He was relieved, however, when Lincoln came to him before returning to the capital. "Good-bye, Captain Holmes," he said. "I'm glad to see you know how to talk to a civilian."

* * *

An excited supporter burst into the private chambers of the old tiger Clemenceau one day and cried, "Your son has just joined the Communist Party." Clemenceau regarded his visitor calmly and remarked, "Monsieur, my son is 22 years old. If he had not become a Communist at 22, I would have disowned him. If he is *still* a Communist at 30, I will do it then."

* * *

William Allen White, lifelong Republican, was inveigled into attending the 1928 Convention of the Democratic Party. Senator Jim Reed of Missouri asked him to give the invocation. White hesitated, then begged off. "I'd better not, Jim," he said. "I don't want God to know I'm here."

* * *

Some years after he had been President, William Howard Taft had to make a sudden trip to Chicago. Only an upper was left. Taft noticed that the lower of his section was assigned to an insignificant Casper Milquetoast, and resorted to a bit of psychology. "Last time I occupied an upper," he announced cheerfully, "it collapsed. I certainly hope this one will hold me." Then he went off to the club car. When he returned the little man was neatly buttoned up in the upper berth.

* * *

Dr. Hugh Hampton Young, eminent surgeon, attended the unveiling of a bust of himself at the University of Virginia. After the ceremony, a fluttery Southern belle came up to him and remarked: "Doctah, Ah hope you appreciate that Ah've come fifty miles in a station wagon to see your bust unveiled." The gallant doctor replied: "Madame, I would gladly return the compliment."

* * *

President Coolidge, "Honest Cal," apostle of normalcy, owed his success to a happy combination of Vermont shrewdness and extraordinary good luck. When, for example, after holding office through such a boom as America had never before experienced, he made his famous announcement, "I do not choose to run," and eased out of the White House just in time to let Mr. Hoover weather the crash in 1929, he was probably guided to some degree by instinctive caution and knowledge that a piper was going to demand payment one day; he also was a lucky, lucky man.

Most of the amusing anecdotes concerning Mr. Coolidge relate to his taciturnity and respect for his bankroll. In Northampton one day his wife fell for the blandishments of a traveling book salesman and bought one of those 1800-page "home medical advisers" for something like fifteen dollars. Misgivings assailed her the moment the salesman's hypnotic presence was removed. "What will Calvin say?" was the thought that plagued her. "How am I going to tell him?" Finally, she decided to put the book down on the centre of the library table, and await the explosion when her husband discovered it. To her amazement he said nothing about it at all—either the first evening or for several days thereafter. Mrs. Coolidge couldn't understand it—until one morning she opened the book and found that he had written a note on the fly-leaf. "I have looked carefully through all 1800 pages of this work," it read, "and find no cure whatever for a sucker."

One day Mr. Coolidge fell asleep while the presidential yacht was cruising down the Potomac. He awoke with a start, grinned sheepishly at his guests, and remarked drily, "Is the country still here?" Another time he found himself addressing a tribe of Indians on a reservation where there had been no rainfall for months. Native medicine men and professional "rain-makers" had practised their wiles in vain. Skies remained cloudless. Crops were going to ruin. The Great White Father rose to address a pretty depressed array of Indians. "Do not think that I in Washington," he said, "have not been worrying too about your lack of rain, and wondering what I could do to help you." Just then a veritable cloudburst descended upon the astonished and delighted audience. The President was soaked before he got under shelter. He watched the rain pour down and said, half to himself, "Gosh, I didn't know I had it in me."

The ambassador of a great nation called at the White House one day for an important and private conversation with the President. Mrs. Coolidge came in as the ambassador was preparing to leave. "Why don't you offer the ambassador a drink?" she suggested. "He's already had one," said the President testily. The next day, correspondents asked if he had anything to say about the conference. "No," said Coolidge. "I have nothing to say to you about anything else either." As they were leaving, he called after them, "And don't quote me!"

President Coolidge once visited the Emily Dickinson house in Amherst, and was shown the poetess' original manuscripts. He examined them casually and made a single comment: "Wrote with a pen, eh? I dictate!" There is a famous anecdote about a Sunday when Mr. Coolidge attended church without his wife. When he returned to the White House, she asked what the subject of the sermon had been. "Adultery," said the President. "What did he say about it?" she persisted. Coolidge thought for a moment. "He's against it," he reported finally. (That always reminds me of the sinner who sat in church, bored and dejected, while the pastor rumbled on about the Ten Commandments. Suddenly he reached Number Seven, and intoned "Thou shalt not commit adultery." The man snapped to attention, brightened visibly, and exclaimed with satisfaction, "*That's* where I left my umbrella!")

When Dorothy Parker heard that Calvin Coolidge was dead, she remarked cruelly, "How can they tell?" Clarence Darrow spoke his perfect epitaph: "The greatest man who ever came out of Plymouth Corner, Vermont!"

* * *

When Cundliffe, the Australian economist, was notified that he had been appointed a professor at Oxford, he went to his children's Australian nurse, and asked if she would accompany the family to England. "England?" she echoed in horror. "Where all the convicts come from? Never!"

* * *

Eamon de Valera, the Irish political leader who was born in Brooklyn, is a serious man today, but in his youth showed flashes of typical Irish wit. Returning to Dublin from a visit to Paris many years ago, he was asked by a friend to give his impression of the French mesdemoiselles. "Gentlemen," de Valera is said to have replied, "I may safely say that sex in Ireland is in its infancy."

Another time, he was arrested in the middle of an inflammatory political tirade, and clapped into prison for a full year. When he was released he went right back to the scene of his arrest, summoned his followers, and began another speech, "As I was saying when I was so rudely interrupted."

* * *

The Governor of Iowa has a name that makes rather a neat mouthful: Bourke Blakemore Hickenlooper. He himself tells about a drugstore clerk who refused to charge ten cents' worth of asafetida to the Hickenlooper account. "Take it for nothing, boss," said the clerk. "I wouldn't write both asafetida and Hickenlooper for a dime."

* * *

During President Hoover's last year in office, he was walking down Pennsylvania Avenue with his Secretary of the Treasury, Andrew Mellon. "Andy," said the President, "I came out this morning without a cent in my pockets. Lend me a nickel, will you? I want to call up a friend." "Here's a dime," volunteered Mellon. "Call both of them!"

* * *

Jane Addams, the famous social worker and founder of Hull-House, told this story on herself. She met an old friend on a train one afternoon, and greeted her cordially, but simply couldn't remember her name. "The conversation is bound to give me a clue," she thought, but for a half-hour she got nowhere. Then the friend said, "My poor brother is working himself to death these days." Miss Addams felt that her moment had come. "Ah yes, your dear brother," she exclaimed. "And what is he doing now?" Her companion glared. "He is still President of the United States," she remarked coldly.

* * *

Somebody once asked the late Huey Long if he thought we would ever have fascism in the United States. "Sure we will," predicted Long, "only *we'll* call it anti-fascism!"

* * *

The last time Thomas Lamont was in London he checked on the story that Lenin, many years ago, spent a long period of study in the British Museum. Mr. Lamont challenged an aged and fragile attendant of the Museum. "Do you remember seeing a little man named Lenin around here several years ago? He had a small, reddish beard, and he probably spent most of his time in the sociology and political philosophy alcoves." "Lenin? Lenin?" mused the old attendant. "Why, yes, now that you mention it, I do remember a gent by that name, sir. Read a powerful lot of deep books, e' did, sir. You know, I've often wondered what became of that little man!"

* * *

Only in China could a thing like this happen, said Ilona Sues, who wrote *Shark's Fins and Millet*.

Two mighty war lords, an uncle and his nephew, both of whom bore the name of Lieu, were engaged in a bloody fight for the supremacy of Szechuan Province. That was several years before the United Front in China. The country's greatest tennis player, Gordon Lum, arrived at the nephew's headquarters. The latter was delighted. His enthusiasm for tennis was matched by that of his uncle. He promptly dispatched an emissary to his uncle's camp, and a three-day truce was arranged to celebrate Lum's visit, and stage an honest-to-goodness tennis tournament.

A couple of hundred soldiers from both camps were detailed to build a first-rate tennis court in the middle of the wilderness. The two armies fraternized, Lieu and his nephew sat side by side at the edge of the court, and everybody got beautifully drunk on the best wines that could be found in the province. When the tournament was over, both armies went back to the exact positions they had occupied, and resumed the war where they had left off.

Gordon Lum said that just as he was about to serve one afternoon, he spotted a human head nailed to a tree behind the court, and became so unnerved he missed one ball completely.

"Why didn't you ask them to take it off?" asked Miss Sues.

"Not on your life," said Lum. "Such a request might have offended either the uncle or nephew or both of them, and spoiled the whole feast. A trophy is a trophy, and must remain where it is put. As a guest of honor, I could not make such a tactless remark. So I pretended that I hadn't even noticed the thing."

* * *

On the day that be-ribboned, be-medaled Higinio Morinigo achieved the presidency of the Republic of Paraguay, his aged mother is quoted as saying, "Hmphff! If I had known they were going to make a president of him, I would have sent him to school."

* * *

John Collier, Commissioner of Indian Affairs, gives some surprising facts in *The Changing Indian*, a new publication of the University of Oklahoma Press. Mr. Collier, no one for vague generalities, avers that there are now 350,397 Indians in the United States, and that this represents an increase of thirty-four percent over the 1890 tabulations; 153,993 are full-blood. Some tribes, notably the Dakotas and the Cherokees, are more numerous today than when the white man first encroached upon their territory, and many reservations are becoming overcrowded.

Maybe you have heard the story of Mrs. Lapidus who saw an honest-to-God Indian for the first time in her life at a basket-weaving exhibition at Wanamaker's. "Is it true dot you are a real, one hundred percent Indian?" she asked him. "Ugh," affirmed the Indian affably. "My, my!" mused Mrs. Lapidus. "How do you like our country?"

* * *

A male penguin proposes, according to Sir Hubert Wilkins, who was in the Antarctic long enough to find out, by placing a pebble at the feet of the lady penguin who has captured his heart. If she is inclined to accept, she picks up the token and carries it to a spot she has no doubt lined up well in advance; the nest is promptly built there and connubial relations established without further fol-de-rol.

There was a painter on one of Sir Hubert's expeditions who was sketching on the rocks when a female penguin came waddling along and rather pointedly deposited a pebble at his feet.

"Did he marry her?" laughed an interviewer. "No," said Sir Hubert pensively. "But don't forget, we had been there only four months at the time!"

* * *

In Hollywood, Carl Sandburg was shown the wonders of the MGM lot and met the most glamorous stars without uttering a syllable. The guide, in desperation, led him to the dressing room of a freakish show girl and said, "Just think, Mr. Sandburg. This girl is six foot two!" Sandburg spoke at last. "Lincoln," he said, "was six foot three and a half."

* * *

The correspondent John Whitaker reports that Mussolini openly sneered at his own lieutenants in the final years that he ruled Italy. Pointing to a painting in the Palazzo Venezia of Count Volpi standing arrogantly with his hands thrust into his pants pockets, Mussolini remarked bitterly to Whitaker, "That is the only time I have caught my own Finance Minister with his hands in his own pockets."

* * *

Within three months of Pearl Harbor, ninety percent of the famous authors in America had journeyed down to Washington trying to get jobs of one sort or another in furtherance of the war effort. Edna Ferber was one of the group. "I want to help the Government in Washington," she is said to have told Archibald MacLeish, "but I don't want to be a writer. I want to do something else. What can I be?" "Well," said Mr. MacLeish, "you can always be a battleship."

* * *

Astute diagnosing by John Gunther in his latest book, *D Day:* "The worst thing about war is that so many men like it. . . . It relieves them of personal responsibilities. . . . There is no worry about frictions at home or the dull necessity of earning a living. Military life is like a perpetual camping trip. I heard one officer say, 'How nice all this would be if only you could eliminate the bloodshed and the killing.' " "Perhaps," adds Orville Prescott, "peace planners who debate problems of frontiers and economics had better give a little more attention to eliminating the pleasures of soldierly comradeship and vast cooperative endeavor, the drama and excitement and the fun of war also."

* * *

The mayors of New York in recent years have supplied copy for every newspaper in the land. First there was John Hylan (called "Red Mike" behind his back) who escorted Queen Marie of Rumania on a tour up Fifth Avenue. "What a wonderful avenue," exclaimed Her Majesty. "You said a mouthful, Queen," agreed His Honor. Hylan seldom bothered to read speeches that trusted ghosts prepared for him ahead of time. In the middle of one speech he came to the phrase, "That reminds me of one of my favorite stories about a traveling salesman." It developed that the Mayor had never heard the joke before, and when he finished reading it, he laughed so hard he broke his glasses. The chairman of the dinner had to finish the speech for him.

Jimmie Walker brought color and gaiety to City Hall, although later he had a little trouble explaining what he took away from it. A pretty girl was once led into his office, worrying audibly whether she should address him as "Your Honor," "Mr. Mayor," or plain "Mr. Walker." Jimmie settled all that by pulling her down on his lap and crooning, "Come to baby, Beautiful," while the camera men clicked away in delight. Asked by a publisher to name his ten favorite novels, the Mayor laughed and declared, "Son, I never read a book in my life!"

A battered wreck of a man accosted Mayor Walker outside the Central Park Casino one night. "Jimmie," he pleaded, "gimme a quarter for something to eat." "Have a Corona," said the Mayor, reaching into his vest pocket. "Don't smoke," asserted the hooligan. "I just want a quarter for something to eat." "Come inside with me," suggested the Mayor, "and I'll stand you to a couple of whiskies. They'll buck you up!" "Don't drink," was the answer. "It's food I want." "I tell you what I'll do," persisted Walker. "I'm going to Belmont tomorrow. I happen to know of a horse that's a sure thing at twenty to one. I'll put a couple of dollars on it for you!" "No, no," cried the beggar. "I wouldn't think of gambling. Please stop all this nonsense and slip me a simple two bits for something to eat." "All right," conceded the Mayor reluctantly. "But first you've got to come over and meet my wife. I want her to see what happens to a guy who doesn't smoke, drink, or gamble."

Tammany Hall decided that New York needed a mayor to follow Walker who would be a different character in every respect.

Jimmie agreed. "Never follow a banjo act with another banjo act," was his dictum. So they bobbed up with John P. O'Brien, who, in his own words, was "a thousand percent different." Mr. O'Brien early endeared himself to his constituents when he referred to "that scientist of scientists, Albert Weinstein," and told delighted

Hizzoner Jimmie Walker and Hizzoner John P. O'Brien,
or an illustration of the old political dictum,
"Never follow a banjo act with another banjo act."

reporters that he was "a slave to literature." Mr. O'Brien's first interview consisted mainly of a declaration that he would make his own decisions and take neither advice nor direction from Tammany. One reporter spoiled everything by asking, "Mr. Mayor, who is going to be your new police commissioner?" O'Brien scratched his head. "I don't know," he answered. "They haven't told me yet."

Mayor LaGuardia, the present incumbent, rates a whole book for himself, but as long as he's mayor of the town we all work in,

I'd better be careful. Besides, he officiated at my marriage, and I owe him a debt of gratitude. He whipped through the ceremony in three seconds flat, mumbled, "Don't blame me for anything that happens," and was off—probably to attend a fire. Here's one nice story about him. He presides occasionally in Police Court. One bitter cold day they brought a trembling old man before him, charged with stealing a loaf of bread. His family, he said, was starving. "I've got to punish you," declared LaGuardia. "The law makes no exception. I can do nothing but sentence you to a fine of ten dollars."

But the Little Flower was reaching into his pocket as he added, "Well, here's the ten dollars to pay your fine. And now I remit the fine." He tossed a ten-dollar bill into his famous sombrero. "Furthermore," he declared, "I'm going to fine everybody in this courtroom fifty cents for living in a town where a man has to steal bread in order to eat. Mr. Bailiff, collect the fines and give them to this defendant!" The hat was passed and an incredulous old man, with a light of heaven in his eyes, left the courtroom with a stake of forty-seven dollars and fifty cents.

Fiorello La Guardia officiates at the author's wedding

Chapter Eleven

THE TRAIL OF THE TINGLING SPINE

IN TIMES of stress there is always a tremendous upsurge of interest in ghost stories and tales that make the heart skip a beat. Several such collections have hit the best-seller lists recently, and Hollywood, which used to produce its so-called "Zombie" pictures at a cost of thirty cents (Confederate money) and regard them as a secret weapon to depopulate theatres, has now turned the attention of some of its fanciest directors and stars to the Trail of the Tingling Spine.

In the following pages I have set down a few of the memorable ghost stories and thrillers that have been told me in the past few years. One of them was narrated in the presence of a man who wears a toupee. He got so excited that in two minutes every hair on the toupee was standing on end.

Probably you have heard about the timid soul who was hurrying down a dark, dark corridor when he suddenly collided with a stout and shadowy personage whom he certainly had not seen approaching him. "Golly," said the timid one, "you gave me a fright! For a second I thought you were a ghost!" "What makes you think I'm not?" answered the other—and promptly vanished.

Try a few of these stories yourself at a dinner party one evening. The results are electrifying. Soon everybody is remembering a macabre story *he's* heard about a haunted house, or an ill-mannered ghost, or a thing that behaved in no fashion that was human. Give the spooks a chance, and they'll pay dividends. I have spooken.

* * *

Two ladies from the faculty of a famous New England college for women decided to spend one of their vacations in an automobile tour to California and back. They traveled westward by way of the Petrified Forest and the Grand Canyon, and headed for home by the Salt Lake City route. They were two normal, unimaginative women, enjoying to the full a tour of their native country.

Late one evening, they were driving through the flat and monotonous fields of Kansas, intent upon reaching a hostel some thirty miles distant, when their car broke down. They were the kind of drivers who know nothing whatever about motors. They had no choice but to wait for some good Samaritan to come driving along and help them—and it soon became obvious that no other car was likely to come that way until the next morning.

It was then that one of the ladies noticed a two-story, unpainted farmhouse, set back some distance from the road. They approached it gingerly, wary of watch-dogs, and knocked timidly on the front door. Nobody answered. The impression grew on them that the house was uninhabited. When they discovered that the door was unlocked, they entered, calling loudly, and flashing their pocket searchlight in every corner. They found the living room and kitchen in good order, but an undisturbed layer of dust indicated that no human being had been in them for days.

The ladies blessed their luck, and decided to spend the night in the living room. The couch was fairly comfortable, and they bundled themselves up in robes which they fetched from the stalled automobile. There were dry logs in the fireplace; the ladies soon had a roaring fire going, and, in the light of the flickering embers, went peacefully to sleep.

Some hours later, one of the ladies awoke with the distinct feeling that somebody had entered the house. Her friend jumped up at precisely the same moment. A chill seemed to run through the room, followed by the unmistakable scent of the salt sea, although the nearest ocean front was over a thousand miles away. Then a young man walked into the room! Rather he *floated* in, because they heard no footsteps. He was dressed in boots and oilskins; sea-spray glistened on his rough stubble of reddish beard. He moved to the dying fire, shivering violently, and knelt down before it.

One of the women screamed. The figure turned slowly, gave a sort of mournful sigh, and slowly dissolved into nothingness. The terrified women clutched each other desperately, and lay there until the morning sun poured through the dusty window panes. "I saw it; I know I did!" said one of them. "Of course you did; I saw it too," the other reassured her, and then pointed dramatically to the fireplace. Before it was a small puddle of brackish water, and a piece of slimy green weed.

The ladies made for the open air, but the bolder of the two snatched up the piece of weed before they bolted, and held it gingerly at arm's length. When it dried, she placed it carefully in her bag.

Eventually a car rattled along the highway, and the driver cheerfully consented to tow the ladies to the nearest garage. While the mechanic tinkered with the engine, the ladies asked him about the deserted house some miles back on the road. "That must have been the Newton place," he said with no special show of interest. "Been empty nigh on to two years now. When Old Man Newton died, he left it lock, stock and barrel to his son Tom, who said he didn't like farming, and lit out one day for the East. Spoke of taking to the sea, like his great-grandfather did. Ain't none of us seen hide nor hair of him since that day!"

When the ladies returned to their college, they took the green weed, which still seemed clammy and damp, to the head of the botany department. He readily confirmed their suspicions. "It's seaweed, all right," he told them. "Furthermore, it's a kind that's only found on dead bodies!" The ship news reporter of the *Evening Sun* reported that a Thomas Newton had sailed as first-class seaman on a freighter called the *Robert B. Anthony* on April 14, 1937. It had gone down with all hands aboard in a storm off the Greenland coast six weeks thereafter.

* * *

One summer evening, just before dark, a man was driving his wife along a lonely country road, when she suddenly complained of a violent headache. One look at her agonized expression convinced him that something was radically wrong. He remembered that about ten miles back, he had passed a little cottage with a doctor's shingle on the gate. He turned the car about in a pasture, and drove back to the doctor's house as quickly as he dared.

A gray-haired, white-jacketed little man with sharp, twinkling eyes, answered his summons. He took one look at the ailing wife, and said simply, "Carry her into my office at once." The man waited impatiently while the doctor made a cursory examination, then followed him into his anteroom when bidden. "Something is pressing on your wife's brain," said the doctor. "I'm afraid she must be operated upon immediately. If you wait even until you get her back to town it probably will be too late." The man gasped. "I'm willing to perform the operation," continued the doctor, "but I'm all alone in this house and you will have to help me. I'll do my best but won't answer for the consequences."

There was something in the doctor's manner that inspired confidence. Besides, the woman's condition was obviously desperate. "Go ahead," said the man grimly.

The operation had reached its most delicate stage when the man became aware of an insistent banging on the front door. As soon as he could, he went to throw it open, and found two uniformed men waiting to enter. One of them had a gun under his arm. "The little doctor slipped away from us again," he said. "We usually find him pottering around here." "Who are you?" asked the man. "Guards at the asylum over the hill," was the answer. "Where's the doctor? Got to get him back before he gets violent!"

"Good God!" said the man. "He's in the middle of an operation on my wife's brain. You'll have to let him finish. Get me an ambulance—quick!"

Fifteen minutes later, the doctor came out of the parlor and declared the operation completed. The ambulance from the asylum was already at the door. One attendant helped the man lift his wife gently into the back, while the other led the unprotesting doctor away.

The ride back to New York was a nightmare for the distracted man. His wife had not regained consciousness when he arrived at the home of his own private physician on Park Avenue. "Be quick," he begged. "Something terrible has happened to her. Tell me if anything can be done before it is too late."

It was a sorely puzzled man who came to him a short while later. "This case baffles me completely," he said. "Your wife will live. She has been saved by an almost miraculous operation. But this is the factor that stops me cold. I know of only one man in this world who has the skill and the knowledge to perform an operation of this character. And that man has been in an insane asylum for the past six years!"

* * *

A young lady dreamed one night that she was walking along a strange country lane. It led her up a wooded hill whose summit was crowned with the loveliest little white frame house and garden she ever had seen. Unable to conceal her delight, she knocked loudly on the door of the house, and finally it was opened by an old, old man with a long white beard. Just as she started to talk to him, she woke up. Every detail of this dream was so vivid in her memory that she carried it about in her head for days. Then, on three successive nights, she had precisely the same dream again. Always she awakened at the point where her conversation with the old man was about to begin.

A few weeks later, the young lady was motoring to Litchfield for a week-end party, when she suddenly tugged at the driver's sleeve, and begged him to stop. There, at the right of the concrete highway, was the country lane of her dreams! "Wait for me a few moments," she pleaded, and, her heart beating wildly, set out on the lane. She was no longer surprised when it wound to the top of the wooded hill, and the house whose every feature was now so familiar to her. The old man responded to her impatient summons. "Tell me," she began, "is this little house for sale?" "That it is," said the man, "but I would scarcely advise you to buy it. You see, young lady, this house is haunted!" "Haunted," echoed the girl. "For heaven's sake, by whom?" "By you," said the old man, and softly closed the door.

* * *

John Sullivan was the only son of a doting mother, widowed during the First World War. He was handsome, richly endowed with Irish charm, and a particular favorite of the ladies. They could not resist his fetching smile. In fact, they never tried.

John couldn't explain how he suddenly came to be walking up Euclid Avenue. He had no memory of how he got there, or of what he had been doing previously that morning. "I must be walking in my sleep," he said to himself in some perplexity. Two lovely young girls were approaching him. John stopped them with the confidence born of years of easy conquest. "Could you be telling me the time?" he asked with his easy smile. To his surprise, one of the girls screamed, and both of them careened past him. Several other people, he noticed, seemed terrified by the sight of him. One man flattened himself against a show window of the Halle Store to get out of his way.

Greatly puzzled, John Sullivan started to climb into a taxi. Just as he was giving the address of his home, however, the driver looked at him for the first time, smothered an exclamation, pushed him out of the cab, and drove off with a grinding of gears.

John's head was spinning. He entered a drugstore, and phoned to his mother. A strange voice answered.

"Mrs. Sullivan?" it echoed. "Now who would be expecting to find her in now? Don't you know that her poor son John was caught in a machine at the bindery yesterday and mangled to death? She's out at the cemetery where they're burying him now!"

* * *

Dick Rodgers, the composer, is also no mean hand at spilling a yarn. He tells of a poker game in which the unfortunate Mr. Jones, with an incurable passion for drawing to inside straights, not only lost his entire bankroll, but had to endure the unmerciful gibes of his companions as well.

"What am I going to use for money until the pay check comes in on Friday?" he wailed. The editor of a weekly magazine fished a five-spot out of his pocket. "Your tears are destroying me," said he. "Take this money and scram." Walking home, the disconsolate Jones was accosted by a bedraggled lady of the streets who burst into tears when he shoved her aside unceremoniously. "I'm starving," she said in a low voice. "If you don't help me, I swear I'm going to kill myself." "Heck," reasoned Jones. "This is my night all right." He handed her the five-dollar bill. "I will never forget you," she assured him. "You've restored some of my faith in humanity!"

The next morning Jones was glancing over the newspaper when he noticed a headline that read "Body of Unknown Woman Taken from River." The description of her dress and hat proved beyond a doubt that the suicide was the woman he had befriended.

He met the editor at lunch. "What did you do after you left us, Jones?" said the editor idly. "Nothing at all. I just walked home," said Jones. "Didn't you spend any money?" "Not a cent. Why?" "Oh," mused the editor, "we were just wondering what would happen to you when you tried to palm off that phony five-dollar bill we gave you."

* * *

When an intelligent, comely girl of twenty-odd summers was invited for the first time to the Carolina estate of some distant relatives, their lovely plantation fulfilled her fondest expectations. She was given a room in the west wing, and prepared to retire for the night in a glow of satisfaction. Her room was drenched with the light of a full moon.

Just as she was climbing into her bed, she was startled by the sound of horses' hooves on the gravel roadway. Curious, she walked to the window and saw, to her astonishment, a magnificent old coach pull up to an abrupt stop directly below her. The coachman jumped from his perch, looked up and pointed a long, bony finger at her. He was hideous. His face was chalk-white. A deep scar ran the length of his left cheek. His nose was beaked. As he pointed at her, he droned in sepulchral tones, "There is room for one more!" Then, as she recoiled in terror, the coach, the horses and the ominous coachman disappeared completely.

The girl slept little, but the next day she was able to convince herself that she had merely had a nightmare.

The next night, however, the horrible experience was repeated. The same coach drove up the roadway. The same coachman pointed at her and intoned, "There is room for one more!" Then, as before, the entire equipage disappeared.

The girl, now panic-stricken, could scarcely wait for morning. She trumped up some excuse to her hosts and left immediately for home.

Upon arrival, she taxied to her doctor from the station and told him her story in tremulous tones. The doctor persuaded her that she had been the victim of a peculiar hallucination, laughed at her terror, and dismissed her in a state of infinite relief. As she rang for the elevator, its door swung open before her.

The elevator was very crowded, but she was about to squeeze her way inside—when a familiar voice rang in her ear. "There is room for one more!" it called. In terror, she stared at the operator.

He was the coachman who had pointed at her! She saw his chalk-white face, the livid scar, the beaked nose! She drew back and screamed . . . the elevator door banged shut.

A moment later the building shook with a terrible crash. The elevator that had gone on without her broke loose from its cables and plunged eighteen stories to the ground. Everybody in it, of course, was crushed to a pulp.

* * *

A macabre story told at a dinner party recently sent everybody scurrying to find its source. Subsequent reports were conflicting, to say the least. One expert claimed it came from the Indian captivity stories. Another said it could be found in Jack London's early tales of the frozen North. The man who had told it at the dinner, however, insisted that the locale was the heart of Africa, and that is where we might as well leave it for the retelling here.

The hero is an intrepid anthropologist who made his way, with one faithful assistant, to the darkest jungle in Africa in the furtherance of his studies. While seeking to record the tribal customs of a band of bloodthirsty savages, the two scientists incurred, first the suspicion, and then the blind hatred, of the tribe. One day they were caught off guard and marched to the tribe's encampment. The doctor's assistant was murdered diabolically, after prolonged and ingenious torture. The chief then strode up to the doctor, spat in his face, and informed him with evident satisfaction that this was just a mild preliminary to what was in store for him, beginning the following morning. It would take them a full week, at least, said the chief, to finish him off. Then he was locked up for the night.

The next morning, when the ordeal was about to begin, the doctor asked for one last word with the cannibal chief. It was too bad, he said, that they were going to kill him before he could tell them about his discovery of a miraculous herb. A single bite of this herb, he explained, made a man immune to death. Furthermore, it grew in abundance in the immediate vicinity. The chief registered disbelief. This obvious stratagem would get the doctor nowhere. "Very well," proposed the doctor. "Let me gather a few of these herbs and swallow them. Then let your headsman take his sharpest sword and try to kill me with it. You will see that the blow will glance harmlessly off my body."

A hasty powwow ensued, and it was agreed that nothing could be lost by testing the doctor's claim. Heavily guarded, he was allowed to hunt for the magic herb. After some poking about the bushes, he announced that he had found what he was searching for. In front of the entire tribe, he swallowed two of the herbs, and cried, "Now I am immune to death! Strike with your sword. You can never kill me!"

He knelt in the clearing. The tribe watched in breathless silence. The headsman raised his sword and brought it down with all his strength. The doctor's head, severed cleanly at the base of the skull, rolled crazily onto the ground.

* * *

André Malraux, the author of that brilliant novel, *Man's Hope*, told me this story in a little workmen's rendezvous in Paris, in the shadow of the Sacré Cœur. A flickering candle dripped a widening stain of acrid grease on the checkered tablecloth while he was talking, and an old man with a red beret was plucking the strings of a guitar in the corner in a sad and aimless fashion. We had been talking about World's Fairs, and the discussion drifted back to the Paris Exposition of the last generation. It was at this Fair, said Malraux, that the fastest scenic railway ever constructed was featured. The old fellow with the guitar, in fact, had helped to build it.

"And rode it, too?" I suggested.

"No," was the answer. "He never rode it. That is what I want to tell you about. The man who owned the concession had a mania for speed. He said this ride they were building for him had to be the fastest in the world. For a long time architects and engineers experimented and conferred on plans for a ride that would outspeed the wind.

"Finally, the blueprints were completed, with all the dips and curves and angles calculated to make the cars whiz around the course at a whirlwind pace. When the structure was still in rude state, the new, shiny red cars were sent shooting along the tracks, equipped with instruments and freighted with sandbags approximating the weight of the human cargoes that would be borne when the Fair was opened.

"The last nail in the structure was driven home. In keeping with the custom in such cases, those who had built the racer were entitled to the first ride. There was a scramble for seats. Our friend wasn't agile enough, and had to wait for the next trip. The car started on its dizzy ride, the men in it laughing and cheering.

"He and the others who were left behind heard the car whirl around the curves and roar down the drops as they jostled one another to get near the head of the line for the next ride. Then it pulled into view and rolled to an automatic stop. But there was no answer to the onlookers' yells and eager questions. Not one of the passengers stirred.

"I don't know who rushed forward first. I know that the old fellow over there found himself shaking the shoulders of his closest friend. The others followed suit. One after another the heads of the passengers wobbled loosely on their chests—or back, too far back—or to one side or the other. Every neck had been broken—snapped like a glass stem—on those sharp curves that had been tested only with sandbags!"

The old man sensed that we were talking about him. He smiled at us—a sad, fleeting smile. His fingers never stopped their aimless plucking of the guitar strings.

* * *

A dozen miles outside of Baltimore, the main road from New York (Route Number One) is crossed by another important highway. It is a dangerous intersection, and there is talk of building an underpass for the east-west road. To date, however, the plans exist only on paper.

Dr. Eckersall was driving home from a country-club dance late one Saturday night. He slowed up for the intersection, and was surprised to see a lovely young girl, dressed in the sheerest of evening gowns, beckoning to him for a lift. He jammed on his brakes, and motioned her to climb into the back seat of his roadster. "All cluttered up with golf clubs and bags up here in front," he explained. "But what on earth is a youngster like you doing out here all alone at this time of night?"

"It's too long a story to tell you now," said the girl. Her voice was sweet and somewhat shrill—like the tinkling of sleigh bells. "Please, please take me home. I'll explain everything there. The address is —— North Charles Street. I do hope it's not too far out of your way."

The doctor grunted, and set the car in motion. He drove rapidly to the address she had given him, and as he pulled up before the shuttered house, he said, "Here we are." Then he turned around. The back seat was empty!

"What the devil?" the doctor muttered to himself. The girl couldn't possibly have fallen from the car. Nor could she simply have vanished. He rang insistently on the house bell, confused as he had never been in his life before. At long last the door opened. A gray-haired, very tired-looking man peered out at him.

"I can't tell you what an amazing thing has happened," began the doctor. "A young girl gave me this address a while back. I drove her here and——"

"Yes, yes, I know," said the man wearily. "This has happened several other Saturday evenings in the past month. That young girl, sir, was my daughter. She was killed in an automobile accident at that intersection where you saw her almost two years ago. . . ."

* * *

A distinguished English typographer, who will be called Francis Johnson in this story, has an insatiable curiosity that got him into trouble one dreary afternoon in London. A distant relative had died, and the body was dispatched to a suburban crematorium. The funeral services were held in town. When the dreary procession of rented sedans headed for the crematorium, Johnson and his wife decided to drive down in their own roadster, thereby arriving fully thirty minutes ahead of the others.

The period of waiting was not too cheering, and Johnson began fidgeting with the gadgets in view. A black button in the wall engaged his attention, and finally he gave it a push. To his horror, the body slid slowly but inexorably into the cremator!

When the funeral party duly arrived, the body, of course, had disappeared. So had the Johnsons.

* * *

Saxe Commins remembers a racing meet at a country fair which was interrupted at the close of the fifth race by an official who carried a large megaphone and bellowed an announcement to the milling spectators.

"Ladies and gentlemen," he began (the day of the loudspeaker had not yet dawned). "At exactly four o'clock our patrons are asked to observe two minutes of silence out of respect to the dead President of the United States, Warren Gamaliel Harding. At that hour his body will be lowered into its grave in Marion, Ohio. The audience is requested to bare heads when taps are blown from this stand and remain silent in prayer for two minutes. I thank you."

At the stroke of four a bugler began to blow the mournful dirge for the dead. Hats were removed everywhere. Gradually, however, all eyes were attracted by one giant of a man, near the centre of the crowd, who failed to remove his hat. It was a straw, encircled with a gay ribbon. He stood straight as a poker, with his arms folded across his breast.

Cries of "Take it off! Take it off!" rose to a louder and louder pitch of anger as the man stood oblivious to the clamor. Someone near him hit him in the back. The hat flew off. The man fell. Instantly he was the centre of a milling mob.

By the time the police rescued him he was a bloody mess, his clothes in tatters, his face a pulp. From deep in his throat came guttural noises of pain, tortured but wordless. Then the crowd learned that, of all the thousands there, it was he alone who had faithfully observed the ritual of the two minutes of silence, for he was deaf and dumb.

There was an incident of the same description in New York about a year after Pearl Harbor. A parade was proceeding down Fifth Avenue. When the flag went by, everybody saluted except a frail young man who stood motionless at the curbstone. A beefy, red-faced citizen behind him pushed him violently into the gutter. "Damn it," he cried. "What do you mean by not saluting when our flag goes by?" The young man turned. On his chest was the Purple Heart. He had no arms.

* * *

A favorite story of New York literary circles a few years ago concerned a beautiful young girl in a white satin dress. It was one of those anecdotes which everybody swore had actually happened to his first cousin or next-door neighbor, and several narrators became very testy when they were informed that several other people's cousins had evidently undergone the same experience just a few weeks before.

At any rate, the legend maintained that a very lovely but poverty-stricken damsel was invited to a formal dance. It was her chance to enter a brand-new world. Who knew but that some rich young man would fall in love with her and lift her out of her life in a box factory? The catch in the matter was that she had no suitable dress to wear for such a great occasion.

"Why don't you rent a costume for the evening?" suggested a friend. Not having thought of this before, the girl became hopeful, and that very night went to a pawnshop near her little flat, where for a surprisingly reasonable sum she rented a beautiful white satin evening gown with all the accessories to match. Miraculously, it fit her like a glove and gave her such radiance that upon her arrival at the party she created a minor sensation. She was cut in on again and again, and as she whirled happily around the floor she felt that her luck indeed had changed for the better.

Soon, however, she began to feel faint and nauseated. She fought against a growing discomfort as long as possible, but finally stole out of the house with barely sufficient strength to stagger into a cab and creep up the stairs to her room. She threw herself onto her bed, broken-hearted, and it was then—possibly in her delirium—that she heard a woman's voice whispering in her ear.

It was harsh and bitter. "Give me back my dress," it said. "Give me back my dress! It belongs to . . . the dead . . ."

The next morning the lifeless body of the young girl was found stretched out on her bed. The unusual circumstances led the coroner to order an autopsy. It was found the girl had been poisoned by embalming fluid which had entered her pores when she became overheated from dancing. The pawnbroker was reluctant to admit that he knew where the dress had come from, but spoke out when he heard that the district attorney's office was involved. It had been sold him by an undertaker's assistant who had taken it from the body of a dead girl just before the casket was nailed down for the last time.

* * *

Carter generally minded his own business on the train, but it was impossible to concentrate on his evening paper after the young man had slumped into the seat beside him. In all his years of commuting between New York and Stamford, Carter had never seen anybody so obviously demoralized and on the verge of collapse. The fellow's hands trembled violently, his body twitched, he gave the air of seeing nothing around him and neither knowing nor caring exactly where he was. He mumbled to himself occasionally too, but when Carter pointedly sighed and folded up his newspaper, he pulled himself together sufficiently to apologize for fidgeting and making a nuisance of himself. Carter did not encourage him in any way, and was rather surprised to find himself suddenly plunged into the middle of the young man's story.

"Nine years ago," the young man said, "I was elected head of my college fraternity. We had a strict rule that only three members of every new freshman class be admitted to membership. That kept our active list to an even dozen. Nobody ever refused our bids. Everyone recognized that we were the kingpins of the campus. In what was probably a subconscious effort to prove to ourselves what superior beings we were, our initiations became more and more elaborate and fantastic as the years went by.

"At initiation time it was my idea to take the three neophytes we had selected and bundle them out to a deserted house about fifteen miles from the campus. It had been unoccupied for years, was windowless, sagging and ugly, and was said by the villagers to be haunted. We picked a black, starless night for the initiation, and all the way out to the place poured tales of horror and the supernatural into the ears of our three apprehensive freshmen.

"I picked the frailest of the kids to go into the house first. He was the son of a famous novelist who had won the Pulitzer Prize the year before, and was by way of being a boy prodigy himself. His eyes betrayed his fear when we shipped him off, but he compressed his lips and set out bravely enough. The rest of us built a bonfire, and relaxed around it.

"I watched him enter the deserted house. It was about two hundred yards from where we were gathered. His instructions were to stay inside for a half-hour, and then come back to us. When forty-five long minutes went by without any sign of him, I experienced my first uneasiness, and dispatched the second freshman to fetch him. Ten minutes more went by. Nothing happened. There wasn't a sound anywhere. The fire was burning low—we just sat there, quietly watching.

" 'These kids are a little too smart for their own good,' I said at last. 'Davis, get in there and bring them back fast.' Davis was our prize conquest—a handsome, two-hundred-pound boy whose scholastic records foreshadowed an almost certain place on the next year's All-American squad. He had already been elected president of the freshman class.

" 'I'll get 'em,' he grinned, and loped toward the house.

"And then we just sat there. I guess it was only ten minutes, but it seemed like hours. 'It looks like my move, fellows,' I said finally. 'We'll have to teach these brats that they can't play tricks on their elders this way.' I got up and walked slowly over to the deserted house.

"The first thing that struck me when I entered was a musty smell like the smell of an attic full of old books and newspapers. I yelled for the boys, and poked my flashlight into every corner but there wasn't a sign of them. Only a faint, steady tap that seemed to come from the roof. Filled with dread, I climbed the creaking stairway to the second floor, and the ladder leading to the roof. I stuck my head through the open skylight. There was Davis, stretched out on his stomach! His hair had turned snow-white. His eyes rolled in his head. He was mad as a hatter. In his hand he held a hammer covered with blood. He was rapping weakly with it on the tin parapet, in a senseless rhythm. I screamed to him, but he paid no attention to me. He just went on tapping with that bloody hammer. I somehow or other got back to the fellows waiting for me and we managed to carry Davis down from the roof. He died in the college hospital the next morning without uttering a single syllable. We never found any trace of the other two boys. . . ."

Carter fidgeted in his seat, not quite certain whether or not he was being gulled. The young man certainly was in a desperate condition. A drunkard, perhaps, or dope fiend? All this had happened nine years ago, according to the young man's story; surely he had not been in such a state all that time! The fellow turned burning eyes upon him.

"On the anniversary of that night every year," he explained, "one of the nine men who were on that hazing party has gone stark, raving mad. Each has been found gibbering nonsense, and tapping the floor with a blood-soaked hammer. Each has died within twenty-four hours' time.

"Tomorrow," he said, in low and precise tones, "is the ninth anniversary of that night. And I'm the only one left. . . ."

* * *

This is a story of a hospital ward and three helplessly crippled and broken men who occupied it. The oldest occupant naturally had the bed by the window; the one who arrived last was next to the door. The man in the middle helped make life bearable for the others by his unfailing liveliness and optimism, although heaven knows he had nothing to be happy about.

One cold winter night the man by the window died, and the other two were moved up a peg. Soon the unquenchable optimist was amusing his equally helpless companion with accounts of the things he could see out of the window—automobiles, flower carts, mysterious strangers, pretty girls with their skirts blowing in the wind. Gradually the people who passed every day were given names, and the man in the second bed heard so many anecdotes of their doings from the lips of the other that he began to feel that he knew them well. It helped pass the dreary hours and he was grateful.

Then, suddenly, a new thought entered his head. If something happened to this man next to him, *he* would get the bed by the window! Lying there helplessly day after day, this idea became an obsession. Within his reach was a spoon and a bottle of medicine. His friend sometimes was seized with heart spasms in the middle of the night when no nurse was at hand; he could barely manage to get a spoonful to his lips and swallow it on such occasions in the nick of time. Gradually the spasm would pass. . . .

The man in the second bed brooded and bided his time. One night the attack came. The stricken man reached for his medicine, but the other, by a superhuman effort, lifted his twisted body from the bed and dashed the bottle to the ground. . . .

The next morning they gave him the bed by the window. "I'll wait to look out of it," he gloated to himself, "until the nurse goes out of the room. Then I can see all these things for myself." Finally he was alone, and trembling with excitement, he turned his head toward the window. A dozen feet from it, he discovered, stretching as far as his eye could follow, was a blank gray wall.

* * *

It never even occurred to Duval that he was breaking a twenty-year-old precedent by accepting the Englishman Rodney's invitation to luncheon on the terrace of the Café de Paris. The impeccably polite, coldly impersonal assistant manager of the Monte Carlo Casino knew intimate details about every guest and every employee, but his own private life was a closed book. He was a lone wolf with no friends and seemingly no avocations.

Rodney, however, had attracted him at sight. He was big, blonde, and handsome, and what was so rare among the grim gamblers who laboriously played their "systems," until inevitably they were cleaned out, he seemed really to enjoy his bouts at the roulette and chemin-de-fer tables. He played in moderation, obviously could afford the trifling losses he had experienced. Every morning, Duval knew, he received a letter in a precise, girlish hand, which pleased him inordinately.

"Those battered old wrecks who haunt the tables in there bother me," said Rodney, over the cocktails. "What happens to them when they lose their last sou? What happens to the big plungers, for that matter, who go broke at Monte Carlo? Don't some of them commit suicide? Why don't I ever read about the penniless victims who kill themselves in your beautiful gardens?"

"We have no penniless suicides in Monte Carlo," said Duval quietly. "If anybody is foolish enough to lose all his money at our tables and then do away with himself on the grounds of the Casino, there are always ten thousand francs in fresh, crisp bank notes on the body when it is found. The coroner often discovers, too, that death came from natural causes. I do not have to tell you that suicides of penniless victims would be a bad advertisement indeed for the interests I represent."

Several days later, Duval was informed that Rodney had received a letter that upset him. It was written in the usual hand, but upon reading it, Rodney, instead of assuming his usual boyish grin, had turned white and swayed on his heels for an instant. Then he had jammed the letter into his pocket and stormed out of the hotel. That night there was a change in Rodney's behavior in the Casino. He shunned the roulette tables entirely and concentrated on chemin-de-fer, where he lost steadily and heavily. His eyes were bloodshot when he rose to go; he barely acknowledged the concerned Duval's salutation. The following two evenings he went from bad to worse. Finally he lost two hundred thousand francs on the turn of a single card, muttered, "Thank you, gentlemen," and left the room. Duval, who had been watching him closely, was busy elsewhere for the moment.

Ten minutes later, one of the doormen whose business it was to listen for such noises, heard the all-too-familiar sound of a pistol shot, ran and summoned Monsieur Duval. They found Rodney crumpled up under a tree, his face a ghastly white, a spreading red stain on his evening shirt. In his clenched hand was a letter.

Duval was very sad when he locked the drawer of his desk an hour later. Why did things like this have to happen to him all the

time? Why did it have to be one of the few people in twenty years whom he had liked instinctively? He looked more sombre even than usual as he took a final turn through the gaming rooms. Suddenly he stopped in his tracks. That voice! That figure! It was Rodney, smiling in a peculiar way at him, with a sizable stock of ten-thousand-franc markers in his hand! Duval passed his hand over his eyes, muttered "Sacré Dieu!" and fled. "I always knew one of them would come back," he said to himself.

The next morning, in the bright sunshine, Duval knew that it was no ghost who stood before him. It was Rodney, wearing his old grin, with the arm of a very beautiful girl tucked into his. "Duval! Duval, my friend," he cried happily. "Look! She's changed her mind! She arrived this morning out of the blue, and tells me she's going to marry me after all!" He seemed to take it for granted that Duval knew everything that had gone before.

"But the suicide?" faltered Duval.

"Oh, that," laughed Rodney. "I really considered it for a moment. You'll notice I had the gun all right! Then I remembered your story about the ten thousand francs you planted on every body. I fired the shot into the air and decided I'd let your casino stake me to one last fling. What a hunch it was! I won back practically everything I had lost. And now my girl has come back to me!"

"But the ashen countenance?" faltered Duval.

"Face powder," said Rodney.

"And the bloodstain on your shirt front?"

"Catsup," said Rodney. "Ordinary catsup."

Chapter Twelve

"HIGHLIGHTS FROM THE WORLD OF SPORTS"

"THAT'S BASEBALL"

THE GREATEST terror on the base paths in all the history of base-ball was Tyrus Raymond Cobb, "The Georgia Peach," who scored from first on singles, and got himself trapped off base on purpose to make fools of his opponents by sliding to safety under their very noses. In one year he stole ninety-six bases. When Cobb slid, it was every man for himself. In the 1909 World Series, Cobb was pitted against another all-time star—"Hans" Wagner. Cobb, on first, hollered, "Hey, Kraut Head, I'm coming down on the next pitch." The easygoing Dutchman didn't say a word, but when Cobb came tearing into him, he blocked the bag like a Giant tank, slapped the ball squarely into Cobb's mouth, and knocked out three teeth.

Wagner was quite a man. Pittsburgh's official scorer was offered ten dollars for a picture of Honus that could be inserted in cigarette packages (the price for that sort of thing has gone up). Wagner wrote, "I don't want my picture in any cigarettes, but I also don't want you to lose the ten dollars, so I'm enclosing my check for that sum."

Baseball was different in those days.

*   *   *

One-pitch-that-lost-a-championship Department: In the last game of the season in 1904, Jack Chesbro, of the New York Highlanders, uncorked a wild pitch at a crucial moment that cost his team a chance to win the pennant. When the fans saw that one all-important run come in to dash their hopes, they probably forgot that the same Chesbro had racked up forty-one victories that year. Today a pitcher who wins twenty games in a season is hailed as a superman. The "Highlanders," incidentally, didn't become the "Yankees" until several years later. In those days they played on a field that is now the site of the Columbia Medical Center.

*   *   *

Most tragic accidental death of a big-league star: In 1903 Ed Delehanty, the only man who ever captured the batting championships of both the National and American Leagues, left a train for no apparent reason at Niagara Falls, started to walk across the Railroad Bridge in the dead of night, evidently never noticed that the draw was open, and disappeared into the swirling waters. Most deeply mourned death: In 1941, in the prime of life, an obscure malady cut down Columbia Lou Gehrig, the so-called "Iron Horse" who only a few years before had completed the incredible record of appearing in 2130 consecutive games for the Yankees. The motion picture based on Gehrig's career was a great tribute to the man and the game he enriched, produced in Holly-

wood by the Samuel Goldwyn who is featured on another page
of this compendium.

* * *

In 1908, the New York Giants paid the then-fantastic price of
$11,000 for a kid pitcher in the bushes at Indianapolis. His name
was Richard Marquard, and because he was a tall, wry-necked
southpaw, was nicknamed "Rube." He tried so hard to live up to
his fancy press notices that he went to pieces, and for two seasons
was referred to scathingly as the "$11,000 lemon." In 1911, how-
ever, "Rube" Marquard hit his stride, and in 1912 hung up his
record of nineteen consecutive wins that has never since been
threatened.

* * *

This is the story of the day "Merkle didn't touch second." The
day was September 23, 1908. The Giants, Cubs, and Pirates, who
used to dominate the National League completely, were practically tied for first; every game was vital. The Cubs and Giants
went into the ninth inning of a humdinger deadlocked at 1-1. In
the home ninth, McCormick was on third with two out, Merkle
was on first. Bridwell singled. McCormick crossed the plate with
the winning run, but Merkle, instead of running down to touch
second, dashed for the clubhouse. This was really no "bonehead"
play; it was quite customary at the time. But the shrewd, heads-up
second-sacker of the Cubs, Johnny Evers, called for the ball,
touched second base, and jawed Umpire Hank O'Day into calling Merkle out on a force play. The crowd was all over the field
by this time, and resumption of play was out of the question. As
luck would have it, the Giants and Cubs finished the season in a
dead tie, and the championship was decided by the play-off of
this one game. The Cubs won it, 4-2. A freak play gave a smart
first-rate player a reputation as a "sap" that he could never live
down. Fred Merkle will always be remembered as "the guy who
didn't touch second."

Incidentally, Roger Bresnahan, the Giant catcher in that game, swears to this day that Evers never did get hold of the ball that was in play. "Joe McGinnity picked it up on his way to the clubhouse," asserts the Rajah, "and tossed it into the left field bleachers. In my book, Merkle hasn't been forced out yet." Unfortunately, Bresnahan's book was unofficial.

* * *

Merkle figured unfortunately again in a Giant tragedy in 1912, and as in the 1908 episode, the great Matty was again the mound victim—which increased the public's resentment. The Giants and the Red Sox met in the World Series that year; it was a grueling set of games with the title resting finally on the eighth game in Boston. The Giants broke a 1-1 tie with a run in their half of the tenth; Matty had to retire only three more men to give the Giants their first World's Championship in seven years. The happenings of the next ten minutes are still too painful to be dwelt upon by an old Giant rooter. First Fred Snodgrass muffed a dinky little fly in centre field, putting a runner on second. The next man flied out. Steve Yerkes walked, and the Boston crowd let out a roar as their idol, "Tris" Speaker, strode to the plate. The roar died when Speaker popped a measly foul outside the first base line. "Chief" Meyers, the Giant catcher, and Merkle, on first, however, went into a trance. The ball fell between them. Speaker wasn't the sort of gent who needed more than one reprieve. He lined out the next pitch for a long single, and Gardner's following sacrifice fly sent in the winning run. Matty strode silently to the clubhouse.

But succor for the heart-broken Giants was on its way from an unexpected source. In the town of Gretna, Louisiana, that dismal afternoon, a three-year-old tot was playing in the lazy October sun. His name was Melvin Ott. In another thirteen years, this boy wonder was to hit the Polo Grounds and lead the Giants back to Glory Road.

* * *

The 1909 series between Detroit and Pittsburgh was played in weather so cold that Umpire Bill Klem wore a heavy winter overcoat. "Doc Cook, the guy who was supposed to have discovered the North Pole," reminisces Klem, "was guest of honor at the first game, and it got so cold that he left in the second inning! I knew then," adds Klem, "that he was a phony bologna!"

* * *

Cy Young won 511 major league games in twenty-two years, a record that has never been approached, and under present playing conditions probably never will. The last game he pitched, he lost 1 to 0. (It was in 1911.) The box score reveals that a raw recruit beat him. The name was Grover Cleveland Alexander. Later, he compiled quite a record too.

Alexander won an amazing number of games for some amazingly bad baseball clubs, but his greatest triumph was scored in the twilight of his career in the 1926 World Series. "Alex" couldn't keep away from the giggle water; frantic coaches would pick him up anywhere from the morgue to a flea circus on 42nd Street. This day, however, he shuffled out of the bull pen with the bases full in the deciding game of the series, and fanned Tony Lazzeri of the Yankees, on four pitched balls, giving the title to the St. Louis Cards.

They're still talking about it.

* * *

On July 8, 1914, the Boston Braves wallowed in last place in the National League standings. Then, while the big guns of the Boches were wiping Belgian fortresses off the map in Europe, while Charlie Chaplin and Mabel Normand were beginning to be noticed by movie fans, while a drama called *On Trial* by an unknown youngster named Elmer Rice electrified Broadway, this Boston team, under the inspiring leadership of "Miracle Man" George Stallings, began to click. Three pitchers spearheaded the drive: Dick Rudolph, Bill James, and George Tyler. Among them they won forty-nine games while losing ten; they galloped through the league like wildfire, ending no fewer than ten and a half games ahead of the second-place Giants! To complete the miracle, this one-year wonder team tore through the heavily favored Athletics in the World Series for four straight victories. Fans remember Catcher Hank Gowdy and Second Baseman Rabbit Maranville from that team. Ever since 1914, managers have tried to rouse lagging aggregations by pointing to the exploits of the Boston Braves. The players know, however, that in baseball miracles like that happen once in a hundred years.

* * *

The story of the 1919 "Black Sox" sell-out, which nearly destroyed organized baseball, is something straight out of gangster movies. Scott Fitzgerald used it in his unsurpassed study of a bootlegger, *The Great Gatsby*. John Lardner's *Satevepost* story on it six years ago is still talked about in sporting circles.

Baseball enjoyed a big season the year after World War One. The Chicago White Sox, one of the great teams of all time, romped through the American League for an easy pennant. Eddie Collins, "Shoeless Joe" Jackson, Ray Schalk, Buck Weaver, Eddie Cicotte, Chick Gandil, and their pals packed too much power for their opposition, even though the club was riddled with dissensions and cliques that the manager, Kid Gleason, could scarcely control. The National League winner, the Cincinnati Reds, on the other hand, was completely lacking in class. It had a star in centre field in Eddie Roush, and a smart hombre in right named "Greasy" Neale (later he became a famous football coach). For the rest, the squad consisted of a bunch of guys named Joe who had managed to nose out some other mediocre teams in a typical National League dog-fight. On paper, the White Sox figured to slaughter the Reds; the first odds in the betting were 5 to 1. It was an ideal set-up for a double-cross, and a gang of smart hoodlums moved in for the kill.

It is generally believed that the evil genius behind the big fix was the notorious gambler, Arnold Rothstein, but there is no evidence to support such a notion. He admitted that he had heard of the goings-on, and won a tidy sum by betting on the Reds, but it was easy to believe that he had no actual part in the plot when the full details were revealed. The affair was manhandled from start to finish. Most of the players involved never got a cent of pay-off money; that's why they were so ready to "sing" when the heat was turned on. The "secret" was so badly kept that on the morning of the first game, the odds had slipped from 5 to 1, where they belonged, to even money—a crystal-clear indication to the gambling fraternity that there was something extremely rotten in the state of Denmark.

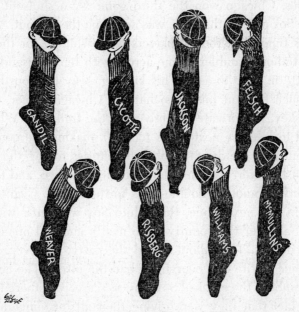

Eight members of the Chicago club were involved in the deal: Gandil, Cicotte, Jackson, Felsch, Weaver, Risberg, Williams and McMullin. They were slated to receive $100,000 for throwing the series; actually they collected a quarter of that sum. The other members of the team knew nothing of the crooked set-up; Collins, Schalk, Kerr, and others played their hearts out in the series; the

manager, Gleason, literally cried on the bench while his charges
kicked games away with bush-league boners that were incompre-
hensible at the time.

The Reds won the first game, 9 to 1. Cicotte, a great pitcher,
hit batsmen in the back, had his offerings hammered to all cor-
ners of the park by third-rate nonentities. In the second game,
the Sox pitcher, Claude Williams, noted for his perfect control,
passed three men in one vital inning, and literally handed the
contest to the Reds by a 4-2 score. The "dope" had been crossed
so thoroughly in these games that the public was confounded.
Not so the professional gamblers, however. They watched the
Cincinnati crowds go delirious with joy, and chuckled grimly to
themselves. Chicago won the third game by a shut-out. Dickie
Kerr, the Sox pitcher that day, was not in on the sell-out.

By this time, the crooked players were whining for their pay-
off. The tinhorn gamblers came across with ten thousand dollars
for Cicotte in time to assure his kicking away the fourth game,
2-0, by such flagrant misplays that the Chicago owner, Charles
A. Comiskey, put private detectives on the trail. The White Sox
managed to lose the next game too, 5-0, making the count four
to one, but in those days it took five victories to bag the world's
championship. Kerr won another game for Chicago, and then the
insiders added another double-cross to the record. Cicotte really
pitched in the next game, the White Sox won in a walk, and
gamblers all over the country were neatly euchred out of thousands of dollars. That about ended the party, however. Rumors
had become so rife that everybody had the jitters. The last game
was a shambles; the crooked Sox players scarcely bothered to conceal the fact that they were giving their all for Cincinnati; the
Reds won the series, five games to three.

The crooked players were exposed publicly some months later.
Their names were expunged from league records; they were
barred from organized baseball for life. Cicotte won jeers with his
dogged assertion that he had "done it for the wife and kiddies."
Joe Jackson, most pathetic of the disgraced players, had gotten at

the most a thousand dollars for his pains; was such a magnificent natural hitter that he hit .375 in the series when he was trying to strike out. "Say it ain't true, Joe," pleaded one of his teen-age fans when the news of the sell-out became public. "Shoeless Joe" hung his head.

That scandal of twenty-five years ago will probably never be repeated in organized baseball. In the first place, controls have been tightened, with doughty old Judge Kenesaw Mountain Landis reading the riot act to any mavericks who stray one step from the fold. In the second place, the 1919 series proved that too many cooks had to be involved in a deal of this sort, with the broth suffering the traditional results. Under the complicated conditions of present-day life, there are a thousand crooked set-ups open to petty chiselers and racketeers; all of them are easier than "fixing" baseball games.

* * *

The speediest pitcher in baseball was Walter Johnson, "The Big Train." Bob Feller was probably the runner-up. When Johnson was right, the batter sometimes never even saw the ball whiz by. Once Chapman of Cleveland watched two strikes zoom by, dropped his bat, and headed for the bench. "You have another strike coming," the umpire reminded him. "Never mind," grunted Chapman. "I don't want it."

* * *

Al Schacht, the inimitable baseball clown, once had a partner named Nick Altrock, but the act broke up because both players suspected each other of deliberately making the rough-and-tumble stuff too realistic. Schacht explained that it was like a pair of old vaudeville comics who did a wooden-shoe number that wound up by their kicking one another in the pants. They began to accuse one another of putting entirely too much behind the kicks, and fought about it so loudly in the dressing room that the acts who followed them complained about the racket.

They were warned that if they created one more disturbance, their act would be canceled. "That very night," says Schacht, "it happened again." They kicked the daylights out of each other, took their bows, and raced to their dressing room. There they carefully closed the door, took off their wooden shoes, and began to beat each other over the head with them. After every wallop, however, each would put a finger to his lips and whisper "sh-sh-sh."

*　*　*

In a World Series game in Chicago in 1932, the crowd, fretful because the home team was taking a shellacking from the Yankees, began to take it out on "Babe" Ruth. The inimitable Bambino strode to the plate, pointed to the flagpole in deepest centre field, and belted the ball out of the lot to the exact spot he had indicated. It was a magnificent performance—the sort of thing only the "Babe" Ruths can ever do—and as he lumbered around the path, the formerly hostile crowd rose and roared out the homage that was due him.

*　*　*

One day Ruth heard about a twelve-year-old kid who lay dying in a local hospital. Babe Ruth was his idol. Maybe an autographed baseball would revive him? The Babe pulled a cap off the rack, and taxied over to the hospital. The kid's eyes popped when his god walked into the room and sat on his bed. "Ya know what I'm going to do this afternoon?" said the Babe. "I'm gonna hit a home run just for you. You watch. It's gonna be your home run. Now you hurry up and get well so you can come out and see me play."

Ruth hit the home run that afternoon, just as he had promised. What's more, the kid got well. Stories like that explain why Babe Ruth was the most popular figure in the history of baseball.

* * *

Bill Dickey's enlistment in the Navy ends the major league career, in all probability, of one of the greatest catchers in baseball history. He wasn't a bad actor either. Remember him in the Lou Gehrig movie?

The Baseball Writers presented Dickey with a plaque as the Player of the Year last winter; Dickey responded with his longest speech on record: "It shore is purty. Much obliged." The night the last World Series ended, the victorious Yankees, including Bill Dickey, went off the wagon with a bang. At the height of the festivities a man he hadn't seen in twenty years, now a beribboned officer, slapped Dickey on the back and chortled, "Remember me, Bill?" "I don't recall the name," mused Dickey. "But you shore were a sucker for a high curve inside!"

* * *

One big-league ball club that always had a playing system— and a band of followers—unique unto itself was the Brooklyn Dodgers—"dem bums" to its loyal but critical supporters on either side of the Gowanus Canal. Brooklyn outfielders caught flies on their beans instead of in their gloves; Brooklyn runners stole second with a man already on the bag; Brooklyn pitchers heaved balls into the grandstand; the crowd roared its disapproval but never stopped coming.

Once Casey Stengel managed the Dodgers. Ejected by the umpires for the steenth time that season, Casey doffed his cap in mock reverence, and a little bird flew out. The ump, his dignity ruffled, fined Casey fifty bucks. In another game, Stengel lifted his pitcher in the fourth in favor of a pinch-hitter, Babe Phelps, with the sacks full of Dodgers. Phelps came through with a juicy home run: four tallies for the Dodgers. In the eighth the Dodgers needed a pinch-hitter again. "Yah bum, yah," cried a typical Dodger strategist to Stengel. "Whyja waste Phelps before? This is when ya need him!"

The last man who tried to figure out the mentality of a typical Brooklyn fan is cutting out paper dolls in Matteawan this very minute.

* * *

Dizzy Dean, famous pitcher of the St. Louis Cardinals, and the game's most distinguished modest violet, has delivered himself of an autobiography. Ol' Diz, as he likes to call himself, is considerably more of a humorist than a lot of tired old gag men who make a living that way. He pops off in print and plays the buffoon for the same reason that led him to act that way on the ball field; he knows exactly what the public wants.

He divides his autobiography into four parts. Part One is entitled "Who's the Greatest Pitcher in the World?" Part Two is devoted to "Who's Got the Greatest Throwin' Arm in the World?" ("Not Countin' Days It Was Sore and How It Got That Way.") Part Three discusses "Who's the Greatest Hitter in the World?" ("When He Wants to Be.") The wind-up is the answer to "Who's the Greatest Pitcher-Runner in the World?" ("Not Countin' Days I Was Tired.") Diz demolishes "house dicks" (players who spend most of their time showing off in hotel lobbies) and "pebble pickers" (infielders who alibi fielding bobbles by picking up imaginary pebbles which, they indicate by pantomime, have caused the ball to take a crazy hop); he lingers lovingly (and who can blame him?) on the season when he and his brother Paul won forty-nine games between them for the Cards, and then went on to mow down the Detroit Tigers single- or double-handed in the World Series.

The Dean Dictionary should never have omitted the classic repartee that featured a tense spot in the first Series game at Detroit. The fans were riding him hard that day, and didn't like it at all when he struck out the entire side in one inning, and came swaggering to the bench. "If I was your wife," hollered one lady enthusiast, "I'd give you poison." "If I wuz your husband," snapped back Mr. Dean, "I'd take it!"

* * *

William Faulkner recalls a ball game once played in Mississippi. It was played in a cow pasture and ended abruptly when a runner slid into what he thought was third base.

* * *

The wonderful saga of Two-Top Gruskin, the two-headed pitcher, is the brain child of Ed Gardner, the incomparable Archie of Duffy's Tavern radio program. It goes something like this:

Duffy's Irish Yankees have mechanical perfection, but no color. "This guy, Athos and Porthos McGinnes, may be your dish," says Dugan, the shortstop, to the disconsolate Duffy. "They call him Two-Top Gruskin for short, I guess, on account of him having two heads."

"A pitcher with two heads?" says Duffy dubiously. "You think it'd be a novelty?"

"What if it ain't?" points out Dugan. "Who else could watch first and third base at the same time? Besides, he's a great guy to pitch double-headers."

So Two-Top is summoned from his home (Walla Walla, of course) and arrives to sign his contract in a dress suit. "What are all you guys staring at?" he asks sourly. "Ain't none of you seen a tuxedo before?"

"Two-Top," says Duffy, "I'm a man of few words. Report tomorrow. There's a uniform and two caps waiting for you. Waiter, bring my new pitcher two beers."

Two-Top wins a masquerade that very night by disguising himself as a pair of bookends with a copy of *My Son, My Son* between the two heads. The next afternoon Duffy introduces him to his catcher, Gorilla Hogan, who measures 6 foot 14 inches and squats standing up. "Most people," says Duffy proudly, "calls Gorilla a monstrosity, and I agree with them—a swell guy." Gorilla soon gets into trouble with Two-Top, however. He signals for a high fast one. Two-Top nods "yes" with one head, but shakes the other one "no." Confused and mortified, Gorilla hurls off his mask and yells to Duffy, "Duffy, you such-and-such, I am sick and tired of two-headed pitchers around this place."

"Take it easy," soothes Duffy. "Talk it over with the guy. After all, three heads is better than one."

But the Gorilla says, "It's no use, Duffy. I got a feeling that the guy ain't normal. Besides, you notice how he's always got those two heads together? Maybe he's cooking up a strike around here. No, sir, one of us will have to go, Duffy—and don't forget who owns the baseball."

Well, that's the end of Two-Top Gruskin's baseball career. For a while he watches tennis matches for the News of the Day. Then the Army gets him. The doctor takes his chart to the colonel. "Lemme see," says the colonel. "Eyes—blue and brown. Hair, blond and brunette. Mustache: yes and no. This guy sounds as if he's got two heads." "He has," says the doc. "Oh," says the colonel.

Two-Top will be a big success in the Army as soon as he can make up his mind which head to salute.

...AND "THAT'S FOOTBALL"

THE OLD Carlisle Indians were a tricky and colorful outfit, especially when they had Jim Thorpe in the backfield. They invaded Cambridge one fall to tussle with a fine Harvard team, and had leather patches sewed on their jerseys that looked exactly like footballs. In the first few scrimmages, the Harvard team thought all eleven opponents had pigskins tucked under their arms, and didn't know whom to tackle. One Carlisle back added to the confusion by slipping the real football under the back of his jersey and galloping unmolested over the goal line. Officials had to change the rules the following season.

* * *

Knute Rockne had a brief whirl at professional football in its early days. In one of his first games, he faced Jim Thorpe and his Canton Bulldogs at the Polo Grounds. The great Indian athlete was long past his prime, growing fat and sluggish, but he was still a great drawing card. Rockne was desperately anxious to make good. On one of the opening plays, Thorpe came lumbering around his end. Rockne spilled him. As he rose, Thorpe whispered, "Listen, Rock. Don't do that no more. People paid to see Old Jim run. Next time, let him go." On the next play, Rockne spilled him again. Thorpe said nothing this time, but on the very next play, he summoned some reserve force, and for a moment was the flailing, irresistible runner of old. Rockne was knocked cold, and Thorpe galloped for a touchdown while the crowd cheered. Then the Indian returned to where Rockne was coming to, helped to pick him up, and grinned. "That's a good boy, Rock. You let old Jim run!"

* * *

Dick Hanley, now a Colonel in the Marines, once coached a subnormal Northwestern team, that gave him many a gray hair. On a certain Saturday the boys surpassed themselves, and fumbled so often that Hanley literally fell off the bench with rage. He signaled his last substitute backfield man to warm up, then promptly forgot about him. A substitute centre kept passing the ball faithfully to the lad on the sidelines, but Hanley never signaled him to enter the game. Finally the boy missed a practice pass. From the silence of the dejected Northwestern rooting section came a raucous voice: "Put him in now, Hanley; he's ready!"

* * *

The most lopsided football game in the record books took place in 1916. Georgia Tech defeated Cumberland College, 220-0. There lives a man who admits he quarterbacked that Cumberland team: George Allen, former commissioner of the District of Columbia. Allen treasures a yellowed clipping which reads, "Allen spearheaded the Cumberland offensive with a brilliant run around left end that resulted in only an eight-yard loss." He tackled one Tech man on the thirty-yard line and hung around his neck all the way to the goal line. "Once I fumbled," he remembers, "and as three Tech ogres bore down, another Cumberland stalwart shied away from the loose ball. 'Pick it up,' I yelled to the guy, but what do you think he answered? 'Pick it up, hell,' he said. 'I didn't drop it!' "

* * *

In a Rose Bowl game at Pasadena some years ago, a California star emerged in something of a daze from a scrimmage with the football cradled in his arms, lowered his head, and went charging gallantly down the field—toward his own goal line! One of his own teammates managed to nail him on the five-yard stripe, temporarily saving the game and averting one of the prize boners in football history.

* * *

Harvard and Princeton once broke off football relations for years because their games were getting too rough and bad feeling was rife. The last game before the split wasn't made any gentler by a joke that appeared in the Harvard *Lampoon*, published the morning of the match. "Are you a Princeton man?" queried a sweet young thing. "No," was the answer, "a horse stepped on my face." The Princeton team didn't forget *that* when the whistle blew.

* * *

The 1935 game between Dartmouth and Princeton was played in a blinding snowstorm. A Dartmouth man was on his way to a touchdown, with no Tiger player within ten feet of him, when from the sidelines a spectator, who had found adequate means of keeping himself warm, suddenly scampered onto the field and made a perfect tackle. The touchdown was allowed, of course, and the doughty tackler was rewarded for his pains by being bounced out of the Palmer Stadium on his ear.

* * *

The mighty football teams of Notre Dame are supported and rooted for by more fans probably than any other five squads put together. Pat O'Brien, the film star, who thinks nothing himself of flying five thousand miles to see a Notre Dame game, explains that "every American college graduate has two alma maters: his own and Notre Dame." Coach Knute Rockne built the first great team for "The Fighting Irish"; his eleven that included "The Four Horsemen" is considered by many the greatest college football aggregation of all time.

A few days before an Army-Notre Dame encounter, the Green's star fullback, who will remain nameless on this page, flunked a chemistry exam and was declared ineligible. The entire student body, not to mention certain influential graduates, bore down on the professor, who relented to the point of offering the player a second examination the night before the squad entrained for the East. His classmates crammed him for the test, and a sizable cheering section waited outside the professor's house when the ordeal began.

"Now, Joe," the professor reassured him. "All I expect is a fifty percent grade for passing, and I'm only going to ask you two questions. All set?"

"Yeah," grunted Joe.

"First, what does the chemical formula H_2O stand for?"

"Sulphuric acid," wavered Joe.

"Now, take your time with the second question, Joe. What is the chemical formula for water?"

"I dunno," was Joe's candid reply.

The professor beamed. "That passes you, Joe. You answered the second question correctly."

Another time (aside to Pat O'Brien: I'm only kidding, mister!) the captain of a great Notre Dame team suddenly burst into tears on the bench before the last game of the season began. The coach was aghast. "What on earth have you got to cry about?" he marveled. "You're the captain of the best team we've had in years. You're handsome, rich, and have just been voted the most popular guy in the senior class. What's wrong, man?" "Oh, Coach," sobbed the player, "if I could only read and write!"

Even Notre Dame teams occasionally experience let-downs and form reversals. One Saturday a supposed push-over played inspired football for two quarters and led a highly favored Notre Dame squad, 7-0, at half time. The Fighting Irish took it for granted that Knute Rockne would flay their hides off in the dressing room, but the great coach never even turned up. The players were nervously awaiting the time to reappear on the field when Rockne finally stuck his head inside the door. "Let's go, girls," he said. Notre Dame scored four touchdowns in the next ten minutes.

Bob Considine tells the story of a Notre Dame star who went to a sterling but absent-minded priest every week for confession. The priest had the habit of marking the number of sins on his sleeve with a piece of chalk in order to mete out the proper penance.

"Father," said the player one day, "I ran clear across the field to clip a player in our last game."

"That was very wrong, my son," said the priest, making a chalk mark.

"When he fell, I kicked him in the teeth."

"How terrible, my son! Will you never learn true Christianity?" (Four more chalk marks.)

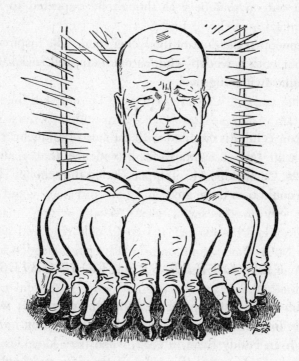

"And then when the referee wasn't looking, I chewed off a piece of his ear."

"Saints preserve us! You're a disgrace to your fine teachers and the college!" By this time the chalk marks were clear up to the priest's elbow. "What was the team you were playing, my son?"

"Southern Methodist," said the player.

"Oh," beamed the priest, rubbing off every mark on his sleeve. "I guess boys will be boys."

A few years ago a forlorn little football squad from a jerkwater college came down to open the season against one of Notre Dame's most powerful elevens. The coach was trying to instil some spirit into his justifiably terrified protégés. "Sure you'll get trimmed," he assured them. "Nobody expects you to do more than your best. At least, show that mob in the stadium that you've got the old moxie—that you can fight to the end for your alma mater. Let's run out on that field as though we expected to win the game!"

He threw open the door of the locker room. The inspired squad dashed out with a whoop—and, as one man, fell smack into the Notre Dame swimming pool.

* * *

Thornton Wilder is credited with the tale of an inebriated Yale student who saw a signpost in Providence that read, "New Haven 126, Cambridge 54." "Yippee," cried the scholar, "I always knew we could trim those guys!"

A FEW OTHER SPORTS STORIES

Probably the most popular heavyweight champion who ever lived was John L. Sullivan, "the Boston Strong Boy," who won the title from Paddy Ryan in 1882, when bare knuckles and unlimited rounds were still the order of the day, and kept it until "Gentleman Jim" Corbett stunned the sporting world by knocking him out in the twenty-first round of a fight in New Orleans ten years later. Liquor and women played a big part in Sullivan's downfall. He drank bourbon by the stein. Whenever he heard there was a good-looking girl on the premises, he would roar,

"Rise her up!" He toured the country offering anybody in the audience a hundred dollars who could stand up to him for three rounds. One punch, of course, generally concluded his evening's work. "My name is John L. Sullivan," was his exit line, "and I can lick any . . . . in the house!" The crowds loved it.

* * *

He was a blacksmith in Australia, and he owned a single race-horse whose dismal record was a series of unvaried lasts. One day he accidentally broke a bottle of whiskey in the horse's stall. The horse lapped some of it up, and then proceeded to confound the form-players by going out and winning a race hands down.

The blacksmith felt that he had made an important discovery. He was sure of it when his horse, after another nip of Scotch, went out and won a second race. Inside of six months, the steed had captured three of the most important races on the Australian calendar, and the blacksmith was in the chips.

Then the story broke that the horse had been given whiskey before each race. There was nothing illegal about it, but the public reacted unfavorably. The owner was booed the next time he appeared at a track. Disconsolate, he sold the horse, and embarked for America, where he began an entirely new career.

You see, in addition to his other accomplishments, this one-time blacksmith was a handy man with his fists. In fact, he was so good that he developed into one of the greatest heavyweight champions in American ring history. His name was Bob Fitzsimmons.

Years after his retirement from the ring, Fitzsimmons became, for reasons of his own, an ardent prohibitionist. He preached fervid sermons on the subject, vowed that he would die a happy man the day prohibition became a law of the land. When the prohibition act was passed, a friend rushed over to Fitzsimmons' house to tell him the news, but there was no answer to his knocks. Bob Fitzsimmons had died peacefully in his sleep during the previous night.

This is a story told by Bill Stern, the well-known radio sports reporter.

* * *

The old adage, "All the world loves a winner," does not always apply in the prize ring. Jack Dempsey, for example, was extremely unpopular in the years from 1919 to 1926, when he was the heavyweight champion. But on September 3, 1926, Gene Tunney licked him at Philadelphia, and from that moment on, the fickle public idolized him.

Dempsey was married to Estelle Taylor in 1926. He wasn't a very pretty picture when he left his dressing room after that Tunney fight. "What happened?" exclaimed his wife. "Honey," said Dempsey. "I forgot to duck." That story got around. People liked it. By the time the same fighters climbed into the ring in Chicago the following summer for a return bout, ninety percent

of the audience of 135,000—the greatest crowd in ring history—
was for Dempsey heart and soul. He almost won back his crown;
in the seventh round, after trailing from the start, he suddenly
launched a terrific attack, and Tunney went down. In the excitement, Dempsey neglected to go to a neutral corner, thus giving
Tunney a "long count." It enabled him to weather the round and
eventually win the fight; Dempsey had shot his last bolt.

In all the history of prize-fighting there have been just five
gates that ran to over a million dollars; Dempsey was one of the
principals in all of them. There were the two bouts with Tunney,

one with Carpentier, one with Sharkey, and the fifth, tops of all
for sheer drama, with Luis Angel Firpo of the Argentine. Firpo
was known as "The Wild Bull of the Pampas." Later it developed
that he had been a drugstore clerk in Buenos Aires. But while
he lasted, he put up a spectacular battle against the champion.
Dempsey knocked him down no fewer than six times in the first
round, but suddenly, Firpo connected with a haymaker that
knocked the champion clear out of the ring. The crowd was so

excited that nobody seems to know how long it took Dempsey to climb back into the arena. He had landed squarely in the laps of a couple of very surprised newspapermen. The referee was so pop-eyed he never even started to count. Dempsey got back in there in time to land one terrific right-hander before the bell sounded. In the second round he knocked Firpo halfway back to the Argentine—but fight fans will never forget that wild first round.

* * *

When Dempsey was training for his first fight with Tunney, he sent a scout named Mike Trent over to his rival's training camp, to pick up some pointers on Tunney's style of hitting power.

Trent returned in high glee. "It's a set-up," he reported. "I seen the lug reading a book!"

* * *

Eleanor Holm, who can swim faster on her back than most readers of this book can navigate on their faces, was the heroine of the 1936 Olympic Games, although she never competed in them.

Besides her aquatic accomplishments, the beautiful Eleanor was a night-club star, and for two years preceding the 1936 Olympic Games expedition had toured the country with a big-name band. In a life of this sort a lady learns how to hold her liquor, also how to stay fresh as a daisy until the wee hours of the morning.

The American team crossed on the *Manhattan* in 1936. Miss Holm, as was her custom, drank plenty of champagne, and danced until four. Other contestants undoubtedly would not have thrived on such a routine, but Miss Holm was something else again. The bluenoses in charge of the American delegation, however, very righteous, very pontifical, bounced her off the squad for "breaking training." Miss Holm got about ten times as much publicity as all the rest of the team put together, the United

States lost a certain "first"—and virtue, I suppose, triumphed. Later Eleanor Holm married Billy Rose, and starred in the Aquacade at the World's Fair. Today she's as popular as ever. The master mind who banned her from the Olympics was forgotten years ago. I hope there's a moral in this story.

* * *

When Quentin Reynolds was an undergraduate at Brown, he became the unexpected hero of an intercollegiate championship swimming meet.

Brown had a renowned plunger on the squad that year who was counted on to bring the first-place trophy home to Providence, but he came down with flu the morning of the meet. The coach was tearing his hair when he spied the two-hundred-pound Quent lumbering across the campus. "Hey, you," he cried, "you look like a guy who can plunge! You gotta plunge your damn head off for Brown tonight."

Reynolds protested weakly that he had never plunged in his life, and then proceeded into town to get most royally plastered. At nine-thirty, sharp, a pistol barked, and five young giants, including Reynolds, took off from the side of the tank. Reynolds went to the bottom like a plummet, and passed out cold. By the time they fished him out of the tank, however—check the records if you don't believe me—he had negotiated the entire length of the pool and broken the intercollegiate record. He had also turned blue. When he came to, they gave him a gold medal and put him on probation for thirty days. He has never plunged since.

* * *

There is a little Italian priest who frequents Mr. Grecco's de luxe barber shop on 59th Street, and likes to lecture the customers and attendants there on the folly of betting on horse races. "Take my own case," he points out. "When I go out to the track, the owners, the trainers, and the jockeys all know me. They tell me just what horses to bet on. The bookies won't take my bets if they know I'm betting on the wrong horse. On the rare occasions when I lose, they refuse to accept my money. And, gentlemen, so far this year, *even I am three hundred dollars behind."*

* * *

Eddie Mead made a classic remark on his way to the track one day: "I hope I break even. I need the money."

* * *

An inveterate race-track gambler went to Saratoga with Tom Cleland, the artist, a few summers ago. Aware of his own weakness, he took the precaution of buying a return ticket for New York before he left. This was one day on which he enjoyed an extraordinary run of luck, and with only one race left to be run, his pockets were bulging with over a thousand dollars in profits. "Let well enough alone," counseled Cleland, but the gambler waved him aside. "This is my lucky day," he exulted—and bet every cent he had on a nag who promptly proceeded to limp home in last place.

The gambler sadly tore his stubs into shreds. Then he came across the return ticket in his pocket. He looked at it a moment— and tore that up too. "Walk home, you dumb idiot!" he mumbled to himself.

* * *

Another yarn of Saratoga concerns a young honeymoon couple who shared a passionate love of gambling. For five hectic days they were dogged by persistent bad luck; on the morning of the final day of the meet, they had only two dollars left between them.

"Let me go out to the track alone today, honey," pleaded the boy. "Wait for me at the hotel. I've got a hunch."

A friend drove him out to the track. He picked a 40-to-1 shot on the first race, and won. Every succeeding race was captured by a rank outsider. He was backing it every time. At the end of the afternoon he had over ten thousand dollars.

On the way back to the hotel, he decided to cash in further on his lucky streak, and stopped at one of the clubs that ran gaming rooms in rather open defiance of the state laws. His luck held. He ran his stake up to forty thousand. He was on the point of leaving when the wheel began spinning once more. Suddenly he put the entire forty thousand on "black."

The ball bounced, and settled. "Number fourteen," called the croupier. "*Red.*"

The boy walked back to the hotel. The girl was waiting for him on the verandah.

"How did you make out?" she called eagerly.

The boy lit a cigarette. "I lost the two dollars," he said.

* * *

José Capablanca, the late Cuban chess wizard, once played sixty-four simultaneous games, vanquished sixty-two opponents, and drew with the other two.

It was he who told me the story of the mighty potentate who was so bored that he offered half of his kingdom to anybody who could find a new way of diverting him. An ancient appeared from nowhere and taught him the game of chess. The potentate was in the seventh heaven.

"You have saved my life," he declared. "Now you must claim your reward."

The ancient's request sounded simple. He asked but a single grain of wheat for the first square on the chess board, double that for the second, double that for the third, and so on down to the sixty-fourth square. The potentate protested. "But I have promised you half my kingdom. Why do you name this paltry reward?" The ancient was adamant, and the potentate ordered the keeper of his granaries to pay off this seemingly modest petitioner. Of course it turned out that there wasn't enough grain in the entire world to pay him off before the fortieth square had been accounted for. If you don't believe it, figure it out for yourself.

There was a time when Charles MacArthur fancied himself as a chess expert. He had run roughshod over the feeble opposition offered by fellow members of the West Side Tennis Club in Hollywood, and was growing pretty insufferable about it. He took to speaking in what he fondly believed was a Spanish accent, and telling newcomers that he was the champion, José Capablanca.

Eventually Capablanca himself visited Los Angeles and Mac-Arthur's lacerated companions sensed the opportunity for a beautiful revenge. They brought him to the West Side Tennis Club, and introduced him to MacArthur as Mr. Spelvin. "Spelvin plays a pretty good game of chess," they said. "Indeed," beamed MacArthur. "I, señor, am Capablanca. We play a game or two, eh?" And so, while the entire membership watched in unalloyed delight, the real Capablanca and the bogus one sat down to play.

Of course, MacArthur was in the soup by the sixth move. To make matters more embarrassing, the champion, by prearrangement, would make his move in one second flat, and then dart off to the swimming pool, leaving MacArthur to sweat over *his* next move for twenty minutes or so. Then he'd saunter back, make another lightning move, and disappear again. MacArthur, perspiring freely, demanded a second game. There is no telling where the gruesome scene would have ended, had not Helen Hayes, MacArthur's wife, arrived, and learned what was afoot. She dashed to an outside telephone and called her husband. "That's the *real* Capablanca you're playing against, you loon!" she cried. "The whole club is laughing at you."

MacArthur claimed feebly that he had known all the time whom he was playing against. "Anything to give you fatheads a laugh," was his attitude. But he never impersonated Capablanca again.

* * *

Frank Crowninshield once played a round of golf with Bobby Jones. It was 1930, the year that Jones won all four major golf titles in America and England. Golf had never known such a popular hero before. Crowninshield was so nervous that he flubbed almost every shot. On the twelfth hole he finally said to Jones: "I hate to bother you, but there must be some dreadful mistake I'm making that you have spotted and possibly can correct. Won't you tell me?"

Bobby Jones gravely replied: "Mr. Crowninshield, I wouldn't change your style of golf for anything in the world. Why, man, you're unique! You make eight errors on your upstroke—and correct four of them coming down!"

When he is golfing with his regular companions, Crowninshield cannot be bothered with any such nonsense as waiting for his turn to play. He plows steadily down the course, ignoring the other players, and often thinks of the cleverest things to say just as somebody else—preferably an opponent—is about to take a shot. Grantland Rice calls him a "floating hazard." "One day," relates Rice, "I was just addressing my ball when Crownie, humming brightly, cut in right ahead of me. I reminded him gently of the lady who asked the station master where she would get the Twentieth Century Limited. The answer was that if she didn't get off the track, she'd get it square in the behind. Crownie got the point and promised to be more careful in the future. On the green of that very hole I had to sink a long putt to stay in the match. I had just lined up the cup when a ball hit my foot. Crownie was essaying a few practice putts while he waited."

* * *

Speaking of golf, did you ever hear the story of the man who came back from the practice tee so visibly unnerved that his friend rushed out of the locker room to ask what was wrong? "What's wrong?" was the bitter retort. "I just killed my wife. That's what's wrong!" "Holy smoke, how did you do that?" "I was out there practising, and didn't see my wife come up behind me. I took a back swing, hit her on the head—and she dropped dead." "Gee, that's bad! What club were you using?" "A niblick," mourned the golfer. "That's the club," said his friend happily.

Chapter Thirteen

THE FIRESIDE BOOK OF
SHAGGY-DOG STORIES

SHAGGY-DOG stories, as almost everybody must know by this time, are the kind of tales in which animals talk, humans do inexplicable things, and the punch lines make no sense at all. They are generally anathema to literal-minded females. There is nothing like a string of shaggy-dog stories to make your wife's Aunt Minnie cut short a visit and go back where she came from. They receive their name from the following legend.

A Kansas City barfly picked up a year-old copy of the London *Times* one day—don't ask me how it got there—and found therein a personal ad offering a ten-pound reward for the return of a very shaggy dog to its bereft owner in Bishop's Bowes, Essex. Ten minutes later he stumbled over the shaggiest darn pup you ever saw. Being a man of decision, he promptly bundled the canine under his arm, took the Twentieth Century to New York, the *Queen Mary* to Southampton, and a limousine to Bishop's Bowes. In keen anticipation, he sought out the lady who had advertised, and rang her bell. She answered herself. "You lost a shaggy dog, madam," he reminded her, holding up the pooch. "Would this be it?" "Good heavens, no," she snapped. "It wasn't *that* shaggy"— and slammed the door in his face.

Well, now that we've settled that, we propose to give you thirty-two examples of the species. We figure that fewer than that would not do the subject full justice; more might set the most avid addicts to baying at the moon. Note that we have numbered the entries. You can't tell the bayers without a number.

1. Two race horses fretted impatiently in adjoining stalls the night before a Kentucky Derby. "You might as well save yourself the effort of competing tomorrow," spoke one, "I've got the Derby sewed up." "Says you," scoffed the other. "What makes you so sure of yourself?" "Didn't you see my owner whispering in my ear just now?" said the first horse. "He was telling me that if I won tomorrow, he'd give me two extra bales of hay. And, brother, that ain't money!"

2. "A quarter's worth of rat poison," ordered the man at the delicatessen store. "Yes, sir," the clerk answered. "Shall I wrap it up for you?" "Oh, you needn't bother," the man said pleasantly. "I'll eat it here."

3. A bat family was flying home from a picnic—Papa Bat, Mama Bat, and Sonny Bat. "Thank heaven that picnic's over," said Sonny Bat. "Now the four of us can have some peace." "Four?" queried Papa. "I only see three." Sonny Bat flared up. "You know very well I can't count," he grumbled.

4. "This dog," Mr. Weber once said to Mr. Fields, "is worth five hundred dollars." To which Mr. Fields replied, "How could a dog save that much money?"

5. A customer entered a saloon and ordered a dozen martinis. He poured the liquor onto the floor, and began munching con-

tentedly on the glasses themselves. The stems, however, he would have no traffic with. A barfly watched the performance with absorbed interest, but pointed to the twelve stems. "You darn fool," he said. "You're leaving the best part."

6. The oysters found a fine new bed several miles up the Sound, and were happily packing their belongings—all except little Mary Oyster, who sat sobbing bitterly in a corner. "What's the matter?" asked her father anxiously. "We'll have a wonderful new home. There's nothing to cry about." "Oh, yes, there is," wailed Mary. "Johnny Bass will never be able to find me now, and I love him with all my heart." "But does Johnny Bass reciprocate your devotion?" inquired the parent. "Indeed he does," Mary assured him. "Last night he took me in his arms at the end of the pier out there. First he kissed me here on the forehead. Then he kissed me here on the lips. And then—my God, my *pearl!*"

7. A very shy young man sat next to a glamorous debutante at a dinner party. In the middle of the main course he seized a bowl of succotash and poured it over the debutante's chic coiffure. The young lady rose indignantly. "How dare you?" she blazed, plucking corn and peas out of her hair. "How dare you throw succotash at me?" The young man blanched. "Good heavens," he stammered. "Was that succotash? I thought it was spinach!"

8. A man's ear was bleeding like a stuck pig. "I bit myself," he explained. "That's impossible," said the doctor. "How can a man bite himself in the ear?" The man said, "I was standing on a chair."

9. Two herrings stopped at a neighborhood café for a couple of snifters. One of them disappeared for a moment, and a puzzled onlooker accosted the one who was left alone at the bar. "Where is your brother?" he challenged. "How in heck should I know," replied the indignant herring. "Am I my brother's kipper?"

10. A man staggered from a railroad car, his complexion a sickly green. "Riding backwards for six hours," he explained. "I never *could* stand that." "Why," his wife inquired, "didn't you ask the party sitting opposite to change seats with you?" "I couldn't do that," said the man. "There wasn't anybody there."

11. A crotchety old bachelor saw a gaily plumed parrot go under the hammer at a country auction, and suddenly decided that the bird might be good company for him on lonely evenings. The bidding grew unexpectedly stiff, but the bachelor was carried away by the spirit of the occasion and before he quite realized what he had done, he bought the Poll for forty-nine dollars. He carried it home, and stood it on the table before him. "Now," he commanded, "talk to me!" The parrot simply drew in its head and glared at him. "I said talk to me," repeated the man. "After all, I bought you to keep me company." Again the parrot glared but said nothing. "Good heavens," cried the exasperated gentleman. "Do you mean to say that after what I paid for you, you can't even *talk?*" "Can't even talk?" echoed the parrot. "Who in hell do you think it was that bid you up to forty-nine dollars?"

12. A cotton-tail rabbit, nibbling thoughtfully at his evening carrot, noticed that his son was in a particularly jovial mood. "What makes Junior so happy?" he asked. Mamma rabbit explained, "He had a wonderful time in school today. He learned how to multiply."

13. At a gala ship concert aboard a liner, a trained parrot did his act, and then teetered excitedly on his perch in the wings while an extraordinary magician performed feats of legerdemain. First he made a goldfish disappear, then a buxom blonde assistant, finally a chest containing three husky sailors. At that moment the liner was struck by a torpedo. The parrot found himself all alone on the Atlantic Ocean, bobbing up and down on a piece of drift-wood, with nothing else in sight. "Amazing," marveled the Poll. "What will he think of next?"

14. (Very, very old.) "Give me a soda," commanded the young sprout, "without flavor." "Without what flavor?" asked the soda jerk. "Without vanilla." "Ain't got no vanilla." "All right, gimme one without strawberry."

15. Two brothers, identical twins, often went fishing together. One twin was always lucky. The other could never catch a thing. They could stand right next to each other and one brother would haul in fish after fish while the other's line dangled idly in the water. One day the unlucky twin decided on a desperate course. He woke in the middle of the night and put on his brother's clothes. He took his brother's rod and went to the very spot where his brother had caught thirty-four trout the day before. For three hours he stood there without getting a nibble. Finally his hopes rose when he saw a magnificent trout swimming his way. The fish ignored the bait and, leaping out of the water, called, "Hey, bud, where's your brother?"

16. Sitting opposite Miss Haas on a northbound subway train one evening sat a man calmly reading his paper with three pigeons resting on top of him—one on his head, the others on his shoulders. Miss Haas contemplated the situation until she could stand it no longer. She tapped his paper, and said, "Pardon me,

but what on earth are you doing with those pigeons in the subway?" "Them?" said the man. "I really don't know, lady. They musta got on at 59th Street."

17. A man dropped in to pay a friend an unexpected visit, and was amazed to find him playing chess with his dog. The man watched in silence for a few minutes, then burst out with "That's the most incredible dog I ever saw in my life!" "Oh, he isn't so smart," was the answer. "I've beaten him three games out of four!"

18. One day a man said to Billy Rose, "Would you like to see me dive into a barrel of water from a thousand feet?" Billy Rose said he certainly would, and next day he called his workmen and had them set up a thousand-foot ladder. Mr. Rose held his breath while the man climbed to the top, and stared fascinated as he took a flying leap and landed, splash, in the barrel of water.

"Magnificent," said Billy Rose. "I'll hire you for $100 a week."

"No," said the man.

"$250 a week," said Billy Rose.

"No," said the man.

"You drive a hard bargain," said Billy Rose, "but your act is worth it. Let's not count pennies. I'll hire you for a thousand a week."

"No," said the man.

"Say, fellow," said Billy Rose, "how much do you want to jump into that barrel?"

"Nothing," said the man. "This is the first time I ever did it, and I don't like it."

19. A worm met another worm coming up from the ground and declared, "You're very beautiful and I'd like to marry you." "Don't be a dope," was the reply. "I'm your other end."

20. (One of the very first.) An elephant looked down at a mouse and exclaimed, "You're about the puniest, most insignificant object I ever laid eyes on." "I'm not always this little," the mouse squeaked angrily. "I've been sick."

21. A dignified old clergyman owned a parrot of whom he was exceedingly fond, but the bird had picked up an appalling vocabulary of cuss words from a previous owner and, after a series of embarrassing episodes, the clergyman decided he would have to kill his pet. A lady in his parish suggested a last-ditch remedy. "I have a female parrot," she said, "who is an absolute saint. She sits quietly on her perch and does nothing but pray from morning until night. Why don't you bring your parrot over and see if my own bird's good influence doesn't reform him?" The clergyman said it was worth a trial, and the next night arrived with his pet tucked under his arm. The bird took one look at the lady parrot and chirped, "Hi, toots. How about a little loving?" "Come to mama," cried the lady parrot gleefully. "What do you think I've been praying for all these years?"

22. A doctor saved a baby elephant's life in the jungle, then returned to America. Years later he was down on his luck, and had to borrow a quarter to see the circus when it came to town. Out came the elephants. One of them saw the doctor, and trumpeted recognition. He wrapped his trunk around the doctor, lifted him out of the twenty-five-cent seat—and planked him down in a box seat worth three dollars.

23. A kangaroo yanked her young one out of her pouch and gave it a healthy smack on the backside. "I'll teach you," she declared, "to eat crackers in bed!"

24. When the manager of the Brooklyn ball club lost his star centre fielder on the eve of a crucial swing through the West, he sent out a frantic call for a replacement. Almost a week went by and there were no applications. The manager sat dejectedly on the bench with his head in his hands. He heard an apologetic whinny behind him, and looking around, saw a horse standing there.

"Go away," he said to the horse. "Can't you see I've got a headache?"

"But I'm applying for that spot in centre field," said the horse.

"That's ridiculous," snapped the manager. "Horses don't play baseball—not even in Brooklyn!"

The horse insisted, however, and finally the manager allowed him to exhibit his wares. It developed that he could field like Tris Speaker and hit like Joe Di Maggio. The delighted manager promptly inserted him into the lineup.

In the ninth inning of that day's game, with the score 0-0, the horse strode to the plate and lashed a wicked liner against the right-field fence.

Then—to everyone's amazement—he stood stock still at the plate, twirling his bat.

"Run, you idiot, run!" beseeched the frantic manager. "This means the game!"

"Don't be silly," said the horse. "Who ever hear ¯ of a horse running bases?"

25. A colony of ostriches—ninety-nine birds in all—had their heads buried neatly in the sand when ostrich number one hundred came galumping onto the scene. He looked about in a puzzled way and inquired, "Where on earth *is* everybody?"

26. A reporter was assigned, a long time ago, to interview Mr. Barnum's favorite midget, Tom Thumb. The hotel clerk directed the reporter to Room 308, but when he knocked on that door, it was opened by a giant fully nine feet tall. "I must have the wrong room," apologized the newsman. "Who were you looking for?"

countered the giant. "Tom Thumb, the dwarf," laughed the reporter. "Well, come in," said the giant. "I'm Tom Thumb." "You Tom Thumb!" the reporter scoffed. "Why, you're nine feet tall!" "I know," said the giant. "But, you see, this is my day off."

27. Mr. Nussbaum was a regular patron of Finkelstein's Shangri-La Bar and Grille. One evening he declared, "I feel like some fried flounder tonight." The waiter brought a generous portion, but just as Nussbaum was about to dive in, the flounder shook his head and threw a warning glance. Nussbaum ran for the sidewalk. A month later he tried again. "We got fresh flounder for you," said the waiter. "Just came in today." But at the last moment it turned out to be the same old flounder, who shook his head even more vigorously than the first time. "This does it," cried Nussbaum. "Never do I come to this joint again!" Some weeks later his wife took him to a swanky Park Avenue hotel. "Here I will get flounder what is flounder," exulted Nussbaum. The waiter brought a steaming platter, beautifully garnished with parsley and lemon. Just as Nussbaum was reaching for his fork the flounder lifted his head from the plate. "Ah ha!" he sneered. "So Finkelstein's ain't good enough for you no more!"

28. "Do you realize," said a man in a cafeteria to a stranger across the table, "that you are reading your newspaper upside down?"

"Of course I realize it," snapped the stranger. "Do you think it's easy?"

29. A pigeon came home very late for dinner one evening, with his feathers bedraggled, and his eyes bloodshot. "I was out minding my own business," he explained, "when bingo! I get caught in a badminton game!"

30. The bartender noticed that his customer had a big carrot behind his ear, but he decided not to mention it. "Probably just waiting for people to ask him what it's for. I'll fool him." For twenty-seven consecutive days the customer appeared, with a carrot always tucked behind his ear. Then, on the twenty-eighth

day, the routine was varied: a banana had replaced the carrot! The bartender could stand it no longer. "What's the idea of that banana behind your ear, fellah?" he demanded, leaning over the counter. "Couldn't find no carrot today," explained the customer.

31. A couple of frogs were dining at the Ritz one evening. "You're angry at me," accused Abdul Amnal (he was a Turkish frog). "You haven't spoken to me all evening." "It isn't that at all," explained the other with some difficulty. "I just can't talk tonight. I've got a man in my throat."

32. A brown horse, hitched to a milk wagon, looked up one morning to see a poster staring her in the face. The Ringling Circus was in town! She calmly trotted over to the stage door of Madison Square Garden, and entered. "Hi, girls!" she neighed, to be greeted with noisy expressions of surprise and delight. "But, Beulah," protested one nag, "what are you doing with that cheesy milk wagon you're hitched to? A year ago you were the star of the show here, with blue plumes over your ears, and beautiful performers somersaulting on your back!" "Aw," answered Beulah, "what can you expect from that darn Hollywood agent of mine?"

Chapter Fourteen

GRAB BAG

THE ORGANIZATION of this book is as loose as the Nevada divorce laws. My purpose was to include as many good anecdotes as I could remember, not to construct a logical and orderly treatise. When I finished pasting the manuscript together, there were some stories left over that simply couldn't be fitted into any definite category. You will find them here, in no logical sequence whatever.

* * *

Frank Case, amiable Boniface of the Algonquin Hotel, tells the story of the day the late DeWolf Hopper protested to him that nowhere in New York could he find his favorite dessert, brown betty, on the menu. "I'd have it here for you," Case said, "if I thought there would be a reasonable demand for it." "You put it on your menu tomorrow night," proposed Hopper, "and I'll see to it personally that the demand develops." The next night brown betty was duly added to the Algonquin bill of fare, and Hopper, much gratified, made a personal tour of every table in the dining room. "I am DeWolf Hopper," he announced to the surprised patrons, "and I personally urge you to sample the brown betty this evening. It's delicious!" Hopper then repaired to his own table, toyed with a beefsteak, and summoned his waiter. "Now,"

333

he said, rubbing his hands in anticipation, "I'll have a double order of brown betty." "I'm very sorry, sir," said the waiter. "It's all gone."

* * *

Do you remember the New England hurricane of 1938?

A commuter who lived in Stamford had always wanted to own a barometer. Two days before the big blow he finally bought one at Abercrombie and Fitch. He tacked it up on his wall, read it, and exploded with anger. There was no phone in his house, so he walked a mile to the nearest drugstore and called up Abercrombie. "Fine barometer you sold me," he snorted. "I put it up in my Stamford house and what do you think it registers? *Hurricane!*"

"Return it," soothed the clerk. "We'll replace it with a perfect one."

He went back to fetch the barometer, but by the time he got there, his house had been blown away.

* * *

Two old friends who had not seen each other in twenty years rediscovered each other recently. "Great to see you, Joe," boomed one of them. "I suppose you are a married man with children by this time." "No," said the other, "I am afraid I never took the plunge." "Joe, you must be crazy," said the first one. "I guess you just don't realize what it means to be married. Take me, for instance. I come home every night from a hard day at the office to a beautiful, warm, comfortable apartment. My wife is waiting to hand me my slippers and the evening paper. Then she runs out to the kitchen, cooks me a luscious dinner. She tops that with my favorite liqueur, plants me in my easy chair by the fire, and hands me my pipe. Then she washes the dishes. Finally, she comes and snuggles down by my side and starts to talk. She talks, and talks, and talks, and talks. *I wish she'd drop dead.*"

* * *

Newman Levy, author of *Opera Guyed*, has a thirteen-year-old daughter who spends endless blissful hours at the movies. "How did you enjoy the picture this afternoon?" he asked her one Saturday. "It was simply awful," she replied. "I could hardly sit through it the second time."

* * *

Deaf people have a little publication called *The Volta Review*. One story that this little magazine made famous concerned three deaf gentlemen aboard a train bound for London. "What station is this?" inquired the first gent at a stop. "Wembley," answered the guard. "Heavens," said the second gent, "I thought it was Thursday!" "So am I," exclaimed the third. "Let's all have a drink!"

* * *

The urbane and witty Frank Crowninshield really surpassed himself on the day that he introduced Amelia Earhart to the members of the Dutch Treat Club.

"Gentlemen," he began, "I mean to tell you a little story about Eliza, a God-fearing and worthy colored girl who died and ascended straight to the Pearly Gates. 'You're in Heaven now, Eliza,' Saint Peter told her, 'and you're an angel in good standing. Just go over to that lot next door and pick yourself out a becoming pair of wings.' 'Wings,' echoed Eliza. 'Lordy me, Mr. Peter, I don't know nothin' 'bout flyin'!' 'You'll learn, you'll learn,' Saint Peter assured her.

"So Eliza picked out a beautiful pair of gossamer wings and made a few tentative flights. She was pretty bad at first, and had a nasty tumble or two, but gradually she caught the knack of the thing, and finally was doing side-slips, Immelmann turns, and the most complicated maneuvers with scarcely any effort whatever. She was so pleased with her progress that she decided to show off a little bit before God.

"God and His Son were on Their thrones, enjoying an after-luncheon nap, when Eliza came zooming into view. God awakened and watched her with mounting astonishment. Finally He shook His sleeping Son. 'Jesus Christ,' He exclaimed, 'can that girl fly!' . . . Gentlemen, Amelia Earhart!"

Another memorable incident at the Dutch Treat Club centred in the appearance of Gertrude Lawrence, who was starring at the time in the very successful *Susan and God*.

Miss Lawrence expressed girlish embarrassment at finding herself the only female in a gathering of some three hundred handsome gentlemen. "Instead of making a silly speech," she suggested, "how would you like it if I raffled off two seats in the fourth row centre for Saturday night's performance of *Susan and God?*" The crowd roared its approval. "O.K.," said Miss Lawrence. "Every one of you has a green hat-check. I'll call out a number at random. The man whose hat-check number corresponds with it gets the ducats." Followed the business of three hundred gentlemen fishing in their jeans for their hat-checks.

"Ready?" asked Miss Lawrence. "The number I pick is 171."

"That's mine," said a happy voice from the back of the room. It belonged to Mr. John Golden, owner and producer of *Susan and God*. Miss Lawrence and Mr. Golden escaped from the room before the stunned audience could translate its mute rage into positive action.

* * *

Clarence Budington Kelland presided the day that Nicholas Murray Butler, Columbia University prexy, was the guest of the Dutch Treat. "For years," said Kelland, gazing fondly at Dr. Butler, "organizations have been besieging this retiring gentleman to address them—with remarkable success."

* * *

Harry Hansen climbed into a taxicab, told the driver where he wanted to go, and added, "Please don't go down Third Avenue. I don't like those El pillars."

"Yessir," said the driver—and went right down Third Avenue.

"Didn't you hear me?" screamed Hansen. "I said not to go weaving in and out around those El pillars. It drives me crazy."

The driver stopped his cab and looked at Hansen reproachfully. "Listen, Buddy," he remarked. "What do you suppose it does to me?"

* * *

The twelve-year-old daughter of a publisher of the *New York Times* volunteered to help her mother pass cocktails at an informal reception whipped up for a visiting General. Everything progressed beautifully until the horrified mother heard her daughter say to the General's wife, "May I serve you your eighth martini?"

* * *

Kid Stuff: A famous composer was questioning his ten-year-old son about his history lesson in school that day. "Was it interesting?" he asked. "I'll say!" declared the boy. "We heard all about Nebacadenza!"

* * *

And Leonard Lyons' young hopeful watched his mother try on a new dress. "You sure are beautiful," he assured her. "You look just like Abraham Lincoln!"

* * *

A Navy J.G., home on leave, took his little daughter on a shopping tour. In a crowded department-store elevator, a stout party gave the J.G. an outraged look, and smacked him squarely in the face. The J.G. compressed his lips, and said nothing. As they emerged on the ground floor, his daughter said, "I hated that woman too, papa. She stepped on my foot, so I pinched her right on the heinie!"

* * *

Paul Whiteman, the famous band leader, never could see why some people thought he was fat—even when he tipped the scales at something in the neighborhood of 250. He likes to tell the story of the *really* stout party who made a million dollars without budging from his comfortable couch. A visitor found him one day wearing a bathrobe with enormous checks, and a number sewed on to each check. "What's the idea of those numbers?" he inquired. "Watch me," said the Croesus. He summoned his butler, yawned, and ordered, "Jeeves, scratch Number 23!"

* * *

In my book, Fredric March's kid story still is tops. He found himself alone with a little seven-year-old one evening and, to pass the time before its parents entered the room, inquired, "What do you want to be when you grow up, sonny?" The boy looked him straight in the eye and replied firmly, "A sex pervert."

* * *

Olin Clark reports the story of a mother who lost her young daughter in the week-end confusion at Penn Station. After a frantic search, she finally located her in the midst of a group of nuns. Both the little girl and the nuns seemed to be having a very good time. "I hope my daughter hasn't been giving you too much trouble," exclaimed the relieved parent. "On the contrary," chuckled the Mother Superior. "Your little girl seems to have the notion that we are penguins."

* * *

When Bob Gilham, Paramount's publicity chief, vacationed in the Blue Ridge country a few summers ago, he noticed one old native who sat rocking on his porch day after day, a shotgun across his knees, staring intently into the hills. Uncle Eph was his name, they told Bob. One day he asked the old man what he was gunning for. "Sly old fox in them hills sneaks down ter steal my chickens, an' I'm aimin' ter dispose of him," said Uncle Eph grimly.

A week later Bob went by the cabin, and noticed that Uncle Eph had put away his gun, and was rocking happily with a look on his face that indicated he was at peace with the entire world. "I'll bet you got the fox!" said Bob. "Yep," said Uncle Eph. "Are you absolutely sure you bagged him?" said Bob. " 'Course I'm sure," said Uncle Eph. "I been lookin' for him steady from the minute I killed him up there, and by cracky, I only seen him once since!"

Later, Bob remarked to Uncle Eph, "I bet you've seen plenty of changes here in your day." "Sure have," agreed the old man, "and I bin against every single one of them!"

* * *

Dialogue overheard on a cannibal island: "Who is that lady I seen you with last night?" "That wasn't no lady. That was my dinner."

* * *

When one famous explorer went on his Antarctic expeditions, report had it that the personnel invariably included the ugliest old crone he could sign up. "She's my yardstick," he explained. "When she starts looking good to me—I know it's time to start for home."

Willie Howard once appeared in a sketch which showed him and a few companions freezing and starving on an Antarctic ice floe. He turned on the radio just in time to hear an announcer describing a Thanksgiving dinner back home. "We'll start with a plate of hot, luscious soup," said the announcer. "With noodles?" groaned Howard. "Yes," said the voice on the radio—"with noodles."

* * *

"Jimmie" Walker, once mayor of New York, tells the story of the drunk who climbed into a taxi and demanded, "Drive me eighteen times around Central Park." The cab had gotten about as far as 86th Street when he banged on the window and cried, "Fashter, you idiot! I'm in a hurry!"

He probably was a brother of the gent who boarded a cab on 42nd Street, and pointing to the revolving electrical news sign on the Times Building, commanded, "Just follow that sign."

* * *

Hamish Hamilton, prominent English publisher, overheard two young ladies who were dining together at Lyons (the English equivalent of Child's). One of the ladies asked, "Is your boy friend a freethinker?" The other replied, "Bless me, 'e 'ardly ever thinks of hanything else."

* * *

There is a bone-dry town in Oklahoma where an honest-to-goodness rattlesnake bite is the only way to get a shot of whiskey. One native came home angry and thirsty and told his wife, "It's about time this burg had more'n one rattler. I stood in line for three hours today and by the time it was my turn the rattler was so tired he wouldn't bite nobody any more."

* * *

You have read a lot about the knights of King Arthur who fared forth on coal-black chargers to rescue beautiful maidens from dragons' clutches, but did you ever know that one of them was mounted on a St. Bernard dog? His name was Sir Marmaduke, and he and the St. Bernard performed many a deed of derring-do. One evening, however, they were caught in a torrential thunderstorm, and sought shelter at a nearby tavern. "Reservation?" asked the room clerk. "No," admitted Sir Marmaduke. "Sorry," said the clerk, "no room without a reservation." It was at this moment that he discovered that Marmaduke was sitting astride his faithful St. Bernard. "Hold on," said the clerk. "We'll have to find *something* for you. I wouldn't put out a knight on a dog like this."

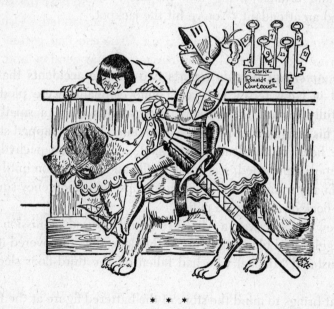

* * *

Barney Greengrass, who sells sturgeon to the White House, is reported to have waited on a customer who ordered a single raisin and one pinch of sugar. "What are you making, Mrs. Geddes?" he inquired. "A cookie?"

* * *

Earl Wilson tells about a well-known Broadway comedian, in his cups as usual, who careened into the 46th Street Automat, changed two dollar bills into nickels, and began inserting them in the pie slots. He had made a neat pile of four slices of apple pie, three of lemon, and five of peach, and was slipping a nickel into his first coconut pie slot when the manager collared him. "What the hell are you doing with our pies?" he cried. "Cut it out!" "Whaaat?" exclaimed the Broadwayite. "Quit now when my luck's running so good?"

Maybe that's how George Price got the notion for his cartoon of the flabbergasted Automat customer who had deposited a single nickel, and found an assortment of sandwiches, cakes, hard-boiled eggs, and crullers flying into his face. "Congratulations, sir," beamed an attendant. "You've hit the jackpot."

* * *

The *American Weekly* reports two strange accidents that occurred in New Jersey last year. Nine elephants were plodding peacefully toward the Newark fair grounds when a small boy urged his insignificant puppy to "sic 'em." The pup yapped shrilly at the heels of the leading elephant, and all nine pachyderms thereupon stampeded, scattering traffic and destruction until they were finally rounded up by six radio cops, two emergency squads, and a flock of motorcycle police.

A few blocks away a Mrs. Fitzgerald refused admission to a bedraggled and bleeding figure at the door, then discovered it was her husband Michael who had fallen off the third-floor sleeping porch.

That brings to mind the story of the battered figure at the Hotel Astor who demanded the key to Room 614.

"Room 614 is occupied by a Mr. James Collins," said the clerk at the desk.

"I know it," rasped the applicant. "I'm James Collins. I just fell out of the window."

* * *

Mabel Jullup, relates Dorothy Sims, was a lady with taste. She bought a lovely vase at an auction and put it on her table. It was Ming, and it made the Grand Rapids furniture look very cheap. She was sad, so she sold the Grand Rapids and bought "period." That made her whole house look cheap. So she sold the house and took an exclusive apartment in town. But the apartment was so exclusive it made Mr. Jullup look cheap. Naturally she got a divorce, and married a Mr. Preston Potter. But here she was stymied. Mr. Preston Potter made her look cheap.

* * *

The Prize for Paralyzing Puns this year falls into the lap of the perpetrator of the following horror:

Waitress: Hawaii, mister? You must be Hungary?

Gent: Yes, Siam. And I can't Rumania long either. Venice lunch ready?

Waitress: I'll Russia table. What'll you Havre? Aix?

Gent: Whatever's ready. But can't Jamaica cook step on the gas?

Waitress: Odessa laugh! But Alaska.

Gent: Don't do me favors. Just put a Cuba sugar in my Java.

Waitress: Don't you be Sicily, big boy. Sweden it yourself. I'm only here to Serbia.

Gent: Denmark my check and call the Bosphorus. I hope he'll Kenya. I don't Bolivia know who I am!

Waitress: Canada noise! I don't Caribbean. You sure Ararat!

Gent: Samoa your wisecracks? What's got India? D'you think this arguing Alps business? Be Nice! Matter of fact, I gotta Smolensk for ya!

Waitress: Attu! Don't Kiev me that Boulogne! Alamein do! Spain in the neck. Pay your check and scram, Abyssinia!

FINNISH

* * *

An old drunkard from the Panhandle saw so many pink elephants and purple snakes that he hired a hall and put up a sign. "25¢ to See the Zoo." A couple of customers resented the fact that they saw nothing but four bare walls, and swore out a complaint. The sheriff took the warrant and set out to make the arrest. The old boy hauled his jug out from under his counter, the sheriff took three snifters—and paid him $600 for a half interest in his show.

* * *

Meyer Levin tells this story about a little eight-year-old girl in a Pennsylvania orphan asylum. She was a gangly, painfully unattractive child, with annoying mannerisms and secretive ways that set her apart from the others. She was shunned by the children and actively disliked by the teachers. The head of the institution longed only for a legitimate excuse to pack her off to a reform school, or get her out of the place some other way.

One afternoon it looked as though her opportunity had arrived. The girl who was the child's very unwilling roommate reported that she was conducting a clandestine correspondence with somebody outside the grounds. "I've seen her write these notes every day for a week now," she reported. "Just a little while ago she took one of them and hid it in a tree near the brick wall."

The head of the asylum and her assistant could scarcely conceal their elation. "We'll soon get to the bottom of this," they agreed. "Show us where she left the note."

Sure enough, they found the note in the branches of the tree. The headmistress pounced on it. Then she hung her head and passed it silently to her assistant.

It read: "To whoever finds this: I love you."

Chapter Fifteen

"THERE'S A WAR GOING ON"

A NEW YORK sports expert covered a series of Army bouts at a nearby training center. The highlight of the evening was a furious and bloody combat between a young giant and a gray-haired gladiator who looked twenty years older than his opponent. The writer wondered what had happened to the Army's sense of fair play when the entire audience sided with the younger man and cheered wildly when he knocked the daylights out of his adversary. He was even more surprised when the loser was the one who came to the loud speaker. Then he understood.

"Top Sergeant Graham speaking," panted the bruised fighter, grinning broadly. "When my son enlisted in this army four months ago, I never knew the day would come when he could lick the hell out of his old man."

* * *

A wedding limousine rolled up Fifth Avenue a few weeks ago with a large placard tied to the rear bumper. It read, "Careless talk caused this."

* * *

345

College courses are being abbreviated daily to cope with the emergency. A Princeton instructor reports a serious incident on the Nassau campus as a result thereof last week. It appears that a student left the room to go to the washroom, and missed his entire sophomore year.

* * *

Major Donald S. Klopfer, stationed in England with the Eighth Air Force, tells of a determined London bookseller who trundled down Charing Cross Road despite the warning blasts of an air-raid alert and a red-faced bobby's command that he seek shelter. "My radio is installed in the bookshop, my dear fellow," he explained, "and alert or no alert, I've simply got to get there to tune in on the eight o'clock news." He had his way. A few moments later the Nazi bombers were over the city, giving it what for. When the raid was over, a taxi driver who had overheard the argument said to the bobby, "I wonder if that there bloke heard his eight o'clock news?" " 'Eard it?" echoed the bobby. " 'E *was* it!"

* * *

An officer on leave from a post in Panama tells a whaling story that's very different from anything in *Moby Dick*.

A mammoth whale was washed up by the tide on the Pacific beach, and a company of coast artillerymen set out to capture it. They discovered, however, that the floundering whale was anticipating a blessed event. Instead of killing it, they waited for high tide and by dint of a prodigious effort, relaunched it. The officer adds that as the grateful whale headed out to sea, it sent out three short spouts and a long one for victory. His pals insinuate that he saw Walt Disney's *Pinocchio* too often and had whales on his mind, but the newspapers printed the yarn, and I pass it on to you for what it's worth.

* * *

Knut Hamsun, author of *Growth of the Soil* and *Hunger*, Nobel Prize winner and erstwhile literary head man of Norway, shocked his countrymen and disgraced himself eternally by throwing in his lot with the Quislingites when the Nazis invaded Norway. Word has reached these shores of how his countrymen have chosen to register their contempt for him. They have piled up every copy of his books that they could in their homes, their shops, and their

libraries, and mailed them back to him without a word of explanation. The little postoffice in his native town was so swamped that it had to take on several extra helpers to handle the flood of books that poured in day after day. At a public auction recently, a complete set of Hamsun's works, autographed, and bound in full morocco, came under the hammer. The auctioneer knocked down the set to the first and only bidder for a sum equivalent to twenty-five cents in American money. The books were added promptly to the pile that was headed back to Hamsun. He must have quite a few thousand of his books by this time.

* * *

The infantry regiment assigned to patrol the Makin atoll in the Gilbert Islands has discovered that there was some truth, after all, in those legends about the beauteous South Sea belles. A sergeant of the 165th conveyed to a Makin glamour girl that he wanted a grass skirt for a souvenir. She politely whipped her own off and handed it to him. The red-faced soldier hastily handed her a large bandana handkerchief. She thanked him prettily—and wrapped it around her head

* * *

The Teheran Conference brought little solace to Lord Louis Mountbatten, anxious to start a big Allied push against the Japs in Burma. "You'll have to wait," Churchill told him. "Supplies intended for you originally have been diverted elsewhere for something more pressing." Mountbatten returned to Delhi, summoned his staff, and told them gloomily, "I've heard all of you say that you wish you had been here six months ago. Gentlemen, you've got your wish!"

* * *

An unprecedented rush of business has made it practically impossible to get a table in a New York restaurant during the dinner hour, and Mr. Garfinkle became increasingly aware of this fact while he tried vainly to fight his way past the lobby of a half-dozen high-class eateries. Finally he staggered into a tiny delicatessen, and planted himself at the solitary marble-topped table in the rear.

To his surprise, a waiter appeared instantly, and said, "What'll you have?"

"A couple of soft-boiled eggs," begged Mr. Garfinkle, "and a few kind words."

Five minutes later the eggs were planked down in front of him. "So here are the eggs," he murmured plaintively. "Now how about the few kind words?"

The waiter leaned over and whispered into Mr. Garfinkle's ear, "Don't eat them eggs!"

* * *

A prominent author up from Washington to attend a session of the Writers' War Board explained his tardy arrival: "I came by bus and the darn thing stopped at every post on the route. It turned out to be a Greyhound."

* * *

A certain number of crooked gamblers are bound to turn up at every army post, and John Scarne, an expert on the subject, has recently toured camps from one end of the country to the other to expose the methods by which card and dice games can be "fixed" in advance. A private at one of his lectures lingered behind to thank him, and tell of his own initiation to the "galloping dominoes." "I had never shot craps before I joined this outfit," he declared. "They told me I could learn in no time. The first time I rolled the dice I got an 'eleven'—a six and a five. 'That's an easy point,' a sergeant assured me. 'Go ahead and try to make it.' I could tell by the looks on the faces of the other fellows that something was being put over on me, but of course I had no idea what it was. Well, sir, I shot fourteen 'elevens' in a row. It's a lucky thing for me I learned how to throw 'em when I was a kid playing parcheesi."

* * *

Clark Lee, author of *Call It Pacific*, tells of an officer, very religious, who insisted on reading a burial service over a hundred Jap soldiers who fell in a pitched battle in New Britain. Fellow officers didn't relish the notion, but he persisted. "They may be Japs," he said, "but they're dead, and I'm going to give them a decent burial." In the middle of the service, one of the "corpses" suddenly rose with a grenade in his hand. The officer dropped his Bible, whipped out a gun, shot the Jap through the temple, calmly reholstered his weapon, and resumed the sermon. "Lord," he declared, "I said I'd give these Japs a funeral, and that goes for every last one of them. Amen!"

* * *

A collector's item from a Lewis Gannett book review: "But the Fortress flew on with her chin up, like Marie Antoinette walking to the scaffold, even when red flames from her pitted gasoline tanks were spreading from her cockpit to her tail."

* * *

When André Maurois went to North Africa late in 1943 on a special mission for the Fighting French, he had heard no word of his son for over two years. This son had been an officer in the French Army. Maurois could only hope that he had been taken prisoner somewhere, unharmed. In Casablanca, he heard that Frenchmen who lived only to lick the Nazis were being smuggled across the Mediterranean by the hundreds each week. "Come with me and watch them when they arrive," suggested a friend. Maurois went with his notebook in hand. The first boy who came in that night was his son!

* * *

A regiment resting up at an undisclosed spot on foreign soil fell to debating noisily over which smelled worse: a goat or a local peasant. Considerable sums were wagered on this vital question, and an agreeable colonel was made judge and stakeholder. First they brought the goat into the tent. The colonel fainted. The men who had bet on the goat reached for the money. Their triumph was short-lived, however. Somebody brought in the peasant—and the goat fainted.

* * *

A reporter who was doing a feature story on Madame Tussaud's Wax Works in London sought out the laundress who had washed for the exhibition for twenty-five years.

"Tell me," said the journalist. "Do the queens and the duchesses in the wax works wear anything under those gorgeous velvet robes?"

"As a matter of fact, they don't," the laundress admitted. "But I'd rather you didn't make it public. As it is, nobody knows but me and a few Australian soldiers!"

* * *

Royal Gunnison was broadcasting from Manila for Mutual when the Japs caught up with him and interned him at Shanghai until he returned to this country on the exchange liner *Gripsholm*. One of his anecdotes concerned what must have been the most unusual soft-ball game ever played. The inmates of the Shanghai concentration camp were lucky enough to dig up some soft-ball equipment, and took the game up avidly to kill time and keep fairly fit. The Jap captain of the guard turned out to be a ball fan. He watched the games for days without comment, then suddenly sent a formal challenge to the internees' committee for a game against his own picked team.

The internees sensed trouble, and tried to duck the game. The captain thought they feared a trouncing, and became more and more insistent. Finally a date was set. A big crowd of internees and Japs turned out for the game. The atmosphere was tense as the Americans prepared to take their first turn at bat.

It was a slaughter. Before the Japs had retired three men, the internees had scored 27 runs, were trying desperately to be put out deliberately for fear of reprisals. The umpires were Japs. At the end of three innings the score was 28-1, and the Jap captain had enough. "It more better we do not play for score," he announced, sucking through his teeth. "After this we play for sportsmanship."

* * *

Eddie Cantor avers that in his bed in an overcrowded Washington hotel he suddenly heard snores emanating from the adjoining bathroom. He investigated, and rushed to the telephone. "Good Heavens," he cried, "there's a midget up here snoring in my bathtub!" "A midget?" echoed the room clerk calmly. "He must have pulled the plug out. There's supposed to be two of them!"

* * *

From David Niven in London comes the story of the RAF pilot who made a forced landing in Belgium and was rescued by a nun. She shepherded him into her convent, handed him a complete set of nun's habiliments, and counseled: "Lie low. Say nothing. Be as inconspicuous as possible. Sooner or later we will find a way to spirit you back to England." For eight weeks the pilot spoke to no one, shaved eight times a day, was a model convent habitant. One evening, however, he spied a beautiful young sister alone in the pantry, and on a sudden but irresistible impulse, swept her into his arms. A moment later he was reeling from a terrific sock on the jaw. "'Ere, 'ere, you rum bloke," spoke a deep masculine voice. "'Old yer 'orses, carn't yer? I been 'ere since Dunkerque."

* * *

Two K.P.'s were staggering under the weight of a steaming kettle they were hauling from the kitchen in Fort Dix, New Jersey. A colonel stopped them. "Get me a ladle," he commanded. One of the K.P.'s rushed for a ladle. The colonel dipped it into the kettle, swallowed a mouthful, gulped, and roared, "Do you call that soup?" "No, sir," came the meek reply. "That's the water we've been washing the dishes in!"

* * *

John Hersey, author of *Into the Valley* and *A Bell for Adano*, writes about a friendly encounter between an American Navy officer and a cannibal chief. The officer visited the chief's village, and, in the course of the ensuing powwow, pleaded, "If you see American soldiers come down from sky in parachutes, you must not eat them. They are here to protect you from Japs." The Chief replied, "No eat white men—too bitter."

* * *

The boys in the South Pacific retain their sense of humor. One writes, "I am raising quite a beard on the instalment plan: a little down at a time." Another explained his plight in a note of exactly four words: "Long time no she."

* * *

If the armed forces ever took a vote for their favorite comedian, Bob Hope would undoubtedly win by something like the 85,000 miles he figures he has traveled to spread sunshine—and Hope— wherever American boys are fighting. Hope does not rely on one or two corny routines. He has fresh and timely gags for every stop on his lightning tours, special quips that only the audience he is playing to can appreciate. That's why most of the beachheads, fox-holes, camps, and hospitals have GI's for Hope alone.

Bob Hope was born in England in 1904, but moved to Cleveland while he was still a choir boy. (He says that his voice changed right in the middle of a beautiful solo.) He was a vaudeville performer for years, crashed Broadway in *Roberta* and *Red, Hot, and Blue,* and then discovered pictures and radio, in both of which he was so riotously successful that producers didn't dare to peep when he treated sacred scripts as something to be ignored. When he and Bing Crosby were making *Road to Singapore,* he told the author, "If you hear any of your own dialogue, yell 'Bingo!'"

In Africa, he reported, "The boys were so happy to see me they actually got down on their knees. What a crap game!" In Edinburgh he told his audience, "This blackout isn't all wasted; I just bumped into eight Scotchmen on Princes Street developing films." In Palermo, the Nazis bombed his hotel. "We did a show," said Hope, "and then ran for our lives. But then, I've never done anything else!" In London, he reported, "I just saw Winston Churchill. Best newsreel I've caught in months!" At a base hospital he was introduced to a soldier who was suffering from anemia and sundry other ailments. "I remember giving a pint of blood last year," cracked Hope. "I've got an idea that I'm shaking hands with the guy who got it!"

* * *

"A Fascist country," opines Robert St. John, "is where they name a street for you one day and chase you down it the next."

* * *

Milton Sperling, one of the best-known writers and producers in Hollywood, now a captain in the U. S. Marines, brings back this story from an island in the South Pacific.

A complete set of motion-picture equipment and fresh prints of a dozen new features were dispatched for the amusement of the five thousand boys on the island. The equipment was landed in fine style, but unfortunately every film but one was lost in the process of unloading. That film was *Action in the North Atlantic,* a rousing action story that starred Humphrey Bogart.

An outdoor theatre of sorts was set up on a hillside and *Action in the North Atlantic* was run over and over again. Some of the boys saw it twenty times. One tough young marine came in from a little sortie, stripped to the waist, with a belt of ammunition still strapped over his shoulder, and watched the picture with evident satisfaction. The point just had been reached where a Nazi wolf pack attacked the convoy when the air-raid alarm sounded. Almost immediately thereafter the first bomb landed less than two hundred yards from the theatre. The Japs had smashed in over hills which had thrown off the radar system.

The picture stopped abruptly and everybody dove madly for shelter. The marine flung down his cigarette in disgust. "The bastards!" he cried. *"Right at the most exciting part!"*

* * *

Some Belgian patriots recently blew up a Nazi vessel docked at Antwerp. Only clue was a guard's statement that he had seen a woman lurking in the shadows just before the explosion. The Gestapo began a search for the woman, felt they were on the right track when an anonymous Belgian mailed in the photo of a curvaceous girl, minus name, or address. The photo was reprinted in all Belgian papers, with a hefty reward offered for her identification. Two thousand delighted Belgians promptly claimed the reward. The girl in the photo was Paulette Goddard.

* * *

St. John was dining in Chicago's Palmer House after his return from the front. A lady at an adjoining table recognized him and said, "Why, there's St. John! I didn't know he was in Chicago." Her companion was impressed. "St. John, eh?" she hazarded. "He's probably here for the Baptist Convention."

* * *

An accountant now serving in the Air Corps came home on leave last week and brought his young son an airedale puppy. The delighted youngster named it "Hurricane." Two days later, by common consent of the entire family, it was rechristened "P-47."

Austin Stevens, of *The Times,* reports that at his Denver base they're trying to cross a carrier pigeon with a woodpecker. The idea is to develop a bird that will not only carry messages but knock on the door when it arrives.

The rarest tale of poetic justice comes from dusty Texas, where an erstwhile *New Yorker* cartoonist is laboring in a camouflage unit. A loud-mouthed and overbearing officer drove up one day last week, and bawled the daylights out of the entire company. Their efforts, he informed them, wouldn't befuddle a Jap with one eye missing entirely and the other closed by a cataract. "Take down this claptrap," he bellowed, "and start all over again." The officer then climbed into his jeep and drove smack into the camouflaged headquarters hut.

* * *

Frank Gervasi brought this story home from the front, but, under pressure, admitted he didn't exactly see it happen.

A comely young WAC was walking alone on a dusty road when she espied a shimmery lake in a grove of beautiful green trees. Not a soul was in sight. On an impulse, she took off all her clothes, and had a fine swim and sun bath in the altogether. Suddenly she saw an officer heading purposefully in her direction. She made a dive for her clothes, and sighed with relief when she got the last button closed before he entered the glade.

The officer paid no attention to her whatever. He walked to the edge of the lake, wheeled about, and barked, "Camouflage battalion, 'tenshun! Forward march!"

Every tree around the lake marched off!

* * *

The Canadian correspondent, Matt Halton, tells a tale of the days when the British Eighth Army, not yet molded into a magnificent fighting machine, was playing hide-and-seek with Rommel in North Africa. An English patrol ventured deep into the Libyan desert, where it encountered a Nazi patrol of comparative strength. In the bloody fight that followed, everybody was killed except two English officers and one Nazi lieutenant. The Nazi was promptly made a prisoner, whereupon it developed that he not only spoke perfect English, but was a graduate (he declared) of Cambridge University. That put a different complexion on the situation, and the two Englishmen, very sportin', very school-tie, forthwith declared him one of themselves, sharing their meagre rations with him on an equal basis. The Nazi waited his chance, and, suddenly catching both of the Englishmen off guard, seized one of their pistols, and turned the tables on them. "Now, you—— English," he grunted, "you are *my* prisoners! Get over there!" The English officers, dumbfounded, hastened to obey, but one of them was heard to mutter, "I'll bet the blighter never went to Cambridge after all."

Eventually, the Englishmen outsmarted the Nazi anyhow, and brought him back alive. "A couple of months later," concluded Halton grimly, "those same English officers had learned what war against the Nazis meant. If you ever think England will be the same after the war, talk to the men or the officers of the British Eighth Army."

* * *

Liddell Hart, the British military expert, has always declared that a strong defense can hold an offensive three times its size. In support of this theory, he likes to tell the story of the young man who spent one entire week going from store to store in New York changing a dollar bill into two half-dollars, the half-dollars into four quarters, the quarters into ten dimes, the dimes into twenty nickels, and the nickels into one hundred pennies. Directly he had the one hundred pennies, he began reversing the process, until he again had a dollar bill. After he had gone through this strange procedure three times, Hart ventured to inquire what on earth his purpose was.

The young man lifted an index finger and smiled craftily. "One of these days," he explained, "somebody is going to make a mistake—and it isn't going to be me."

* * *

An Australian infantry division, recalls George Johnston in *Pacific Partner*, was stationed in England during the blitz in 1940. The boys were invited by the city corporation to visit Manchester, and were given a wonderful time.

At the end of their stay, a huge-muscled sergeant respectfully asked the Mayor to attend a little gathering in the City Hall. The Australian, he explained, would like to make a little presentation as a gesture of thanks to the people of Manchester.

The Mayor, touched by the request, attended the function. The sergeant, speaking on behalf of the assembled Australians, made the usual remarks of appreciation and then handed the Mayor a most magnificent collection of Australian curios and native weapons.

The Mayor, stuttering with emotion, pride and gratitude, mumbled his thanks. The Australians marched out of the hall and filed solemnly to the train that would take them back to camp.

It was not until the next day that the Police Department reported the great burglary of the Manchester Museum, a burglary notable for the fact that the theft was confined to the entire Australian aboriginal art collection.

DR. CHRISTIAN'S RING

THE BEST-KNOWN bibliophile in the Hollywood colony is Jean Hersholt, well-loved Danish actor who created the role of Dr. Christian on the screen and radio. Hersholt's collection of "firsts" ranks with the country's finest. When the late Dr. Dafoe (the man who took care of the Dionne quintuplets) visited Hersholt last winter, he picked out five or six of the rarest items in the library (they were worth, conservatively, $20,000) and horrified the collector with the casual, "Jean, I have lots of time for reading during those long nights in Canada. Do you mind if I cart these worn-out-looking books home with me? They are too shabby for a fine library like yours, anyhow."

Every year Jean Hersholt's radio program offers a prize for the best original script involving a new adventure of Dr. Christian. Last year's winner was submitted by Nelson Bond, of Roanoke, Virginia. Dr. Christian, according to Mr. Bond's story, was an ineffectual, namby-pamby young man when he was graduated from Berlin's finest medical college years ago. His sister kept house for him, but was out of patience with his lack of initiative. The roof of their flat leaked, the plaster was cracked, the paper was flaking from the walls, but the landlord pooh-poohed Dr. Christian's pleas for renovation on the grounds that labor was unobtainable, and that the inflation had ruined his business, anyway. As a matter of fact, this was the very height of the German Republic's disastrous inflation spiral. One American dollar was worth a million marks.

One afternoon the young doctor dropped in at a public auction in Wilhelmstrasse, and his eye was caught by an ornate, curiously fashioned ring that came under the hammer. He found himself bidding heatedly for it, in competition with an old priest, who was very agitated. The priest shook his head helplessly when Dr.

Christian bid thirty million marks. The doctor slipped the ring onto his finger, and walked toward his home. Unusual things began to happen immediately.

First, a pair of bandits, brandishing guns and running pell-mell to escape pursuing police, catapulted into Dr. Christian's arms. Strangely unafraid, the doctor seized and disarmed them, and turned them over to the policeman, who complimented him on his bravery and presence of mind. Then, when he arrived at his home, he read of the arrival in Berlin of the head of a famous American research institute. Dr. Christian, formerly so lacking in initiative, called the great specialist, and talked his way into a job at five times the salary he had envisioned in his wildest dreams. "You sound mighty cocky and sure of yourself," the American said on the phone. "I like young men of your stripe around me." Dr. Christian next collared his landlord, and cowed that individual so completely that he promised to have a crew redecorating the apartment the very next day. "Suddenly I feel able to make everybody do what I want," said the doctor in a somewhat surprised tone.

Two days later there came a knock at the front door, and Dr. Christian discovered that his visitor was the selfsame priest who had bid against him for the old ring. "Doctor," began the priest, "let us not beat about the bush. I've got to have that ring! I couldn't meet your bid of thirty million marks at the auction, but now I'm prepared to give you a hundred million for it!"

"I cannot understand your insistence on possessing that trifling bauble," wondered Dr. Christian.

"Ah, but it's the farthest thing possible from a trifling bauble," the priest said gravely. "That ring is a terrible force for evil. It must be destroyed at all costs, before it does further injury to the entire human race. It belonged originally to Judas Iscariot. Centuries later it fell into the hands of Genghis Khan, and then Napoleon. The last man who owned it was the Kaiser. It gives everyone who owns it overwhelming delusions of grandeur, and the ability to make whole peoples do his bidding."

"I've noticed myself," said the doctor, "that ever since I've worn the ring I've been imbued with a strange power over people."

"Get rid of it before it is too late," pleaded the priest. "Soon you will find it making you do terrible things. Not only you, but the whole world will suffer."

The doctor could not help being impressed by the priest's passionate plea. "The ring is on the bureau in my bedroom," he said. "I've got some men putting new paper on the walls there, but, if I can get past the scaffolding, I'll fetch the cursed ring for you."

But the ring was nowhere to be found. Dr. Christian searched high and low for it. Finally he summoned the foreman, who clapped his hand to his head when he heard that the ring had disappeared. "Ach," he exclaimed, "it's that schweinhund I threw off the job this morning! I'll bet he stole it! He was worthless from the day he started to work for me!"

"It is vitally important that I get that ring back at once!" cried Dr. Christian. "What was your workman's name? Where does he live?"

The foreman opened his record book. "I never did get his address," he said, "but I remember that he had a queer sort of name. I don't think he even was a German. Ah, yes, here it is, sir . . . *Adolf Schicklgruber!*"

* * *

When the Americans cleaned the Nips out of Attu, they found all sorts of booty which was divided up by avid souvenir hunters. One corporal found what looked like the Japanese equivalent of a ten-cent candy bar. "This stuff doesn't taste bad," he said to a buddy who could read Japanese. "What does the wrapper say?" The translator read it. "Brother," he reported, "you are eating a stick of dynamite."

* * *

Colonel Rex Smith, first editor of *The Chicago Sun,* relays the latest sergeant-rookie variation. The sergeant spoke his piece on the shoes the rookie wore to assembly. The rookie explained that he had worn them in private life. "So what?" snapped the sarge. "Did you have a high silk hat when you were a civilian, too?" "Why, yes, Sergeant, I did," was the reply. "Then why don't you wear that here, too?" "Don't be silly," snapped the private. "Who ever heard of wearing a top hat with brown shoes?"

* * *

The engineering department of a defense plant at Newburgh, New York, has been experimenting with steel wire, drawing it out very fine. They finally produced a piece of 120-gauge wire—practically invisible. The boys were proud—so proud, in fact, that they cut off a strand and sent it to a rival defense plant farther upstate. "This is just to show you what we are doing in Newburgh," they wrote.

Weeks went by. Recently, a package arrived at the Newburgh plant. The boys opened it with great care. Inside was a steel block; mounted on the block were two steel standards, and strung between the standards was the same piece of 120-gauge wire. At one end of the block was mounted a small microscope delicately focused on a certain spot on the wire. One by one the engineers placed an eye to the microscope and examined in silence the work of their rivals, who had bored, in the wire, a rather handsome little hole!

* * *

A correspondent who is writing a book about the Flying Tigers tells of a speech made to a group of Army fliers in Burma by their briefing officer on the eve of a bombing raid on distant Jap installations. "Men," said the officer, "tomorrow's stint is one of the toughest we've ever tackled. The enemy has received reinforcements. Our planes are falling apart. There is a hell of a storm brewing. We'll be lucky if one out of four of us ever gets back alive. We take off at seven sharp. And if any one of you is thirty seconds late, damn it—he can't go with us."

* * *

"In Southern Italy," reports Vincent Sheean, "an American flier won a coveted Free French decoration, but he was so ugly they couldn't find a French General who was willing to kiss him."

* * *

From London comes the story of the two Yanks who wanted to see the War Office, but didn't know on what side of the street it was located. They hailed a passing Tommy, and asked, "Which side is the War Office on?" The Tommy thought hard for a moment, then replied, "Gorblimey! Ours—I think!"

* * *

A marine sergeant led his men to the crest of a ridge, and spotted a whole company of Japs peacefully eating chow in the clearing below. "Jack," he called in a stage whisper to a corporal behind him, "bring up the guns on the left flank."

"No! Better on the right flank," a voice answered.

"I said the *left* flank—and on the double," rasped the sergeant.

"And I said the *right*," came the voice.

The infuriated sergeant plunged into the bush behind him with murder in his heart, but instead of the expected corporal, he came face to face with a smiling, English-speaking Jap.

The sergeant shook a finger in his face and hollered, "Damn it, Mac, you run *your* outfit and I'll run *mine!*"

REYNOLDS, THE FUN-LOVING ROVER

ONE OF THE most popular figures in the war book industry, which must be about the third biggest in the country by this time, is Quentin Reynolds. This towering, six-foot-something, burly 220-pound hunk of all-round good guy has a way of making you feel you are sharing every one of his adventures. He loves practically everybody and vice versa. When Quent Reynolds starts waving that American flag, it is like standing on the summit of a mountain at sunrise, with a ten-thousand-voice chorus of *The Star-Spangled Banner* ringing in your ears.

Reynolds began his literary career as a baseball writer. What is there about working on a sports page that makes men learn to write so well? Look at Lardner, Broun, Pegler, Runyon, Rice and Considine. Quent had a tougher job than any of them, though, because the team he was assigned to cover was the Brooklyn Dodgers. In those days the Dodgers played a brand of ball that was positively unique. Quent himself tells about the day he was sitting in the last row of the grandstand at Ebbets Field and, glancing into the street behind him, saw a rabid rooter running lickety-split for the entrance gate. "Hurry up," yelled Quent, "you're missing something big. The Dodgers have three men on base." "Holy mackerel," panted the rooter. "Which base?" Two years with the Dodgers provided ideal training for a career of hair-raising and death-defying experiences.

In 1930, the International News Service sent Reynolds to Berlin, where he saw the Nazis take over. He left Germany by their special request—but fast. "It was those babies," he says, "that made everybody else seem so attractive by comparison." *Collier's* signed him as a sort of reporter-at-large, and his list of "intimate friends" and pals began to stretch into the thousands—from diplomats to taxi drivers, from society queens to broken-down pugilists. The late Charlie Colebaugh, editor of *Collier's,* said that Quent came back from an interview with a steel magnate and declared, "He's a great guy! A wonderful man!" After a day at Hyde Park with the President, he reported, "He's a great guy! A wonderful man!" Then he visited the Tombs to build a story around a confessed killer. "He's really a great guy," he told the staff later. "A wonderful man! Can that boy cut throats!"

At a recent testimonial banquet to Reynolds in New York, one of the speakers referred to the guest of honor as "Quent, the fun-loving Rover." The Rover was too busy lining up the shortest route to Myrna Loy to pay heed; when the speeches were ended, Wendell Willkie, Deems Taylor, and Quent broke from the barrier as one. "Darling!" cried Myrna, and threw her arms about Mr. Reynolds' rotund bay. "Hell," Mr. Willkie was heard to mutter, "who can buck competition like that?"

No foreign correspondent has the right to have a wife as beautiful as Quent's "Ginny." It makes leaving for the front just that much harder. The day that Virginia Peine became Mrs. Reynolds, the President happened to be in New York. The police cleared Park Avenue for him just as the Reynolds nuptials were about to begin. Quent's father observed the host of motorcycle cops and the suspended traffic and said quite seriously, "I never realized how important my boy has become."

Quent Reynolds' description of the American landing in Salerno, Italy, and the establishment of the beachheads there will, I think, be reprinted in anthologies for years to come. At dawn of D-Day at Salerno he found himself on a boat with Vincent Sheean, now a Lieutenant Colonel. Sheean looked at the gray hills just beginning to be visible behind the town, and said, "Just around that promontory, the road dips sharply and goes by a tiny inn that serves the best damn fettucini in the entire world." Reynolds was deeply impressed. "I didn't know," he said, "that our Intelligence sent back reports in such incredible detail." "Intelligence, my eye," answered Sheean. "Salerno is where Dina and I spent our honeymoon."

Just before Reynolds returned to America, he interviewed General Montgomery. The first thing the General asked him was, "Is it true that back in the States the girls are wearing a beret they've named after me?" He ate one of his last meals in Italy in a little spaghetti joint that had a big sign over the door reading "GUERRA CONTRA LA MOSCA" ("War Against Flies"). When the waiter brought him his "spaghet," the plate was rimmed with flies. A few of them were even struggling in the spaghetti. "Hey," said Quent, "how about that sign, 'War Against Flies'?" "It's true," sighed the waiter. "We had the war here once—but the flies won."

A "welcome home" dinner—one of an endless series—was tossed for Quent at Toots Shor's elegant chop-house. Quent gave Toots an advance copy of *The Curtain Rises,* and wrote on the fly-leaf, "Too bad you are iliterate, otherwise you would enjoy this book." It was Toots who informed the scholar Reynolds (with two honorary degrees) that he had misspelled "illiterate."

* * *

Clark Gable brought back from abroad the story of a radio dialogue between a Swiss anti-aircraft battery and a U. S. bomber that was flying over forbidden Swiss territory, overheard by an enraged but impotent German radio station. "You are over neutral Swiss territory," said the officer on the ground. "We know," said the radio man in the bomber. "If you don't turn back, we'll have to shoot!" "We know. Go ahead!" The German station heard the sound of intermittent ack-ack, and then the voice of the man in the plane came back on the air. "Your fire is a thousand feet too low," he said. The Swiss answered, "We know!"

* * *

Washington is laughing over the malicious proposal that directly the war is concluded, a plaque be affixed to the Pentagon Building, reading "Washington slept here."

A new cocktail bar on Pennsylvania Avenue is named "Chez When."

A play opened at the National Theatre. One critic pronounced it a phony. "Act two," he explained, "takes place three weeks after Act One—and the heroine *has the same servants!*"

* * *

Are you going in for chicken-raising this year? If so, here are a few anecdotes that may amuse you.

A rooster was reading the morning paper aloud to a group of hens. "It says here," he reported, "that Mayor LaGuardia laid a cornerstone yesterday." "My, my," clucked a hen. "I didn't know he had it in him!"

In the next county, an arrogant red rooster was giving chase to a fluttery little hen. She scrambled into the highway to escape him, and was run down by a truck. Two old maids on a nearby porch witnessed the tragedy. "You see," one of them said with an approving nod, "she'd rather die!"

George Price drew a cartoon of a chicken farmer who fell for a box of feed that carried a caption, "Lay or Bust," on the carton. He scattered the feed on the ground; the picture shows the hens exploding all over the place.

* * *

Before she returned to Russia, Mrs. Maxim Litvinoff lunched with a publisher to discuss the possibility of bringing out her autobiography. "I need a notebook," said Mrs. Litvinoff, "in which to jot down little bits of my life as they come to mind." The publisher took her to a stationery shop around the corner, where she found just the notebook she wanted. When the clerk informed her that the price was a dollar, however, Mrs. Litvinoff protested. "That's outrageous," she said. "I will do without it." "Let me buy it for you," suggested the publisher. "We'll call it part of the luncheon." "Really," beamed Mrs. Litvinoff. "In that case, I will take two."

* * *

Leonard Lyons reports that one die-hard professor at Oxford still chooses to ignore the fact that, because of the war, female students at the university far outnumber the males. He began all lectures to mixed classes, "Gentlemen." Even when there were forty girls and ten men, he stubbornly addressed them as "Gentlemen." This Spring he found that his class consisted of forty-six girls and one lone man. He gritted his teeth, sighed, and began his lecture, "Sir."

* * *

Ed Wynn, "the Perfect Fool," has proven to be just what the doctors ordered for wounded soldiers at U. S. Army hospitals. They roared at his pole eleven feet four inches long, to be used for people you wouldn't touch with a ten-foot pole. They loved his cigarette lighter: when he pushed down on a little wheel an arrow jumped up and pointed to the nearest man with matches. But the biggest laugh of all came when he demanded of a colonel, "Say, have you seen the morning papers?"; the obliging colonel answered, "No, what's in them?" Wynn cracked, "My lunch, and I'm getting mighty hungry."

Old Wynn enthusiasts believe that he reached his greatest height in a show called *Manhattan Mary*. Wynn was a waiter in one scene. "I don't like all the flies in here," complained one patron.

"Show me the ones you don't like," suggested Wynn, "and I'll throw 'em out." When the patron said, "I'm so hungry I could eat a horse," Wynn led a live nag on to the stage. Then he sold it to the customer. "This horse has only one peculiarity," he told the befuddled buyer. "He loves to sit on potatoes. Remember that!" The man made off with his horse, but was back a moment later. "You fraud," he screamed. "I no sooner got that horse to the bridge down the road, when he bolted out of my control, and jumped over the bridge into the river." "Oh, I forgot to tell you," said the contrite Wynn. "That horse loves to sit on fish, too!"

In another scene, Wynn was busy painting a ship. An old dowager entered and asserted, "Mr. Wynn, I have decided to commission you to paint my ancestors." "Oh, I couldn't do that," he protested. "I'm just a ship painter." "Nevertheless," insisted the dowager, "you are the man I want for the job." "But I tell you," he wailed, "I only paint ships." "The question is closed," she announced. "You, and you alone, are going to paint my ancestors." "All right," agreed Wynn finally. "I'll paint your darn ancestors. But I want to warn you now: they're going to look like ships!"

* * *

One of the heads of the European propaganda division of the British Broadcasting Corporation submitted a letter of resignation recently. "Doing foreign propaganda for the BBC," he averred, "is like making love to a female elephant. There is no pleasure in it, you run the risk of being crushed to death, and it is years before you see any results!"

* * *

An English bomber flushed a flock of FW-190's over the Channel on the way home from a raid on Berlin, and the crew had to parachute to safety. The pilot, a chap named Donald, had long been prepared for this, and had always worried about freezing, so he never went up without tucking a bottle of brandy in his Mae West. After an hour or so in the water, he was picked up by a destroyer—but not until he had consumed the entire bottle of brandy.

As he climbed aboard the destroyer, the captain said jokingly, "Sir, you're dripping water all over my clean deck."

Donald haughtily answered, "I never stay where I'm not wanted," and promptly walked overboard. It took them fifteen minutes to fish him up again.

* * *

Lt. Col. Rogers writes from the Pacific area that the most striking personality in those parts is a cannibal chief with nine Jap flags tattooed on his stomach. And a hand-lettered sign tacked to the officers' bulletin board reads, "Hats altered to fit any promotion."

A biologist was taken into the army as a captain, and then proceeded to go right on doing the things he always had done before. They let him use his own laboratory, and he didn't even wear an officer's uniform. "Has your life changed in any way?" a reporter asked him. "Well," he answered, "I work the same. I live the same, and I even think the same; but now if a guinea pig bites me, I get the Purple Heart."

* * *

A nervous lieutenant had been informed that General Eisenhower was due on an inspection tour. Three times he popped out of his tent to ask Private Nussbaum, "Has General Eisenhower arrived yet?" "No, sir," said Nussbaum each time. Finally he looked at his watch, barked, "When the General comes, let me know at once. It's important," and re-entered his tent. A few minutes later the General drove up. "Are you General Eisenhower?" asked Nussbaum. "Yes, I am," said the General. "Oy," sighed the private. "Are you going to get it from the lieutenant!"

* * *

A Waco major who had co-piloted a B-26 allowed that the war would last another five years: "One to lick the Nazis, another to take the Nips, and three more to get the Yankees out of Texas!" A fellow officer declared, "The only things these boys are interested in are Death and Texas. Whenever a juke box plays 'There's a Bit of Texas in my Walk' they stand at attention."

* * *

One of the prize tidbits of the year concerns the Boston author who was scheduled to lecture in Louisville, but was bounced off his plane in Washington to make room for a colonel with a priority. The author couldn't make Louisville in time by train, so he returned in disgust to Boston. The colonel, it developed, had flown to Louisville for the sole purpose of hearing his lecture.

* * *

Ernie Pyle tells about a sergeant who had been a three-striper for over a year and had passed up numerous chances to enter an officers' candidate school. A pal asked him why. "Remember Sergeant York in the last war?" queried the sarge. "Sure do," was the answer. "Chum," said the sergeant, "name me just one of the second lieutenants in that war!"

* * *

An officer, home from strenuous service overseas, was assigned to a desk job in the Pentagon Building. Each day for a week he shifted the location of his desk—next to the window, away from the window, into a corridor, and finally into the men's wash room. "He must be shell-shocked," the authorities figured, but the officer had a different explanation. "It's the only place around here," he said grimly, "where people seem to know what they're doing."

INDEX OF NAMES

NOTE ABOUT THE AUTHOR

THAT REDDISH *glow you may notice in the atmosphere is caused by all those irons Bennett Cerf has in the fire. He is, at the moment, publisher, editor, columnist, book reviewer and radio commentator.*

He was editor of The Jester *at Columbia University. He received his B.A. in 1919, with a Phi Beta Kappa key, and his Litt.B. in 1920 from the School of Journalism. It was a mere hop, skip and jump from college to Wall Street to the publishing house of Boni and Liveright, from whom he and his lifelong friend, Donald Klopfer, bought the Modern Library in 1925.*

In 1927 Random House was launched. From 1933, when Eugene O'Neill brought his plays to Random House, to the present day, Bennett Cerf has guided the fortunes of his company to a place of national prominence in the publishing field. Among the authors represented in its list, in addition to O'Neill, are Robinson Jeffers, Sinclair Lewis, Vincent Sheean, Edgar Snow, William Faulkner, Maritta Wolff, Budd Schulberg, Walter Van Tilburg Clark, William McFee, André Malraux, Mignon Eberhart, Elliot Paul and Ward Greene. Among its wartime best sellers are Guadalcanal Diary, Thirty Seconds Over Tokyo, Suez to Singapore *and the increasingly popular books of Quentin Reynolds.*

In his odd moments Bennett Cerf writes a weekly column, "Trade Winds," for The Saturday Review of Literature *and a monthly book-review section, "Esquire's Five-Minute Bookshelf." His weekly radio broadcast, "Books Are Bullets," has been a feature of the Council on Books in Wartime on Station WQXR for more than two years. His published anthologies include:* The Bedside Book of Famous American Stories, *with Angus Burrell (1936),* The Bedside Book of Famous British Stories, *with H. C. Moriarty*

(1940), Three Famous Murder Novels *(1941) and four collections of famous plays, with Van Cartmell, since that date. In addition, he has edited* The Pocket Book of War Humor *and* The Pocket Book of Cartoons, *each of which has sold well over a million copies.*

No one underrates his ability to make the twelve Herculean labors seem like light housework. When we say no one, we include Mr. Cerf.